"THE EVENTS OF OCTOBER"

"THE EVENTS OF OCTOBER"

Murder-Suicide on a Small Campus

GAIL GRIFFIN

A PAINTED TURTLE BOOK
Detroit, Michigan

14 13 12 11 10   5 4 3 2 1

LIBRARY OF CONGRESS CATALOGING-IN-PUBLICATION DATA

GRIFFIN, GAIL B.

"THE EVENTS OF OCTOBER" : MURDER-SUICIDE ON A SMALL CAMPUS / GAIL GRIFFIN.

P. CM.

"A PAINTED TURTLE BOOK."

INCLUDES BIBLIOGRAPHICAL REFERENCES.

ISBN 978-0-8143-3472-0 (PBK. : ALK. PAPER)

1. MURDER—MICHIGAN—KALAMAZOO. 2. SUICIDE—MICHIGAN—KALAMAZOO.

3. WARDLE, MAGGIE, D. 1999. 4. ODAH, NEENEF, D. 1999. 5. KALAMAZOO COLLEGE.

6. KALAMAZOO (MICH.)—HISTORY. I. TITLE.

HV6534.K17G75 2010

364.152'309277417—DC22

2010007829

LYRICS FROM "RUN FOR YOUR LIFE" (LENNON/MCCARTNEY) © 1965 SONY/ATV MUSIC PUBLISHING LLC. ALL RIGHTS ADMINISTERED BY SONY/ATV MUSIC PUBLISHING LLA, 8 MUSIC SQUARE WEST, NASHVILLE, TN, 37203. ALL RIGHTS RESERVED. USED BY PERMISSION.

A PORTION OF THE AUTHOR'S ROYALTIES WILL FUND PROJECTS AIMED AT PREVENTING VIOLENCE AGAINST WOMEN.

Adapted from a design by Isaac Tobin
Typeset by Maya Rhodes
Composed in Sabon and Gotham

for **Bob**,
who almost made it
to the end of this with me

and in memory of
Marilyn J. LaPlante,
who got us through

What we remember, wrote the poet who was my first teacher of the art, *can be changed. What we forget we are always.* Dick was right: we live the stories we tell; the stories we don't tell live us. What you don't allow yourself to know controls and determines; whatever's held to the light "can be changed"—not the facts, of course, but how we understand them, how we live with them. Everyone will be filled by grief, distorted by sorrow; that's the nature of being a daughter or a son, as our parents are also. What matters is what we learn to make of what happens to us.

And we learn to make, I think, by telling.

—Mark Doty, *Firebird*

There is really nothing more to say—except why. But since *why* is too difficult to handle, one must take refuge in *how*.

—Toni Morrison, *The Bluest Eye*

CONTENTS

A ringing phone in the middle of the night is aggressive, even violent. It drills into sleep; it jars like a collision.

That early Monday morning I was deeply asleep. The phone jerked me awake. The clock read three-something. On the other end of the line I heard the high tenor of a student in my first-year seminar at Kalamazoo College, now four weeks underway. A sensitive, needy kid, he was struggling with the transition from thirteenth-grader to college student. My adrenaline rush came out as anger. "Do you know what time it is?" I snapped, heart thumping hard.

A student had been killed, he said, his voice watery and thin. Shot by her ex-boyfriend, who then had shot himself. They had evacuated DeWaters, the dorm where it happened.

"Do you know who it was?" I asked, now very awake. I didn't recognize either of the names he gave. "Are you OK? Where are you?"

"We're in Trowbridge. They brought us over here. The police are here. We're OK, I guess . . ."

We talked a few moments more. I asked who was with him and heard some other names from our seminar. Finally I told him I would be in my office later in the morning if he or any of the others needed me, and I hung up.

The pattern was grimly familiar: the jealous man who murders his former girlfriend and then "turns the gun on himself," as the papers always say.

I rolled onto my back in bed. My cat, annoyed at being disturbed, rearranged herself and dropped down beside me again.

It was like watching those silent films of an atomic explosion, a flash and then, after a delay, the mushroom cloud, blooming out and out. Lying there watching the windows lighten to gray, I began to feel the weight of all that would come.

1

FAIR ARCADIAN HILL

"If you were a painter and wanted to paint the ideal college, you'd go out there and paint that quad," mused President James F. Jones, always known as Jimmy.

Everyone says much the same thing on seeing the Kalamazoo College campus for the first time; it looks the part, brilliantly. It's what I thought when I first drove onto the campus on a snowy December day in 1976. It is set on one of several high hills above the Kalamazoo River valley. The central quadrangle slopes eastward from the chapel, whose bell tower with its gilded dome rises up like a benedictory hand. Big oaks and maples shade the grass and shelter overfed squirrels that lost their fear of humans generations ago. The architectural unity of the place would gladden an eighteenth-century eye: Georgian red-brick buildings with white trim, nothing over four stories high. Classrooms and the administration building line the north side of the quad, and the student center borders the south side. At the foot of the quad is Hoben Hall, which, along with Harmon Hall next door, was a men's dorm when I arrived. The original women's dorms sit up behind the chapel: Trowbridge, the oldest on campus, and DeWaters. Gender segregation in the residence halls evaporated in the eighties.

Beyond the north side of the quad runs Academy Street, and across it are the library, the Dow Science Center, the Light Fine Arts complex, and Humphrey House, the fine old 1915 manse that houses the humanities departments, including my own, English. Down Academy Street a block or two are the Anderson Athletic Center and the two other residence halls, Crissey and Severn, remarkably nondescript, soulless echoes of the seventies.

From the chapel steps, you can look out over downtown Kalamazoo to the east and beyond across the river valley. The reigning theory around here is that the Potawatomi gave the river its name, *Kikalamazoo*, which describes water boiling in a pot. (The college yearbook is *The Boiling Pot*, the literary magazine *The Cauldron*. Unaccountably, the newspaper is *The Index*.) White people moved into the valley in the 1820s. By 1833 the American Baptists, those freethinking, education-minded, abolitionist folks, had founded the Michigan and Huron Institute, later renamed the Kalamazoo Literary Institute, the first institution of higher learning in the Michigan Territory (exclusively for young men, of course).

Meanwhile, in preparation for the state university at Ann Arbor, yet only a vision, the Michigan legislature mandated that branches of the university be established in several Michigan communities, a plan designed to create a student body for the university-to-be. Each branch was to have a Female Department with a largely separate curriculum, its purpose to educate the sisters of said university students to be the teachers who would play a critical role in the settlement of the "West." One of those branches was created in Kalamazoo. Seeing the obvious redundancy of physical and human resources, leaders of the Kalamazoo Literary Institute and the Kalamazoo branch of the University of Michigan merged the two institutions, although the Baptists from the Institute maintained administrative control.

Many of the Baptist founders of the Literary Institute were New England exiles, pilgrims to the promising wilderness of the Michigan Territory. Under the inspired leadership of two such pilgrims, James and Lucinda Stone, the University of Michigan Kalamazoo branch thrived and grew into what became Kalamazoo College in 1855, when it received the first charter given to a private college by the state legislature.

The city of Kalamazoo, located roughly halfway between Detroit and Chicago, burgeoned into an important stagecoach and then train stop. Lincoln spoke in Bronson Park downtown. Visitors to the college included Ralph Waldo Emerson, Frederick Douglass, Elizabeth Cady Stanton, Wendell Phillips, Bronson Alcott—the radicals on the burning edge of nineteenth-century American thought. It is within this context that coeducation began at Kalamazoo College, informally and surreptitiously. At the time, coeducation was regarded as far more radical than the single-sex model of higher education that emerged in the east in the 1860s and 70s. Regardless, coeducational programs at Kalamazoo College gradually became official, as happened at many denominational colleges throughout the Midwest, although they remained associated with the dangerous unorthodoxy of the frontier.

It's a double-edged word, "frontier." It means the edge of the future; it also signifies an uncivilized backwater. When I landed in Kalamazoo in 1977, I wasn't quite sure which definition was more pertinent. I was toting a spanking-new doctorate from an east-coast university, where the educational philosophy rested on the Enlightenment principle of laissez-faire (also known as the law of the jungle), and where teaching was something you did when you had to in order to support your research. If you were lucky or powerful, you avoided undergraduate classes. "Academic advising" meant signing a form as quickly as possible. You worked for the day when you could deliver lectures twice a week while some graduate-student wage-slave led the discussions, met with the students, and graded the papers.

Now I found myself not only back in my home state but in a town that no one believes exists outside of one entirely too famous song, at a college of less than fifteen hundred students and a hundred faculty. Everybody on campus and locally called the place by its nickname, "K." Classes of thirty were considered large. No grad students or teaching assistants in sight. Faculty were in their offices constantly, five days a week. People talked about teaching, and about their students, all the time. In any given discussion involving three or more faculty members, any student mentioned would be known by two of them and her progress through the college reliably charted. In fact, no one at the college is more than two degrees of separation from anyone else, and you find yourself saying you know people you've never met because you've heard about them so often. For me, true culture shock.

Recently a young colleague who had taught as a graduate student at the University of Michigan gave me two great insights about teaching at

Kalamazoo. First, you don't have to work overtime to endear yourself to students at a megaversity like the University of Michigan; any humane gesture, any personal attention is rare enough to elicit profound devotion and gratitude (not to mention stellar evaluations). At Kalamazoo, that kind of interaction with students is the norm, and students learn quickly to take it for granted. Second, whereas at Michigan you might teach a student in his first year and never see him again, at Kalamazoo your path is more than likely to cross a given student's several times, if not in another course, then at campus events or as the result of some extracurricular project. What I came to understand shortly after arriving at K is that the experience known as "higher education" changes substantially when the development of undergraduates moves to the exact center of the map.

Another reason students often occupy faculty conversations at Kalamazoo is that their four-year journeys tend to get so interesting. I discovered this as I realized that students were often discussed in their relation to the distinct educational plan that had brought Kalamazoo from the brink of extinction to national prominence. Called the K-Plan, it was developed in the late 1950s, implemented in the early sixties. It combined a traditional on-campus liberal-arts curriculum with off-campus career preparation, a junior-year study-abroad experience lasting three to nine months, and a senior independent project required of all students. No single facet of the plan was unique to K, but the way in which the four were integrated certainly was. And the jewel in the crown was Study Abroad, as a result of which Kalamazoo soon became the acknowledged national gold standard. The program is exceptional first because it is endowed, enabling all students to take part. Second, wherever possible, it sends students into indigenous universities and provides home stays rather than sequestering them in floating American islands as many other programs do. Third, whereas many study abroad programs effectively exclude science majors because of the pressures of the premed curriculum, the Kalamazoo faculty bought into a fundamental principle of universal availability, jerking the curriculum around such that a student in any major can be absent for two-thirds of the junior year. Finally, students have many choices beyond Europe, including Africa, Latin America, and Asia, allowing white-bread midwestern kids to travel much farther from home, culturally speaking.

Study Abroad has evolved significantly, but it is still the watershed, the Great Divide, in the Kalamazoo student experience. The "before and after" comparison can be stunning, and it often drives faculty discussions of students, as do senior project ordeals and forays into experiential learning. For those of us educated firmly within the classroom's four walls, teaching these kids is a juicy, endlessly challenging experience.

Faculty usually say that the best thing about working at K is the students. Generally they're smart, curious, highly motivated academically (often too motivated, as in driven, as in unable to digest a B-minus). K's admissions office competes with U of M for the academic stars in the state. Because of our longstanding reputation for premedical education, fully fifty percent of any entering class will indicate at least an interest in pursuing the sciences, though many jump ship after the first rigorous year. Many of the students come from small places—small towns, self-enclosed suburbs. Most come from racial and economic privilege and thus have been successfully insulated from certain discomforting realities. Often they are champing at the bit, ready to take risks and brave the unknown. Many were the stars of their high schools, with high test scores and two-page résumés, but frequently they were the misfits—geeks of various flavors; gay/lesbian/bi; feminists and peaceniks; socially marginal; or merely curious and intellectually vital kids who struggled to breath in an asphyxiating community or a numbing school. They bring all their unexamined baggage and spend the next four years unpacking and repacking it in forays to, away from, and back to that green quad.

The progressive legacy of freethinking American Baptists and New England renegades still lives at Kalamazoo College, though sometimes one has to check for a pulse. On more conservative Michigan campuses we are apparently known as "gay K," and locally we are regarded as a leftist utopia—or dystopia, depending on the angle of vision. I often tell prospective students and their parents that I wish I'd gone to K. I think I would have become more confident, less cautious, more engaged and assertive—because I have seen students like me become so. I could have used the care, the attention, the opportunity to be known by my professors. Had I not had to wait in line behind seniors and juniors to get into choir or join the newspaper staff, I might not have abandoned two high-school passions. Had I found myself negotiating six months in another culture, or finding an internship in a big city, or researching and completing a senior thesis largely on my own, certainly I would have vanquished some of the demons that were still waiting for me after college ended.

I once said to a graduating class that K is a place where, on the one hand, when you're in trouble, people close around you like a comforting hand, and on the other, everybody knows who you're sleeping with. (It got a huge laugh.) It's a remarkably cosmopolitan place, where in any given class discussion students might make reference to their experiences in Senegal or Thailand, in a sustainable-development initiative, or in a local-foods movement. It's also a painfully parochial place, where two-thirds of the students are from Michigan, virtually all of them are eighteen to twenty-two years old, and a large portion of them are white. Unlike most private midwestern liberal arts colleges, K is in the middle of a midsize, very diverse city, and yet it often feels like a bubble in which we're all encased while the world goes on around us. Students' hands get held all too tightly, yet their level of initiative and imagination regularly dazzles me. It's a warmly supportive place and an inordinately demanding, competitive one. It can be sharply alienating for students of color and for the children of the working class. Does it contradict itself? Daily. Hourly. Above all, it's intense, and so can be atomizing: it's easy to go through your day utterly consumed with your singular priorities. But the place is also a tensile web, and when one strand is plucked, the whole entity hums; if one filament tears, the entire design shudders.

The view from the chapel steps down the quad doesn't reveal all this complexity and contradiction, of course. It's a provocative, eloquent view. When parents accompany their high school juniors and seniors to check out the college, I can see in their eyes when the quad has seduced them. They have heard it whisper all manner of stories about college and what it will do for their kids. These stories, which neither parents nor prospective students could possibly articulate, are products of hope, memory, fantasy, and bad movies—all of which tend to supply happy endings. Indeed, on an October morning, the serene beauty of the campus is enough to make even a seasoned student or faculty member start singing the truly embarrassing "Kalamazoo Alma Mater":

Each tree upon thy fair Arcadian hill
Is dear to us for aye.

Dark storms may come, cold blasts may chill
But friendship e'er will stay.

What follows is a chronicle of the days leading up to a particular October morning in 1999, and the days that came after. It's a fusion of fact, memory, testimony, impression, and one other ingredient, a potent and dangerous catalyst: imagination. There is no invented dialogue or character, no fictional scene-making, but there is indeed interpretation.

We teachers of literature struggle to bring our students to the crucial recognition that there is, in fact, no reading without interpretation. Reading is a collaborative act between text and reader, so no text is read "objectively," and none gives up pure meaning. We bring ourselves to everything we read—including the people around us, the most complicated texts of all. We perceive patterns and connections; we foreground some things and subordinate others; some details we fail to see altogether. The best we can do is to try diligently, continually to expand our vision. This is where imagination collaborates with fact, taking us toward some kind of truth.

The greatest of the Victorian sages, Marian Evans, a.k.a. George Eliot, believed that the imagination is a moral agent that enables us to transcend the limits of our little selves and enter with sympathy (her favorite word, used with its original meaning) the realities of the lonely and wounded who walk the earth alongside us—just as it allows us to enter into the lives of characters on a page. She inherited that idea, in part, from her forebears, the Romantics, who believed that imagination is not so much a creative force as a power of perception—of seeing deeply into what Wordsworth called "the life of things," but through particular eyes, from a specific vantage point.

So it is that I've begun with myself, with the moment the story began for me, and with my imaginings of how the story would continue. When we struggle with how to tell a story, it's because we know that how we tell it—indeed how we have read it—influences what it will mean to those listening. For me, the question of how to tell the story became an inextricable part of the story itself, the story of what happened at Kalamazoo College just after midnight on October 18, 1999. "What happened?" may be the hardest question of all.

2

MILLENNIUM GIRL

1

I have blond hair, green eyes, My favorit amnils are dog and cats, I like to roller-skate, I have a brother, my favorit season is spring, and I like swimming.

This is Maggie Wardle in third grade, as seen through those same green eyes. The words are printed carefully in pencil on soft, buff-colored paper lined in blue. The letters are shaped beautifully, even if the mysteries of commas and capital letters still elude her. She stays assiduously between the lines.

Maggie produced this self-assessment at Cooper Elementary, a small school halfway between Kalamazoo and Plainwell. Maggie's family had moved to Plainwell a year earlier from Portage, the burgeoning southern suburb of Kalamazoo where Maggie was born in August of 1980. Her mother, Martha, was a psychiatric nurse at the Kalamazoo State Hospital, the imposing old structure riding one of Kalamazoo's high hills, its massive cone-topped tower visible all over town, its primary claim to fame that Malcolm X's mother was hospitalized there. Maggie's father,

Robert Wardle, a brilliant engineer, was the scion of a wealthy east-coast family. Maggie followed their first child, Rob, nineteen months later. By the time she was two, her parents had divorced, and her mother had married Rick Omilian, director of special education in the Plainwell school system. When Maggie was seven, they moved from Portage up to Plainwell, ten miles north of Kalamazoo, into a light-filled octagonal house on a lot enclosed in trees. Martha surrounded the house with lush gardens.

The move took the family across lines of class and local culture. A white offshoot of a midsize, multiracial midwestern city, Portage is where Kalamazooans head to do their serious shopping; "Por-TAHGE," it's sometimes sardonically called. Plainwell, originally a farming town in the rich fruit belt of western Michigan, still strikes one as the definitive Village, with small shops, a renowned ice-cream parlor, and neat clapboard houses on shady streets. There is nothing hip about it. With some set dressing, it could serve as the location for a TV series set in the fifties.

The schoolyards and backyards of such a place were perhaps as idyllic as America got in the eighties, at least for little kids. A happy, gregarious child, Maggie "seemed to instinctively know how to share and play with others . . . rarely choosing solitary activities," Rick recalls. The only shadow on Maggie's life was her brother's struggle with Asperger's Syndrome. He had been diagnosed early, when Asperger's was still little understood; in fact, when Martha took him to an autism specialist at Western Michigan University, she was advised to institutionalize him.

In Rob, the obsessiveness, egocentrism, distractibility, and inability to master tasks that often mark the autistic spectrum combined with the ingeniousness that is also so often part of the package: Rob came to be able to fix anything—but he learned to do it by taking things apart. "It was a little bit rough at times," Martha recalls, with the understatement characteristic of one who accepted long ago that life would be difficult. Rob was "a handful," and Maggie was devoted to him, "always covering for him, pulling him along and out of things." He quickly manifested his father's engineering proclivities, and the two children spent hours in the backyard sandbox creating land- and cityscapes. "He says there's many things buried under the yard," Rick laughs. Rob ran with the rest of the neighborhood kids, but his behavior often ignited conflicts. "Just send him home," Martha would tell the neighbors. "We'll take care of it." Rob's inability to master simple tasks baffled his sister. "Why doesn't he just *get it?*" she'd ask. But she also became his teacher, watching Martha and Rick interact with him and then repeating their lessons. Little sister became big brother's caretaker.

Rob was undoubtedly Maggie's most profound early lesson in nurturance, the centerpiece of the female role, as much so in 1989 as in 1959. Maggie Wardle was born at a highly charged moment in American women's history. It might be seen as the instant before feminism's Second Wave crested and crashed on the sands of so-called post-feminism. The girls of her generation came to womanhood with conflicting voices buzzing in their heads: the voices chanting about aspiration, power, self-determination, and a sharp analysis of gendered behavior, countered by the voices of the antifeminist backlash documented in detail by Susan Faludi. One of the arenas in which the backlash manifested itself was toy stores, in which the products seemed even more gendered than in previous years. Maggie learned femininity, as millions of other girls did, through the things she loved to play with: Pound Puppies and Cabbage Patch dolls (carefully designed to evoke pity for the unclaimed and unwanted), Barbies, old gowns and dresses discarded by female relatives—rehearsals for womanhood.

But there were other forces at work in Maggie, too, forces that do not traditionally belong to the female realm. First and foremost, from earliest childhood, she was, in Rick's words, "enthralled by small organisms"—or as one of her college friends put it, a "bug geek." Unable to bear killing the hornworms on the tomato plants, Maggie was hired to remove them, for a dollar apiece. With a seriousness and persistence bespeaking a genuine scientific bent, she studied the fauna of the midwestern backyard. In daylight hours, she chased flying creatures from flower to flower. She trapped spiders and installed them in cardboard boxes turned into "habitats" in which she studied their behavior. After dark on summer nights she would take lawn chairs into the yard, hang a white sheet over them, place a light under it, and then identify the bugs that flocked to the sheet. As she got older, she killed insects progressively, with scientific detachment, moving them from jar to jar in graduated phases, carefully arranged in advance. She taught herself to mount and preserve them. An early reader, she devoured books on snakes, spiders, and insects. She became an avid nature photographer. "She was into a lot of different things," her mother recalls, "and really wanted to *know stuff*." Rick echoes, "She was always just very curious."

In fifth grade, Maggie wrote two brief articles for her school paper, *The Cooper Snooper*. One is a recipe for "Cookie Paints," using evaporated milk and food coloring. The other describes a school club: "Future Problem Solvers is a group of third, fourth, and fifth graders at Cooper Elementary that solve problems for the state of Michigan. Mrs. Van Gorder is running this program. Our goal is to try to come up with as many solutions that we can that might stop the ozone from depleting. The state might use our solutions and put them in action."

On the one hand, ten-year-old Maggie Wardle was going to help the state of Michigan solve the environmental crisis. On the other, she was going to decorate cookies. On one side, Barbies; on the other, entomology. In one moment, protecting and caretaking; in the next, happily killing bugs. There is, of course, no inherent reason why these different impulses should conflict. But in many women, for many reasons, they do. And they exerted cross-pressures on American girls in the eighties and nineties.

As she grew, Maggie thrived on all the benefits of a remarkable extended-blended family and struggled with its complexities, the geographic and emotional distances she had to cross. Rick's family had embraced her as their own immediately. Martha's German mother, Doris, Maggie's cherished Oma, was nearby in Kalamazoo. Bob Wardle now owned a structural engineering firm near Philadelphia, where he lived with his second wife, Sandi. The populous Wardle clan in Pennsylvania and South Carolina eagerly awaited Maggie and Rob's arrival each summer. When they were small, Bob Wardle would come to Kalamazoo to collect them. In later years, they made the trip by themselves, with Maggie watching out for Rob, as ever. This journey took them across the major divide in Maggie's life, one she worked hard to negotiate. Every time she went southeast, Maggie crossed pronounced lines of class, regional culture, and, predictably, politics: The Wardles were hard-core Republicans, the Omilians classic liberals. The Wardles had the family foundation and the private island. Rick and Martha were hardworking members of service professions not known for being lucrative. East coast/urban versus Midwest/small town. Between these worlds Maggie oscillated on her way to adulthood, trying to reconcile them in herself, imagining whom she might become.

In a town like Plainwell, you can actually survive until middle school without being pinned like one of Maggie's insects by the social politics of your peers. But not much longer. In middle school "you start to realize who the groups are," says Brooke Nobis, who met Maggie in seventh grade. "I remember knowing in middle school that she was the smart girl who lived in the octagon house." The Smart Girl: there are worse things to be—and there are also easier things to be. Maggie was also a musician, having studied piano in elementary school and now taking up French horn to play in the school band. And she was an athlete. The little girl who loved to swim now joined the basketball team. There is a picture of the team, eight girls, with Rick, their coach, standing beside them. Maggie is in the front row, grinning, wearing huge glasses. Her hair—the blonde now darkened to light brown—is yanked gracelessly back, and her long legs don't seem to know where to go. In this awkward girl, it's hard to see the pretty, confident young woman trying to claw her way out in time to pose for her senior pictures five years down the pike. Bug geek, band geek, b-ball geek: no question that middle school was Maggie's time in limbo before a remarkable emergence.

Part of what fueled that emergence was Maggie's own competitive drive, increasingly in evidence as she matured. Rick remembers her becoming "an avid player at board games and card games," inexhaustibly recruiting competition until it "became hard to find volunteers to play with her as she mastered the moves and tricks of the game." Her taste in jigsaw puzzles ran to those with "the most shades of one color and the most pieces." For band "she didn't care if she had to practice her heart out," her mother remembers, "because she wanted to be first chair." And in the classroom she was intensely competitive with her friends, even her dearest friend, Sarah Ayres, whom she met in middle school. In high school, they were "almost inseparable. . . . Sarah was almost identical to her, equally intelligent, really lanky. So they really clicked," as Brooke Nobis recalls it. Ultimately Maggie and Sarah would agree to go to different colleges to avoid carrying that competition into adulthood.

When Maggie hit the court with the Plainwell High School girls' basketball team, her ferocity startled her friends because her usual affect tended toward shyness and even self-effacement. Brooke Nobis saw a sharp divide: "Maggie was really quiet, but you got her on the basketball court and she was really aggressive. A very, very aggressive girl, really feisty." Maggie was tall and thus became her team's main rebounder and a serious threat—sometimes even to her own teammates. "As a short, squatty girl myself," Brooke says, "I was underneath Maggie a lot. . . . I remember looking up during practice [at] these bony elbows." The team wasn't much good, but it afforded Maggie an outlet for that fierce energy, and it provided something else as well, something that would feature prominently in Maggie's life at college: a tight group of girlfriends, including Sarah. Brooke remembers:

> We had a losing streak of a season, and I think that somehow made us become really close with one another. And we had all these silly rituals, because we knew we just *sucked*. And we had these horrible uniforms for freshman girls—there were these really short shorts. . . . But we had a really great coach who had a great attitude about us being a group of girls together. We would go [out for] pizza together; we would all do our hair the same on the bus; we'd wear these really obnoxious socks up to our knees and just really have fun, even though we were pretty bad.

The sisterhood, according to Brooke, stopped at the classroom door, where Maggie and Sarah differentiated themselves from the pack: "I played sports with her, I got along with her really well, but academically I never saw her in a classroom," as Maggie "was always placed in upper-level courses. She was incredibly intelligent and shot right above the rest of us."

"She never seemed to want to be caught not knowing something," Rick Omilian observes—a description that captures both her genuinely hungry mind and her need to measure up, to please, not to be found wanting. A curious mind and competitive drive, swaddled in humility and shyness: the conundrum of the Smart Girl.

According to Brooke Nobis, their talks on the bus rides to and from basketball games during freshman and sophomore years brought Maggie and her friends to a stunning realization: "Whoa! There's *boys!*" Maggie began to shed her geekiness. She begged her mother not to talk about the bug thing outside of the family. She began to cultivate her long hair with all the dedication girls bring to that most evocative feature, with which they so often play out their crises of identity. Brooke remembers her conditioning it religiously, leaving the conditioner in for a certain span of time to ensure silkiness. Finally, when she ditched the glasses for contacts, "that was the demise," according to Rick, of "hiding her from the boys. We were pretty strict—I mean, we kept her under wraps, [but] she still managed to do the things she felt she needed to do." They monitored her time carefully. She experimented socially with Plainwell High's "alternative group" as a freshman, dating a guitar player named Andrew who was "cool and sophisticated." Then, as a sophomore, she began dating a senior named Sean. Rick immediately vetted him among the teachers and administrators in the Plainwell system, and he passed muster. Martha remembers it as "more of a friendship," with the two of them hitting golf balls in the yard. As a junior, with Sean now at Western Michigan University in Kalamazoo, she dated Brad Ascherman, who was a year younger and whom she would later term "the love of her life." "She was the only girl I knew as stubborn in her views as me," he remembers. "She was also the only girl that has ever beaten me at golf. She would do whatever it took to win." The next year they decided to be "just friends," and Maggie was back with Scan, who now had the allure of the College Man.

The off-and-on relationship with Sean probably had to do with his neediness, a quality that is both attractive and repellant to a girl like Maggie. "Sean wanted someone to take care of him," says Rick. The sister of an impaired, troubled brother responded immediately to that kind of need, but her nurturance had its limits, he explains. After a point, she wanted out. "She always picked decent kids who were a good match for her," Rick continues. "But she was a competitive person." Martha adds, "Maggie was very strong, and it takes a different kind of guy . . ."

Brooke remembers that toward the end of high school Maggie "grew into herself—was realizing she was a very pretty woman, and she was very smart about the way that she handled herself with men. . . . I'm pretty sure she knew exactly what she wanted with guys and knew how to kind of tease them." She had discovered that her sexuality, like her mind and her muscles, could be a fascinating source of power.

In childhood, Rick recalls, Maggie strove to please her Plainwell parents. When she crossed the great divide into adolescence, the wind shifted. Not surprisingly, her energy now went toward ingratiating herself with a biological father who had been absent since her infancy and was somewhat emotionally distant. She and Rick became adversaries. Martha says Maggie took up golf at this point mostly to please the Wardles, and Maggie's college friends remember hearing her say so. She was now in charge of the trips to her father's side of the world each summer, and between Kalamazoo and South Carolina there were countless opportunities for Rob to disappear or lag behind. The summer she turned seventeen, she called from the Atlanta airport, distraught because Rob had wandered off and couldn't be found, and the flight was boarding. Finally, Martha said, "You've got to get on the plane, Maggie. Just *go*." Maggie often played peacemaker in the conflicts between Rob and his father, who was unused to the daily struggle of dealing with Rob's condition and tended to erupt when Rob would, for example, dismantle the stereo.

A particular draw for Maggie to her father's world was his sister Megan, who, with her husband, Mike, had adopted eight children from around the world. Something about this multiracial family galvanized Maggie. She was "very attached to them," says Rick, who believes that this familial microcosm "opened her eyes to the world a lot." She loved visiting the huge family, taking photos, imagining herself as the mother of a brood of kids. As an interesting counterpoint to Aunt Megan on the Omilian side was Rick's sister, Aunt Susan, who lives in Connecticut and shares Maggie's birthday: a single woman, a lawyer specializing in sexual harassment and violence against women. If indeed Maggie felt the pull of two distinctly different paths for women, they were embodied very clearly, very close to home.

The class differences that shaded Maggie's extended family also came at her sideways from her peers. Rick remembers the social landscape of the high school as rugged, with nasty cliques running the show. The rich kids at Plainwell High migrate in from nearby Lake Doster, and their brand-consciousness sometimes found its perfect victim in Maggie. She talked to her mother about being teased. Martha stresses the irony: "Nobody ever knew what Maggie was worth."

A potential heiress in the guise of a high-school nerd. A girl described by friends as "quiet," who nonetheless "giggled a lot and had this really infectious laugh." A gentle, nurturing soul inside a ferocious competitor. A shy girl with a "feisty and sometimes catty side to her. . . . Her opinion was made known very quickly." A star student who minimized her own accomplishments and abilities. A girl with the chops for a high-powered career and fantasies of mothering a brood of kids. A girl both drawn to and exasperated by neediness and dependence in boys. Maggie's contradictions only point to her complexity—and to the larger complexities of being a girl in her time and place.

That spring the Plainwell High School *Trojan Torch* featured an article on the top ten seniors, with a group photo and biographical sketches of each student. Maggie stands just behind Sarah Ayres, wearing a long skirt and short-sleeved sweater, her hair swept over one shoulder. Her accomplishments are listed, and then: "Her life ambition is to have a family and be happy."

In contrast, the résumé Maggie presented to prospective colleges was unambiguous, and it was a record to make admissions counselors drool: Impeccable 4.0 grade-point average, heavy in science. Three instruments: piano in the school jazz band, first-chair French horn in the symphonic band, mellophone in the marching band. Basketball and golf teams. A year in student senate. Assistant editor and feature editor of *The Trojan Torch*. A National Honor Society peer tutor in science. Jobs at the local funeral home, owned by Sarah's father, and at the construction firm owned by Martha's brother, Maggie's uncle Pete, along with the usual babysitting gigs. In her final year at Plainwell High, Maggie earned certificates for outstanding achievement in science, journalism, and jazz band; a Trustees' Award of Excellence from Kellogg Community College; a Michigan Interscholastic Press Association Award of Merit; a President's Award for Educational Excellence; a National Student-Athlete Day Award; and her school's award from the American Chemical Society. To clinch the deal, she also received a Michigan Competitive Scholarship to help with tuition. When she graduated in June of 1998, Margaret Lynn Wardle was a shining arrow, aimed into the twenty-first century and far beyond Plainwell, Michigan.

Her admission essay for Kalamazoo College, which describes the most influential person in her life, portrays Sarah's mother, dying of cancer at the time Maggie was applying to colleges. "Though her body is dying, her spirit is still thriving," she writes. "Every time I see her, I am impressed with her inner strength. She makes me think about the value of life—when I talk to her she revives my love of life." Kalamazoo awarded Maggie a forty-thousand-dollar merit scholarship. Perhaps this tipped the scales away from the eastern schools she was considering, some of which would have taken her closer to the Wardles. Instead—perhaps significantly—she chose proximity to her mother and the stepfather who had functioned as her father for sixteen years. As a talented young scientist, certified by the ACS, she was also drawn to Kalamazoo's powerful academic reputation. Her journey, then, would start with a ten-mile trip down the road, along with her comrade from Plainwell High's class of 1998, Brooke Nobis. While Martha and Rick had encouraged Maggie's far-reaching college search, they were secretly relieved when she chose the tiny campus close to home. "We were glad when Maggie decided on K," says Rick. "We thought she'd be safer."

2

Like a large portion of her class, Maggie came to K intending to major in the sciences, "to become a doctor, because that was something [her father] would approve of," according to Martha Omilian. Martha thinks Maggie joined the golf team, as well, "to please that side of the family." Maggie's friend Kelly Schulte says, "Golf was important to her, but had it not been important to her dad," she might not have played. But the team was Maggie's entrée to the college and became a significant sisterhood for her. One of its members was Heidi Fahrenbacher, who had transferred out of Plainwell High as a freshman. She and Maggie renewed their friendship, but Maggie quickly began running with another crowd. In the weeks of practice before the other students arrived on campus, Maggie and teammate Leza Frederickson, from Brighton, north of Ann Arbor, became tight very quickly. Shortly before the academic year began, Leza became friends with a group of four young women, Michigan girls who, as Leza and Maggie were practicing their golf swings and putts, were rappelling down cliffs and hiking through the Canadian woods as part of Land/Sea, Kalamazoo College's powerful wilderness experience.

"I remember we went over to Crissey [Hall] to pick up Leza for dinner," Kelly Schulte recalls, "and she said, 'Oh, do you mind if Maggie comes along?'" Maggie lived in a single room in a suite in Severn Hall, just a few steps away. "It just seems like that was the first moment we [all] became friends," Kelly says, "and after that we were pretty much inseparable."

Leza Frederickson and the Land/Sea contingent—Kelly Schulte, Erin Rome, Nandini Sonnad, and J'nai Leafers—all saw Maggie as somehow more mature than the rest of them. Erin Rome didn't realize for a while that Maggie was a first-year. Compared to "some of us who were still figuring things out," Nandini Sonnad says, Maggie "really had her act together. She was that ridiculous person who could do everything."

Maggie was one of the first people Dan Poskey met at Kalamazoo. "She had a great sense of humor and a beautiful smile," he says. One of the first things she said to him was "I never stress," and he subsequently discovered, to his amazement, that it was true. "I remember Maggie being very calm," he says. "I never once heard her yell or even raise her voice." She maintained an even keel in the face of both academic pressures and the dramas in her friends' lives. Kelly Schulte says, "It's like she was eighteen, but she was thirty. When you go to college, you're thrown in with all these new people, and you have no boundaries and no limits. She never lost sight of her priorities."

That sense of firm priorities—family, friends, school, golf, in that order—is something many people underscore in describing Maggie, distinguishing her from the general first-year population. "She was so confident. . . that I was intimidated by her," says Leza, yet in Kelly's words, "she just exuded gentleness." Her new friends discovered only gradually that Maggie was an academic star, because she never talked about it: "She was very humble about all of her accomplishments, about how smart she was, and talented. Once you got to know her you found that out about her, but she was never overt."

As this group of six young women coalesced, what emerged as Maggie's particular gift was an extraordinary quality of attention—which probably accounts for her uncanny ability to keep her priorities straight. Leza says, "I looked forward to practice every day because I knew that I could have Maggie all to myself for two hours. She had the ability to make me feel like I was the only person in the world." J'nai Leafers puts it in strikingly similar terms: "She had this way of making whoever she was talking to feel like you two were best friends, like she knew about everything in your life ever and she wanted to be the one to fix whatever the problem was. She listened to every word and gave you very straightforward advice, no matter how brutal it was." Leza agrees that Maggie could be blunt, saying, "She told me the truth about any situation I found myself in, and that was very refreshing to me."

As far as the other five girls were concerned, Maggie had only one flaw: she had brought with her from Plainwell a deplorable sense of fashion, which they immediately set out to correct. "Maggie was always really nerdy in high school," Heidi Fahrenbacher reminds us. "She was in band." When Maggie first arrived on campus, "the girls on the golf team made fun of her pants because they were tapered, so they made her get rid of them and buy boot-cut jeans." The pumps and loafers also had to go. Kelly Schulte remembers "the khaki pants and the blue shoes, her little tennis shoes." Her bouncing ponytail became a kind of trademark. "God love her," Erin Rome laughs, "she was so cute." One night these daughters of the great age of makeovers took Maggie on, with stunning results. Just before dinner, Erin recalls, "We sat her down and said, 'We're going to do your hair and put you in some different clothes.' We cut her hair, we put her in some outfit, we took her to the caf[eteria], and *all* the guys were like, 'Who's THAT?!' It was *insane*!"

There is no denying the rush Maggie must have felt upon walking into the cafeteria and drawing a virtual tsunami of male attention. But she and J'nai—who was from Muskegon, on the west coast of Michigan—both saw a distinct divide between the girls from the wealthy suburbs of Detroit and the west-Michigan crowd, and they were stunned by the "easterners'" emphasis on fancy cars and clothing labels. The wealthier east-Michigan girls were the more avid partiers, too, says J'nai, who saw herself and Maggie striving to be dutiful students. In all of J'nai's photos, Maggie is dressed in borrowed clothes. Maggie loathed snobbery and materialism as much as ever—in fact, she complained about it to her parents—but she also borrowed more fashionable clothes and let the girls cut her hair. She bought a leather jacket, which became her signature article of clothing, even in the coldest weather.

People who knew Maggie in high school tend to speak of this time in her life as an emergence, a flowering, and these cosmetic and sartorial adjustments were certainly part of that process. Her initial shyness started to drop away. Family friend Beth Green, a Kalamazoo College alumna, wrote, "She blossomed from a shy, quiet academic into a shining, accomplished young woman . . . brimming with potential and yet so humble."

The old geekiness was gone—if you don't count the French horn, which she played in the K concert band despite the sarcasm of her friends, who nonetheless faithfully showed up for the concerts. "Oftentimes," says Dan Poskey, "I think people as smart as Maggie are 'off balance' in college—either by being socially inept or demonstrating a superiority complex. Maggie, however, went to the bar and partied as easily as she got As on exams." As she got to know the Kalamazoo bars, she also started smoking, in true college-student style. As a fellow student put it, she was "getting away from being a girl from Plainwell," trying on a worldlier, sexier persona, cultivating the unexplored territory beyond the bounds of the Smart Girl, the Good Girl. But she did her exploring without falling off the edge of the map. She could party with the best of them and then get serious, focused, and academic, says J'nai, "in a heartbeat."

You might say Maggie was honing that edge that Brooke Nobis had seen in her back home, that snarky, sarcastic, outspoken part of her. It's visible in one of her senior pictures, where she stands, in jeans and a black sweater, arms folded across her chest, her head slightly tilted, smiling insouciantly, her silky brown-blonde hair falling over her shoulders. Her golf coach, Lyn Maurer, sketches a memory that captures, among other features, this insouciance:

> I see her walking jauntily down the fairway with her ponytail bouncing from the back of her golf cap. I see her walking a little slower at the end of a long, hot eighteen-hole match, her prized Taylor Made clubs slung over her shoulder, but still with that mischievous little smile creeping across her face. I see her arriving at practice angered by unfair or unjust circumstances she had observed. I can picture that little quirk in her lip as

she tried to hide her smile and appear serious when she was teasing me.

Stephanie Schrift knew the sly side of Maggie, too. They met in a calculus class that first fall and wound up in a study group together. They all struggled with the coursework, but Maggie struggled less. "She was never behind," Stephanie marveled. Stephanie, a serious feminist, says, "I remember her joking me, saying, 'I'm getting my MRS degree.' I was like, 'Maggie, come *on!*' She would say, 'I just think it's funny that people say that.'"

For Maggie's first term at K, Sean was still very much in the picture. In fact, initially, Erin Rome remembers, "She didn't hang out with us a lot because . . . he was in a fraternity over at Western, and she was spending a lot of time over there." Maggie & Co. would trek over to the frat house to hang out. But Maggie and Sean "were kind of on-and-off," Erin continues, because he was "unstable." The dependency that had troubled their relationship in high school intensified: Maggie broke the relationship off; Sean wouldn't let go. One night when he showed up at her dorm and Maggie wouldn't see him, he refused to leave, calling repeatedly on the house phone until finally Maggie called the college's security office and had him removed. "When he got back to his fraternity house, he said he was going to handcuff himself to his car," Kelly Schulte recalls. "He was a little nutty in the head, too." According to Erin, "He was a little strange. I never could really understand it: she was so pretty, so smart, so much fun—and these *guys!* Her taste was *odd*. But he was fine," she hastens to add. "He was harmless."

So "harmless" that, on another occasion, when he was scheduled to drop something off for Maggie, she enlisted two guys in a neighboring dorm to stand by, ready to intervene if Sean got difficult. One of them was Nick Duiker. A burly sophomore football player, Nick shared a kitchenette suite on the ground floor of Severn. "We never closed our door, so people just kind of showed up and hung out in our room," he recalls. Leza, Maggie, and Kelly were frequent visitors. After the episode with Sean, Maggie "kind of made it known that she liked me," says Nick. "She was pretty persuasive. I had a girlfriend at the time, and I said, 'Maggie, I'm flattered, but I'm going with someone.' She kind of pursued me. It was more like joking and fun, not like she was throwing herself at me." "Come on," she'd tease him, "you don't need to be with her!" But Nick insisted that he wanted to give his new relationship a chance. With Sean now out of the picture, says Nick, "I think she was on the rebound."

It's a familiar story: the Hometown Honey carried over into the first year of college, like the teddy bear brought from home but soon relegated to history. In this way, Maggie, while an exceptional young woman, was also a sister to the thousands of Michigan girls I have taught at Kalamazoo over the past thirty years: Girls from small communities in Michigan, where they emerged as stars in their schools. Girls who are barely on speaking terms with a B grade and are completely unacquainted with Cs. Girls who were "geeks" for some period, sometimes precisely because of their academic success or uncool extracurricular interests. Girls privileged by class, most by race. Many of them come from split and reconfigured families that complicate their lives. They have long lists of awards and certificates, records of lively civic participation. And so many of them are torn by those cross-currents at the center of female adolescence in the United States: the burning desire to do something in the world, to be self-reliant and self-respecting, versus the driving need to be seen as attractive, to be liked, to be sure of male attention and desire, to escape solitude, to feel oneself in a nexus of deep, sustaining relationships. That tension comes partly from adolescence, partly from femininity, partly from American culture, and probably a great many other factors as well.

To "hook up" as soon as possible is almost a requirement of a first-year, affirming that one will succeed socially in this new world, that one belongs. With Sean in the past, Maggie seemed to feel a pressing need to find a replacement. Nick—a year older, an athlete, a gregarious host, someone who had already served as a knight-protector—presented a very attractive possibility. For a while, Maggie and Nick remained friends. Then one night in the winter of 1999, Maggie showed up and raised the issue again, and again Nick gently turned her down. At that point—almost as if she were offering Nick a last chance, or asking for one herself—she disclosed that she was considering dating someone else. "I like this Neenef guy," Nick remembers her saying. "And I said, 'Honestly, you need to stay away from Neenef. *Don't*. Just don't.'"

—

3

WOUNDED BIRD

1

It's difficult to find a picture of Neenef Odah smiling, though the first thing his good friends mention is his comedy. Dan Poskey says he often smiled, but "more like a half-smile." The photo that comes closest, among those I've seen, is the photo on his green card, taken when he was around twelve. And even there, it's not quite a smile; it's more a hopeful upturning of eyes and lips, as if something good might just be coming. Perhaps he thought it waited in the United States.

Neenef was born in Iraq in May of 1979, the second son of Assyrian parents, Wilson Odah, a physician, and Susan Aprim Shima Odah. "Assyrian," a transnational term, refers to a particular Christian ethnic group in the Middle East, descendents of the earliest Christians. Their first language is Aramaic, the language spoken by Jesus. In the sixteenth century, Assyrians joined with the Roman Catholic Church and remain under its jurisdiction today, while retaining their ancient language and rites. Within Iraq, Assyrians often identify as Chaldean Catholics, descendents of the Babylonian Empire, though the Odahs apparently do not; while Iraqi Chaldeans are not taught at home to speak Arabic, Neenef apparently spoke and wrote the language.

Assyrians in Iraq did not generally fare well under Saddam Hussein, although some Iraqi Christians, such as Foreign Minister Tariq Assiz, were able to achieve prominence. For the most part, however, Saddam and his Baath party were pan-Arab and secularist in orientation, intent on unifying Iraq within an Arab national identity. Assyrians, then, felt pressure to assimilate. Saddam's policies toward minorities were undoubtedly a factor in Neenef's family's decision to emigrate, not to mention the fact that the region was in turmoil that would culminate in the first Gulf War. Neenef also told friends that his family's priority on education was a primary motivation for their leaving. Safety, freedom, opportunity—the traditional immigrant mix.

Neenef told Martha and Rick Omilian that his family had been very wealthy but had had to leave much of their wealth behind. He said that they had been on vacation in London when the situation at home suddenly became critical—perhaps at the outset of the first Gulf War—and they simply never returned. From England they moved to the United States when Neenef was about twelve. They went to Seattle, where Neenef attended Seattle Preparatory Academy, a Jesuit secondary school, graduating in 1997.

By the time Neenef was ready for college, the family had developed a Kalamazoo connection, most likely through the large Chaldean community in southeastern Michigan. A cousin attended Western Michigan University, where an old family friend and distant relation also taught. It may have been this professor who told the Odahs about Kalamazoo College; he was sending his own daughter, Neenef's age, to K. It had been decided that Neenef would study science, preparatory to becoming a physician like his father, so K's reputation for premedical education and medical-school placement probably figured in the decision as well.

The first thing his peers at K tell you about Neenef will probably have to do with his family. The friends who loved him clearly saw him against a dark, troubled backdrop of family life characterized by patriarchal domination and intense pressure to succeed. According to one story, by the time Neenef arrived at K, his older brother had in fact jumped ship: unable or unwilling to sustain the role of Eldest Son in such a context, he was estranged from the family, living on his own. If true, this would have left Neenef heir apparent to all the expectations—about grades, career, masculinity, culture—that his brother had fled.

German professor and soccer coach Hardy Fuchs met the Odah family when they visited K in the spring of 1997, Neenef's senior year in high school. Above all, he recalls Neenef's father, a tall man, well dressed, who emphasized the family's being Assyrian and explained that this meant they were Christian. Even in those days before 9/11, Neenef's father felt it was important to counter assumptions that the family was Muslim, especially in such a midwestern Protestant enclave.

Greg Mahler, provost and academic vice president at K at the time, met Wilson Odah and son on Neenef's first day of college. "I was right in front of Mandelle [Administration Building] and they were walking up the hill, looking like they were lost, and I got into a conversation with them. Neenef was a scared, quiet incoming freshman. And the father was a very nice Middle Eastern father who was very excited about the adventures that his son was going to have at Kalamazoo College. And we talked about the West Coast, him coming so far away from home." Mahler, who had gone to Oberlin after a childhood in California, empathized.

Unfortunately, Neenef would remain that scared, quiet boy long past orientation week. Heidi Fahrenbacher remembers, "His eyes always looked sad." Neenef was a regular visitor to the suite where the math and computer science faculty have their offices. Its manager for many years has been Peggy Cauchy, who remembers him as "slight, tense, quiet and with rather sad, haunting eyes."

In the fall of 1997, Neenef was enrolled in the double whammy of the premed curriculum at K: Evolution and Introductory Chemistry. In the latter, his lab partner was Nick Duiker. They were friendly at first, but Nick rapidly smelled trouble: "He reminded me of some of the guys I used to hang out with in Cleveland and why I actually went to college somewhere *outside* of Cleveland. He was just kind of bad news— wanted to fight. Talked about how he was a black belt in karate and whatever. He was a little twerp who wanted to get into fights." Nick understood the dynamics of machismo at work: the smaller, insecure kid—Neenef was much shorter, and very slight—spots the alpha male and needs to take him on. For Nick, that scenario represented a past-life regression: "I didn't want that part of life anymore. [When I came to college] I made a conscious decision to get away from that." In what would become a pattern in Neenef's life, he pursued Nick, calling and attempting to sustain a friendship, but Nick wasn't having any. "I just kind of backed away from him. . . . He was one I really didn't want to have anything to do with."

But plenty of Neenef's friends never saw the darkness Nick spotted in him. For Frank Church, Neenef was, first of all, "warm, sympathetic, funny." Along with many others, he recalls Neenef playing soccer by himself, up and down the narrow linoleum hallways of his dorm, the ball smacking the walls and doors. From anybody else it would have been annoying, says Frank. But apart from yelling, "Take it outside, Neenef!" the other residents seem to have tolerated it with good humor. Neenef struck up a lasting friendship with Nick Duiker's roommate, Nick Porada, with whom he developed a traveling ritual: wherever they were on campus, if someone yelled, "Handstand!" they had to drop and kick their feet into the air immediately, and he who balanced longest won.

LaVange Barth, a year behind Neenef, was "immediately struck by him." Neenef called her "cousin," his term of endearment for particularly beloved friends. It is a common immigrant gesture, creating extended family in an adopted country. LaVange also saw Neenef's sexual appeal: "He had a very cute, teasing way about him and was a natural flirt." Lavange describes Neenef as "very kind to women and drawn to them socially. Not in a creepy manner, but it was obvious that he'd been raised around women and was perhaps most comfortable around them. The first time we went to his room he showed me the family pictures on the wall and spoke with great love for his mother and sisters. He clearly treasured these women." Other friends also recall his being especially drawn to women for friendship and emotional sustenance.

One of Neenef's warmest friendships was with another premed, Nancy El-Shamaa. "I found out he was Iraqi," she says, "and I am Egyptian; there's not a whole lot of other Middle Eastern people [at K]. He was a cool guy, and we became friends pretty soon. We began having a lot of mutual friends. We just started catching dinner together every once in a while; he'd walk me to class or whatever." Friends recall the two of them talking over issues of race and ethnicity. But Nancy also confirms the Neenef that Frank saw. "All the times that I hung out with him it was like nonstop laughter," she recalls. "He wasn't one of those friends that I'd go to to talk about deep, dark issues. He was someone I'd go to after a long day of studying just [for] having a very pleasant time. . . . I don't know if I'd use 'charismatic' as a word. He was introverted and he did keep a lot to himself. But when he was with a few close friends, he was just a riot."

Nancy introduced Neenef to Caitlin Gilmet, whose first recollection of him is a crucial part of the warm memory of her first year at college:

> K is small enough that everyone hung out in the same cafeteria, but it was divided by invisible lines for its cliques—jocks on the "other side," theater and philosophy geeks in the smoking room, our motley crew over by the juice machine. Nancy knew everyone and was always inviting new people to sit with us at lunch or dinner. I think we all liked those afternoons or nights in the cafeteria—to me, at least, it was one of the first times I'd ever felt cool. We genuinely appreciated each other, and it was so easy to meet interesting friends, students who were equally as excited to be living away from home and learning about the world. It was one of the best parts of college for me.
>
> Neenef was shy, but he had a terrific sense of humor—it was kind of sly. He'd listen to the wild chorus of voices for a while, then wait for the perfect moment to drop some wry response. He knew he was funny, and he'd sit there smirking, enjoying himself. He loved to tease and to be teased, loved sarcastic humor. He listened well and picked up on nuances in language.
>
> One of the only clear pictures of Neenef I can recall is him at the juice machine with a plastic glass, turning toward our table to joke back and forth with Nancy. He was wearing jeans and Adidas sneakers, and he had a huge smile on his face. I think I remember it because when I look back at that time in my life, I remember being amazed at how happy I felt all the time and how happy everyone around me also seemed to feel.

Caitlin was living in DeWaters Hall, K's smallest dorm, "known also as the 'Alice DeWaters Retirement Community and Convent' because it was the quietest residence hall on campus. The halls echoed, and something about the place seemed more sterile than the other dorms. I remember living in a corner and feeling isolated, something that changed completely when I moved into Trowbridge later that year and came to love its messy, noisy circus."

Neenef lived in the dorm next door to DeWaters, Trowbridge, known locally as "Trow." "There are intentional communities and then those communities that come together by coincidence," Caitlin says, "and this was the latter—a group of boys that all seemed to fit, different as they certainly were." She and her roommate "spent lots of time procrastinating down there, since they always seemed to be playing music, goofing off in the hallway, or plotting some kind of adventure."

Frank Church says Neenef rarely talked about his family. On a campus full of kids from midwestern white-bread families, "He was from somewhere else," says Frank—and he doesn't mean Seattle. But in fact, as soon as you got past Neenef's initial reserve or his comic antics and earned his trust, you heard about his family. Neenef told Nick Duiker that his dad dominated the family, and he explained the subordination of women as a traditional part of Middle Eastern cultures. In the picture of his family he gave Nancy El-Shamaa, "his mom was just trying to make peace in the house," comforting the children after her husband disciplined them. Neenef told Maggie's parents that when his father was displeased with his mother, he sent her away to visit her sister. To Nancy, as to LaVange, it was clear that the place at the center of his heart was reserved for his younger brothers and sisters. "He *loved* his siblings," LaVange says. "He was very close to his brothers and sisters [and] they *adored* him. I think they really idolized him. He was their big brother; he always shopped for gifts to take home with him for Thanksgiving or Christmas. . . . If there was any sort of happiness in his family for him, it was his siblings." He could love them completely, without reservation; in return, he could see himself reflected in their eyes at twice his size. Nowhere else in Neenef Odah's life would he find this combination.

I once asked a class of first-year students about the most important thing they'd learned in their first year at college. "Humility," one young man fired back, seconded ruefully by the rest of the class. When someone who got a 3.5 or 4.0 in high school without breaking a sweat hits a demanding collegiate curriculum, what usually gives is his or her sense of identity, particularly if it's deeply rooted in being the Smart Kid. Among those who tend to bounce back most quickly are the athletes; they understand what it means to move from the minors to the majors, third string to first. But they all die a little when they see that first C. Even Maggie Wardle had to learn to accept less than As—"but not much less," says Rick Omilian. Most of them have to swallow much more disappointment and self-doubt. Usually, as I tell them after the first Evolution exam, their grades pop up again when they acclimate to the waters in which they're now swimming. But that kind of patience with the process comes hard at eighteen—especially if you're already obsessed with grad school or med school or law school. And even more so if your parents are on your back.

It doesn't really matter what Neenef's first-term grade point average looked like. The pertinent fact is that it wasn't good enough for his father. Nor did Wilson Odah like it that Neenef's initial academic advisor was Ahmed Hussen in Economics. At K, like many liberal arts colleges, students usually have academic advisors outside their prospective majors for their first two years, a strategy designed to encourage exploration. But for many, if not most people coming from educational contexts outside the first world, higher education—a terrific luxury—is fundamentally about preparing for professional life, not about exploration, self-discovery, or learning for learning's sake. Mr. Odah was one of these. He began to call Ahmed, upset about his son's performance. Parental phone calls are not unheard of, especially in recent years, but they are rare, since parents generally know that faculty are prohibited by the Family Education Rights and Privacy Act from discussing a student's academic performance. Ahmed, who came to the United States from Ethiopia as a high-school exchange student, returned for college, and stayed to begin his career, saw another factor in Odah's dissatisfaction with his advising. "I was not exactly a white person," he says. At the end of the winter term, Neenef told Ahmed that his father wanted him to switch advisors.

Ahmed and Neenef had been discussing abandoning the premed curriculum for computer science; Ahmed thought that as a devoted gamer maybe Neenef would find his academic groove there. Alyce Brady, the director of the computer science program, became his new advisor. To many parents in contemporary culture, computer science represents a practical and potentially lucrative area of study. But Wilson Odah had the patriarch's sense of tradition combined with the immigrant's eye on status and prestige in a new culture, where physician easily trumps computer programmer. His son's defection from the paternal footpath was yet another sign that this expensive college might be a mistake and that Neenef was not living up to expectations.

So it was only with his father's misgivings that Neenef was sent back to Kalamazoo for a second year. Misgivings and an ultimatum: a 4.0, or else financial support would be withdrawn.

According to LaVange Barth, "It was clear to all of us who were close to Neenef that he was not doing well psychologically" during the winter term of his sophomore year. "Prior to exams," she remembers, "Neenef took an absurd number of NoDoz and stayed up for a few days. Needless to say, his grades did not improve with such tactics!" The NoDoz overdose landed him in the emergency room and entered the campus lore as a suicide attempt. NoDoz might represent an unusual way to die, but at the very least the overdose points to Neenef's desperation.

And his grades did not improve: Bs, Cs and sometimes Ds, even in computer science. Marigene Arnold, Neenef's professor for an anthropology class, recalls, "He and I had some *hard* conversations when he was my student, because he didn't do very well, and he was under tremendous pressure from his father to do well. He would come and sit in my office for, it seemed like, hours and hours, just kind of paralyzed, under a tremendous amount of pressure." His academic advisor, Alyce Brady, remembers that same paralysis:

We sometimes talk about the stereotypical students slumped way back in their chairs, and that's how I think of him. So he was *slumped*. Very quiet. And not contributing. . . . My impression was that he wasn't the kind of natural student who loves to be here, wants to be learning. Almost as if this was someone else's idea, as if he was doing it but he was sort of checked out. And as his advisor, I learned that it was very definitely [due to] parental pressure that he was here. I learned that he had thought about maybe transferring to Western, where he had a cousin, and I tried to be really open about it—"That seems like more of a natural place for you, you are more comfortable there"—because I had this very strong feeling that he was not . . . happy here, not comfortable here. And so I didn't quite say, "Yeah, I think that would be a really good idea—you should leave K and go to Western," but I did try to support him if he thought this was a good idea, to follow through on that. The more I worked with him, the more I felt . . . that he was doing what he was doing because he was told to do that.

Among Neenef's friends, the long shadow of Wilson Odah was well known. Nancy El-Shamaa says his father would "threaten him constantly. Almost every other time I would talk to Neenef he would talk about" his father's demands, mostly laughing them off: "Oh, I talked to my dad the other day, and he's pissed off that I'm getting Bs and Cs, so if I'm not here next semester, don't be shocked; my dad's going to pull me out of here and make me go home." Nancy interpreted it as the usual student hyperbole, until Neenef's jocularity finally broke. "I was using his computer," she remembers, "and he'd just gotten a grade back and it wasn't that good, and he said, 'Oh, my dad's going to kill me!'" And then the dam burst. "I honestly don't give a shit anymore," Neenef said to Nancy. "I hate him! He's a fucking psychopath! He thinks I'm going to get straight As at K, and I'm working my ass off, and he's still not happy with it!"

Nancy was shocked by "this unbelievable amount of control his dad had over him. The first thought in his head wasn't, 'Oh, I got this kind of bad grade, and I want to get into this grad school, so I have to improve it.' It was 'My dad's going to kill me.' Like he was a three-year-old. He was a twenty-year-old man at that point—or guy or young kid—and he was *terrified* about what his dad would say about his grades! Not upset—he was *scared*." What still angers Nancy is that Neenef's father never did make good on his ultimatums. "So why that emotional threat, emotional abuse?" The blade simply hung over his head, reminding him constantly of his inadequacy and making him feel even more the outsider at K, a temporary "resident alien."

Much as his friends sympathized, few of them could really understand the cultural context for Neenef's struggle. "Neenef described his father in terms that I can now see are very culturally specific," says LaVange Barth.

> He had much higher expectations for Neenef than his sisters: that Neenef was to be a doctor was a matter of course. The family had immigrated to the U.S. [to] ensure quality higher education. The family looked to Neenef for financial support in their future. Neenef was very proud of his family and his ancestry, making sure that people understood that he was not Syrian and patiently explaining the difference for those with little understanding of the Middle East. Words like "obligation" and "duty"

were prominent in Neenef's familial experience in a way that few Waspy American children understand.

Neenef told LaVange his father said that if he failed, "You will be dead to me." Whether or not such threats were sincere, she says, "Neenef took them very seriously."

This second year, Neenef was rooming with Nick Porada, and among Nick's circle was Maggie's buddy Erin Rome. In her, Neenef initially found another empathetic, receptive woman to hear him. "He and I had some pretty in-depth conversations," Erin says. Like Nancy, Erin saw the power and danger of Neenef's father. She says, "I *know* his dad was abusive. Well, abusive by our standards, but they come from Iraq—I mean, maybe the way he treated his family was normal over there, but I know he was *very* hard on the kids." In an era when the term "abusive" tends to be applied to an extremely wide range of parental behavior, it becomes difficult to know what it means and where it genuinely applies, especially across cultures. In any case, while it may follow that Wilson Odah treated Neenef and his sisters differently because of his cultural beliefs, it is dangerous to assume that he was abusive toward Neenef simply because he was Assyrian. Nancy El-Shamaa, coming from a cultural background that she saw as similar to Neenef's in many ways, was outraged by the pressure on him, and actually uses the term "abuse." When do parental expectations and empty threats become abuse? When they so badly damage a child that he himself becomes an abuser?

———

Twenty-year-old man, or guy, or young kid: Neenef was, of course, all of the above. Is it any wonder that his fury at his father, his self-loathing, his cultural outsider status, and his thwarted masculinity expressed themselves in crude, immature ways, such as through looking for fights with other men, often authority figures like his father? His friend Chris Wilson recalls being in Neenef's room just after he had received a bad grade. Chris knew about the academic pressure from home. Suddenly Neenef said, "You know what I want to do? I want to go over to my professor's house, and I actually want to shoot him." Chris laughed it off, but Neenef insisted, "No, no, I'm gonna do it!"

It's only in retrospect that the incident becomes chilling for Chris. "I didn't take it too seriously, but the fact that he reiterated it . . . If you're kidding, just drop it. He was really excited, very impassioned in the moment because he had gotten the grade, so he was very upset. It didn't occur to me that he would do it or that he would be able to procure the means to do it." Not to mention that Neenef blamed the grade wholly on the professor, as if he himself bore none of the responsibility for earning it.

It is probably no more surprising, given the picture emerging here, that in his first year-and-a-half at college, Neenef became known for intense, quick infatuations that never worked out. "He developed a crush on every girl he met," says Caitlin Gilmet. "It was me one week, someone else another—but it felt harmless, and he certainly wasn't the only guy at K who couldn't believe his luck, living so close to so many pretty, interesting women. Like all of us, he was figuring himself out." Others recall spurned advances followed by sulking, resentment, or rage.

Erin Rome believes that Neenef's dysfunctional family system also helps to explain his anxiety about securing a girlfriend—including the sexual anxiety—and his difficulty accepting breakups. Along with the 4.0 ultimatum from his father came a demand that Neenef have no women in his life—an even less reasonable demand, if that's possible, to make of a young man at a tough college. Says Erin, "Obviously that's the reason he was so keen on having a girlfriend, you know?" Two of Neenef's friends of color, Nancy El-Shamaa and Chris Wilson, remember the edict as being more specific: "Especially no white girls."

Of Neenef's relationship with Maggie, her friend Kelly Schulte says, "The fact that he was dating a white girl, instead of someone of his own ethnicity, would have been unheard of for his dad." But whether in defiance of the parental edict or in pursuit of the racial ideal, Neenef continued to seek out white women. One of them was Stephanie Miller. In three dates with Neenef, she learned all she needed to know about him. Stephanie came to Kalamazoo with something none of her peers brought to college: a nine-month-old son, Andrew. The boy's father had wanted nothing to do with either of them and had then suddenly died of a heart attack at age nineteen, four months after Andrew's birth. Stephanie faced down abundant prejudice and contumely as a pregnant teenager. But with an exceptionally supportive family behind her, she headed to Kalamazoo, "more determined than ever to get an above average education and raise an above average child—just to prove everyone wrong." She lived in St. Joseph, Michigan, about forty-five minutes west of Kalamazoo on the Lake Michigan shore, with her parents, who cared for Andrew while she was in class. Sometimes Andrew came with her, becoming a popular campus character. On a campus where children are rare, they are treated like celebrities.

In a religion course in the winter term of 1998, Stephanie met Neenef. "When he showed an interest in me," she relates, "I assumed he was like most other students there—open to the idea that my raising a child while going to college wasn't insane or a repercussion of not getting an abortion soon enough or classlessness, etc." Male attention was particularly reassuring to Stephanie: "After having Andrew, I was convinced no man my age would want me." Knowing all about Andrew, Neenef asked her out, and they subsequently went to hear a speaker on campus. As they walked back toward the dorms, Neenef held her hand and kissed her. They wound up hanging out with mutual friends—Neenef's arm around her the whole evening. Even given how speedily college "relationships" can develop, it's clear that what Stephanie accepted as gratifying physical attention, reassurance that she could lead something like a normal college student's life, Neenef interpreted as skipping over the preliminaries and establishing Stephanie as his "girlfriend."

After a week of phone calls and e-mails, they went out again, on a Thursday night, this time to a restaurant. As Neenef had no car, Stephanie drove. To her astonishment, he made it clear that it was very difficult for him to be in a car with a woman at the wheel. "He didn't want me to be in control, clearly," she says. "But he made some effort to let me know he was trying to change his attitude about women driving and being independent. I was stunned: women driving? He had to be kidding." Neenef explained the overt sexism in terms of his family background, which he then began to unfold for her.

He had found another mother figure—this time an actual mother. Stephanie describes herself as "that person with a sign on my forehead that reads, 'Will Listen and Comfort All Who Approach.'" She was a bit taken aback by how much Neenef revealed about his home life, given the brevity of their acquaintance. But that kind of intimate disclosure, common among young people, also works to speed other forms of intimacy. He told her that his father beat him, his brothers and cousins, and his mother. When Neenef brought home a bad grade, he told her, "He would be first beaten [and] then would have to have a long discussion about honor and obligation." Stephanie recognized the duality of Neenef's feelings for the dominant figure in his life. "He hated yet revered his father," she says. "He'd tell me, with hate in his voice, about some such incident and then end with something like, 'But I know why he did it, and it's made me a better person. It's why I could come to Kalamazoo for my education.'"

Neenef pressed for a third date on Saturday. When Stephanie explained that she had to be home in St. Joseph with Andrew on weekends, he offered to come home with her on Friday and stay over. She recognized that he was moving fast, but agreed—after all, her parents' house was safe. So there he was at family dinner—her parents skeptical but friendly, and Neenef responding to Andrew like the big brother he loved to be. After dinner they went to see *Titanic*. If Stephanie had had her doubts about the future of a relationship in which women driving was a problem, those doubts increased when Neenef read the film as the story of a "loose bitch" who gives up an upper-class life for one night with a lowlife who draws an erotic picture of her. After the film, Stephanie showed him around picturesque St. Joe, and they walked on the Lake Michigan pier in the winter darkness. Neenef had been studying her home and her town as a picture of middle-American tranquility that he couldn't quite understand; it seemed, he said, that she'd had a storybook childhood. Then he asked, "Weren't your parents mad when you ruined your future?"

Taken aback, Stephanie laughed and told him that her parents were beyond wonderful with her pregnancy. Neenef was incredulous. "Don't you feel guilty, not being punished?" he asked.

"I probably [did] at the time," Stephanie says, "but he shouldn't have been the person to say it out loud. As I was trying to steer the conversation in a new direction, he finished [it] for me, saying (an approximate quote), 'I guess the life you lead is punishment enough.'" But not enough for Neenef: he went on to surmise that Stephanie's "transgression" had incurred Andrew's father's death. "The person I am now would have smacked him," she says. "The younger version of Stephanie felt guilty, embarrassed, and forlorn."

The two of them stand there on the concrete pier at the edge of a little midwestern city, the big lake lashing away, the winter wind searing their faces. The American girl is thrust back into the hole she's been clawing her way out of for two years, the hole labeled "Slut," a century before labeled "Fallen Woman." America's adopted son, meanwhile, thrashes back and forth in his own mind, trying to assimilate the idea of a world where children's missteps meet with parental kindness and support. Could it be possible that sins don't incur severe punishment, that sinners don't *need* that punishment in order to vanquish their own guilt? The child of a father he at once adores and loathes like some terrible deity, Neenef can't believe in Stephanie's life without relinquishing the entire, deeply ingrained world view according to which he has been raised. He can't figure out whether this girl next to him is Lady Liberty or the whore of Babylon.

Back at Stephanie's parents' home again, they decided to watch TV, whereupon, in Stephanie's words, "mild making out ensued." Suddenly Neenef asked if she had a condom. Stephanie was struck by the contradiction embedded in his morality: "Hadn't he just been talking about what a mistake I'd made, and how it'd ruined not only my life, but many others' as well?" After a few minutes of discussion, she realized how, in Neenef's mind, this all made sense. "He could bed me without feeling guilty—I was already 'used,' and sex with someone who'd already had a baby could be exciting, clandestine, or even naughty-dirty." Exit Stephanie, who went upstairs to her bedroom and locked the door.

Maybe her analysis is correct; certainly that line of thinking isn't anomalous even among traditional American men. But perhaps the same cultural conflict that Neenef was struggling so clumsily and offensively to articulate on the pier was there on the family-room sofa as well. If the dissonance between home and school, Iraq and America remained a low hum in his daily life, it rose to a shriek around American women—with their sex-before-marriage, their "supportive" parents, their out-of-wedlock children, their infinite second chances, and their ready supplies of condoms.

On Saturday morning Stephanie hustled Neenef into the car, grabbed Andrew for security and comfort, and drove back to Kalamazoo in silence. As she pulled up behind Trowbridge, Neenef asked, "What's wrong with you this morning?"

"Nothing's wrong," she responded. "I just think we both know this isn't going to work out between us. It was fun, but I think we're looking for different things."

Neenef was surprised—and Stephanie was surprised to see it. He argued with her for several minutes, and then Andrew began to cry. Stephanie hushed Neenef, who brought his fist down on her dashboard. At this point she urged him to get out of the car, promising friendship but no more dates, ever. He kissed her cheek and held her face in his hands, got out of the car, and walked into the dorm. Stephanie headed back west, relieved.

On Sunday, she discovered through mutual friends that Neenef was MIA. Arriving on campus on Monday, she checked at his room, but he wasn't there. Neither did he show up for their religion class. Finally, around 6:00 p.m. Monday, she spotted him on the quad, his hand thick with bandages. He said he'd been walking around Kalamazoo since Sunday morning. After she had dropped him off, he had put his fist through a window. "Because you didn't want to be with me," he said. "I am always angry when I'm not wanted."

Stephanie urged him to get counseling, and that was the last she saw of him, except in passing. Winter turned to spring, and Stephanie began dating another student, Ben. To her astonishment, Neenef showed up at Ben's room one evening, challenging him to a fight later that night. News spread, as it tends to do in a small community, and finally reached Stephanie, who quickly came to campus. "I didn't know what to do. I went first to Neenef's, to ask him what on earth he was thinking. He told me he'd missed me, and that he was willing to fight over it. He also told me he'd heard Ben saying some nasty things about me—things that made him realize how he felt about me. I told him I was perfectly able to defend myself against Ben, and asked him not to take any action." Then she checked in on Ben, "a non-violent type," who said, "I'll let him hit me if it makes him feel better, but I'm a pussy; I can't fight. I don't need to, anyway." Neenef, meanwhile, called a mutual friend and told her "he was going to hit a brick wall" unless Stephanie would talk to him again. The friend went to Neenef in person. According to Stephanie, the friend said, "We all want you to get help." Neenef reassured her that he'd recover, but when she left, he did indeed go out and punch a brick wall, injuring his hand further. After charging that Ben had said "nasty" things about Stephanie, Neenef himself now told friends that she had "begged for sex" on one of their dates.

Today, Stephanie sees this absurd, heartrending episode in the context of having been an anomaly at K, a freshman mother. "Ultimately, I realized that I was somewhat of a freakish attraction for the culturally bound young man," she says, with empathetic perception. But I wonder if her motherhood was actually the factor that attracted Neenef. For Neenef, maybe every American woman was a freakish attraction, tapping all his raging, conflicted needs: comfort, sympathy, romance, sex, mothering, cultural assimilation, cultural authenticity, affirmed masculinity, social status—everything that would come with the magical Girlfriend, redeemer of his sad, confused life.

Neenef's fist-through-the-window story became well known on campus. When Neenef talked with Nancy El-Shamaa about it, he told her that college authorities stipulated anger-management counseling. "I don't know if he followed through," says Nancy. "I don't know if they made him follow through; I don't know any of the details on that. . . . Neenef and [Neenef's roommate] Nick [Porada] were the ones who told me this, and Nick was kind of laughing about it, and I said, 'You guys, that's not funny! That's really sad.'" Nick Porada turned the blame on the woman: "Oh, she was crazy; she was a bitch!" Nancy pressed on, urging Neenef, as others had done, to take advantage of the therapy the college provided: "Because I cared about him, and he was my friend, and I didn't think he had it in him to do really serious harm."

The aggression Nick Duiker immediately spotted in Neenef appeared more slowly to others, like Stephanie and Nancy—and Maggie's friend Erin Rome. At a party early in the fall of 1998, before Neenef and Maggie met, Erin asked Neenef to play the same protector's role that Maggie had assigned Nick Duiker. Pursued by a guy who was relentlessly coming on to her, she asked Neenef to pretend to be her boyfriend, "and we palled around the whole night, just so this other dude would leave me alone." But shortly thereafter, Neenef submarined their friendship, as he had his initial connection with Nick Duiker. Erin says, "He used to tease me that I liked Nick [Porada], which I truly didn't. It was very juvenile, but he said something that was really mean—I don't remember what—and I wouldn't speak to him. And he was so upset, [he] got all his friends to come up and say, 'Please forgive Neenef; he's so upset that you guys are having a fight!'" But for Erin, it was a turning point, similar to Nick Duiker's flash of insight. "I liked him a lot in the beginning," she says, but "after he said that really mean thing, I remember a red flag went up in my own mind, like 'Maybe he's not the type of guy I should be hanging around with.'"

Quick intimacy, then aggression, followed by the other party's withdrawal, followed by Neenef's repeated supplications: this pattern by no means characterized all of Neenef's relationships, but it was pronounced enough in his history at K to help define him—his neediness and loneliness, his interpersonal clumsiness, and above all, the lurking aggression that would suddenly fly out of him, just like that fist through the window or the explosive fantasy of blowing his professor away.

Neenef frequently made the claim that he had a black belt in karate. He told people that he was not legally allowed to use karate in a fight "because he knew how to kill people with one move," recalls LaVange Barth. She also remembers a tale that now strikes her as wildly improbable. "One weekend he went to Chicago to blow off steam following an argument with his father over bad grades," she relates, "and [he] was jumped in an alley. He claims he kicked the man in the head and left him for dead." At the time, she says, "his charm and boyishness normalized this story."

Neenef's warmth and vulnerability most likely offset the glimpses of darkness that many of his friends saw. Caitlin Gilmet recalls that

> After he died, I felt like people tried to paint Neenef as a recluse—the crazy computer science major plotting obsessively in his basement room. He wasn't like that at all. He was loving and exceptionally loyal to mutual friends like Nancy [El-Shamaa] and Alana Askew, whom he treated like family. He could be goofy, maybe immature, and I think it made people want to take care of him. He could be charming, but you also knew he wasn't terribly confident, and sometimes he'd get into grumpy funks and want to be left alone.

No one saw those "grumpy funks" or the tales of the hand through the window or the man left for dead in the alley as cause for serious alarm, perhaps because they seemed like aberrations in an otherwise kind and generous person. And as Neenef labored through his own personal purgatory, he still held his hand out to fellow travelers. "He was a good friend," Nancy El-Shamaa affirms:

I don't remember how many times I was upset [and] he bent over backwards trying to make me feel better. I had put a lot of academic pressure on myself because I was premed, and in high school I was at the top of my class, and all of a sudden I was at K. . . . And there were endless times, even with his struggle and his dad putting all that pressure on him, even if he had an inkling that I'd had a bad day, he'd joke around with me. And if I still looked sad, he'd say, "Oh, kid,"—he called me "kid" all the time—"get over it; you're going to be fine; you're going to be a great doctor!" There's friends that actually go through things with each other, and he was a *good friend*.

2

By the end of the fall term, in December of 1998, Maggie, like most of her first-year peers, had hit The Wall. She wasn't easily acing all her courses, as was her tradition. The materialism and class snobbery among women students depressed and hurt her. She and Kelly Schulte even investigated joining a sorority at Western Michigan University in order to establish a social life apart from the hothouse environment of K, where everyone knew your business and had already dated everyone else anyway. She conveyed to her parents her resentment of the way women seemed to be regarded in her science courses: one professor in particular always addressed women students' questions or responses with a degree of flirtatiousness that she and her fellow golfer Heidi Fahrenbacher found disturbing. She didn't know about returning to K next year, she said. Sometimes she just wanted to drop out, get a job, get married, and have kids: the Aunt Megan fantasy in which the conflicting values and pressures of being both a woman and a scholar would go away.

That winter Erin Rome and Kelly Schulte were hanging out a lot in Neenef and Nick's room up in Trowbridge Hall. Erin and Neenef were friends again, and Kelly and Nick had begun to date, so Kelly and Erin sometimes made the trek to the room together. Kelly describes Neenef as "a man of few words. When I first met him, I thought he was kind of quiet and shy, like a . . . I don't want to say a computer nerd, because he wasn't a computer nerd. Just an introvert, in every sense of the word. And I don't want to say he was socially inept," but she found talking to him "kind of uncomfortable, like you didn't know what to talk about."

Erin remembers that Maggie and Neenef "hit it off *right* off the bat." Breakneck speed isn't unheard of in campus relationships. A ten-week academic term, as opposed to a fifteen-week semester, will accelerate just about everything. Neither is quick romantic intensity rare among people who are either insecure or on the rebound. J'nai Leafers confirms that it was always important to Maggie to have a boyfriend. It's easy to disparage or discredit the need for male validation in a young woman of Maggie's caliber. But very few eighteen-year-olds have a clear sense of themselves apart from the reinforcement of relationships.

Even so, the sudden intensity of the relationship surprised Erin Rome. "Those two," she remembers, "I mean, I think it was within two weeks they were saying, 'I love you.' Like, it was very quick. I remember exactly: we were walking home from a party and she said, 'Neenef said he loves me.' And I was, like, 'Uhhh . . . that's weird.' And I *liked* him—I was unique; I was really the only one of our girlfriends who knew him." Neneef would later recall that Maggie said the three magic words first, taking him by surprise and disrupting his assumptions about a relationship he assumed would be casual.

Kelly "was really surprised when they dated. The attraction—it still puzzles me." To her, Neenef was "kind of scrawny—and some of the other people that she dated—I don't know, he didn't fit the mold, he didn't fit the type." Erin, however, saw him as another Sean, fitting the type entirely too snugly. Maggie was, in Kelly's terms, "a total catch": beautiful, athletic, smart, outgoing, warm, funny. So of all the men on campus available to her, why Neenef?

There is that cute flirtatiousness that LaVange noted in him—and that Maggie shared. There is Neenef's clowning, which would have appealed to a girl who loved to laugh. But beyond these fairly superficial traits, Maggie clearly responded to something deeper. "Wounded bird syndrome," Erin terms it. The empathetic Maggie who grew up caring for and covering for a beloved, damaged brother seemed to respond instinctively to Neenef's sadness, his victimization, his need. J'nai Leafer wasn't the only one of Maggie's friends who saw her as wanting "to be the one to fix whatever the problem was." Maggie the go-to girlfriend, the intense, compassionate listener, responded to this boy who had a story that needed hearing. Maggie the high-school tutor, for whom K's academic challenges were a mere bump in the road, might have even thought she could help Neenef meet his father's demands. Nandini Sonnad saw the attraction in a more general framework of gender relations: "A lot of girls, and especially a lot of very successful girls who have a lot going on for themselves, seem to have this kind of messiah complex" that draws them to guys who need saving.

Those guys often tend to be great romantics. They fall in love quickly and intensely; they sweep women off their feet; they make the romantic relationship their haven in a heartless world, their raft in a sea of cruelty and indifference. And they are desperately needy. Erin says that Neenef wrote Maggie poetry in Arabic and told her she was the most beautiful woman he'd ever seen. He probably felt that he had waited all his short, painful life for her. And here she was. A heavy dose of romantic mythology for a young woman to resist.

Leza Frederickson sees Maggie's attraction to Neenef differently, in light of Maggie's own sense of inadequacy, on grounds of both gender and class. "A lot of people at K, and a lot of the group we hung around with, their parents have money; they were brought up with money," she says. "Maggie and I didn't come from the same type of background that the others did. You were always trying to fit in, always felt like you didn't have the same as everyone else did." Neenef, on the other hand, was what admissions officers call a "full pay": despite whatever fortune had to be left behind in Iraq, his father was wealthy enough to send him to K without benefit of financial aid. In Leza's view, Neenef proved that someone "who had this background liked her, and it made her feel good. . . . I don't believe that she saw herself the way the rest of us saw her," says Leza. "I mean, she was an absolutely beautiful person inside and out, and I don't think she saw that about herself. I really don't."

Maggie and Neenef had enough in common to draw them together. Both had "family issues"—what college student doesn't? But for both, family was an equal source of great pride and deep pain. Both came to K as premeds in order to please difficult fathers. They shared a sarcastic sense of humor and a love of computer games. But Maggie was also undoubtedly drawn to Neenef by his Otherness. He was a slightly dangerous outsider, coming, as Frank Church put it, from "somewhere else," certainly not Plainwell, Michigan. Neenef spoke with a slight accent, which he seems to have accentuated with a Donnie Brasco "fugged-aboutit" gangster affectation. There was the black-belt story, the man left for dead in a Chicago alley. Rick Omilian calls it "the lure of his danger. I didn't really see Maggie doing that, but obviously she did have that" in her. For a Good Girl trying on her leather jacket, Neenef Odah was a walk on the wild side.

As for him, as Kelly puts it, "He had this gorgeous, talented, friendly, social person who was interested in him." Not to mention really smart. For an immigrant kid, she was in many ways the American Dream walking around in a very lovely female body. And although she was exactly the girl his father had designated forbidden fruit, maybe she would be his portal into a brighter, happier college life and a shining future.

Retrospect makes explanation easy. Sufficiently complicated reasons can always be found to explain why two unlikely people are drawn to each other. But the beginning is usually much simpler. What Erin remembers is Maggie saying to her one day, as they walked across campus, "I think he's kind of cute!"

Chris Wilson, one of Neenef's closest friends during the winter of 1999, had a car and often chauffeured Neenef around town on errands. Of Neenef and Maggie, he says, "When they were together, at first they were like any other couple. You know: 'Yum, yum, love, love.'" When the honeymoon phase ended and they began bickering, Chris thought, "Oh, they must love each other, because they're arguing about *this* again."

Throughout the winter and spring, Maggie took Neenef home for dinner in Plainwell four or five times. Rick Omilian comes from Dearborn, Michigan, a suburb just west of Detroit with a huge Middle Eastern population, which includes a large number of Chaldeans. He grew up around Chaldean families, and he met Neenef with considerable esteem for his home culture and his family's values. "He was respectful here," Rick remembers. "He was very quiet, very reserved. He opened up to Martha more than to me." To her Neenef confided his family stories—leaving Iraq, the struggle with his father, his mother's role in the family, his love for his younger siblings.

"I can understand Maggie feeling sorry for him," Martha says, or feeling "that somehow she's going to make him better or change him. Because I tend to be that way—not so much now, but when I was younger. You know, 'If I do blah-blah-blah, then this person will . . .' Doesn't happen, but that's something you have to learn. And so I guess that's why Rick and I never really worried too much about Maggie, because she had sense."

But on campus, as the relationship intensified, Maggie's posse watched their bright, sensible, solid girlfriend begin to disappear.

When Maggie opted out of parties to be with Neenef, they initially thought it was because he didn't drink or smoke or enjoy the party scene and emphatically disapproved of all three. But then Maggie stopped going to meals with her crew as usual. "He hated us," says Kelly Schulte bluntly. "And he was very up front in telling her that she wasn't supposed to hang out with us." Erin remembers that "the isolation began rather quickly. It was gradual, but it happened quickly. It got to the point where she was just having dinner with him, by himself." He and Maggie would sometimes join his friends but never hers. Neenef was friendly to Erin, as a friend from the fall, but the rest of the group were unwelcome at his and Maggie's table. They began to realize that he was cutting her out of the herd.

Her friends viewed him with increasing animosity. Leza Frederickson was the most severe: "He deceived a lot of people, he really did. And there was something about him that always really kind of put me off. . . . You didn't see anything; it was kind of a gut feeling. You couldn't really put your finger on it, but something just wasn't right." The mutual animosity was immediate, and Leza's deepened when she saw what the relationship was doing to Maggie. "I did not really like him, and he did not really like me," she says. "I didn't like the way he talked to her. I didn't like the way he didn't want her to be who she was. She had to hide a lot of things so that he didn't know, and I just didn't feel that that was very healthy."

In order to sustain her friendships without losing Neenef, Maggie made a frightening accommodation: she split herself in two, conducting a clandestine life outside Neenef's scrutiny. Before long, Maggie was torn between boyfriend and girlfriends. Kelly Schulte remembers Maggie as one who, like so many women, "wanted to make everyone happy." If she met one of the other girls outside for a cigarette, "she would wear gloves and a hat and carry perfume spray on her," so that her hair and skin wouldn't smell like smoke, "and it was absolutely horrible to watch." If she went out at night with her friends, she went in disguise. Kelly explains, "She would have to put on a coat or a sweatshirt and gloves and a hat to try to hide everything about who she was and what she was doing." Even if the social plan involved simply hanging out in someone's dorm room, says Kelly Schulte, Maggie "would have to lie and say she was going home to spend the night with her folks. I didn't like the relationship. I'm not going to mince words about it." Erin, too, noted that Maggie was "terrified" while sneaking a cigarette with her. "She got very skinny," Erin says. "She lost a lot of weight."

Alarming as Maggie's situation clearly was, her periodic escapes from Neenef can also be seen as evidence that she was refusing to be swallowed up in his claustrophobic obsession. In Erin's words, "she was still keeping her own life." An image Erin recalls from this time, the winter or spring of 1999, captures the texture of Maggie's "own life": Maggie wedged into a skinny dorm-room bed with a gay male friend, the two of them "smoking Newports and listening to George Michael." It's an image where sophistication and innocence commingle—as often they do in the college years. It's at once edgy and cuddly, transgressive and cozily safe. It's intimate without the promise or threat of sex. It's a scene Neenef could never have understood.

How did Maggie get to this place, where her own life had to be enjoyed surreptitiously, in snatches, like the forbidden cigarettes? Kelly Schulte surmises that initially Neenef probably "showed Maggie a side that none of us saw"—the side that Neenef's friends attest to. "And once he knew that he could control her," a more menacing person emerged and the restraints tightened. Nandini wondered if, like all too many women, Maggie saw Neenef's possessiveness and jealousy as romantic, flattering, compelling. It was certainly dramatic. Meanwhile, Kelly says, in words that echo Martha Omilian's insight, Maggie was operating from the conviction "that everyone is innately good, and [that] they have the best intentions, and that you *can* change them."

––––––––

No matter how many springs you've lived through in the upper Midwest, each one comes as a surprise at least, a miracle at best. When the Kalamazoo College campus breaks into bloom and tender green, it can be dazzling. The grounds crew clears and plants and prunes like a group of frenzied artists. If the thin sunlight finds an opening, students will appear on the quad to soak it in, reading under the trees or gathering in clutches at the intersections of walkways. The juniors are back from overseas, bringing with them a different energy, eyes full of inarticulate, inchoate experience. The seniors get wacky, desperate to be done and gone. The sophomores feel old, the first-years humbled.

In the spring of 1999 Neenef's partnership with Nick Porada exploded according to the usual pattern: Neenef said or did something offensive, fists were thrown, and the duo was officially separated and installed in separate living quarters. Neenef moved in with Jeff Basta, a good friend of Maggie's crew, who also nursed a famous crush on Maggie. Kelly Schulte's roommate left, and Maggie moved in with her in Hoben Hall, at the foot of the quad. But Kelly soon discovered she might as well have had a single.

"It's not that I didn't get to see her easily," she says. "I *never* saw her." Maggie virtually lived in Neenef's room, occasionally appearing to grab something and then leaving again quickly. Kelly's friend Katherine Chamberlain, who often spent time in Kelly's room in Maggie's absence, says that when Maggie showed up, Neenef would wait in the hallway. Katherine saw him as small, always looking frightened, "desperately seeking approval." But in the same breath, she said he was "creepy," as if he had "something up his sleeve." She described him with Nick Duiker's word, as a "punk." One of Katherine's impressions is deeply revealing: "I remember not seeing him full figure." He seemed "always in the background, always crouching, not coming fully into the doorway."

Even Erin, the only one of the group whom Neenef tolerated because of their previous friendship, saw less and less of Maggie. "I chose not to be around them all that often just because their relationship was strange, you know, and they fought a lot." Their fights became famous throughout the spring. If they weren't about Maggie's friends, they were about men. Needless to say, the man who was so frightened of his girl-friend's involvement with her female friends was positively obsessive where other men were concerned—straight men, that is. Gay friends were safe. Maggie, who had plenty of male friends, had to be particularly circumspect around them. Erin remembers being with Maggie in their friend Thomas's room: "This is something that Neenef would have just gone through the roof [about] if he'd known. . . . And I remember Thomas saying, 'Wow, if Neenef ever finds out that we're all hanging out, he'll come after me with a crowbar.' And I remember thinking that was strange for him to say. [Neenef] had a violent temper, and people knew that."

Predictably, Neenef's deep insecurity generated an obsession with Maggie's sexuality. Mostly she kept the nature of their fights secret from her friends, knowing how they would respond and so desperately trying to maintain the separateness that had made her double life viable. But occasionally, when she was with her friends, she would open up. Neenef called her a whore. He wrote her notes in a class they took together. Erin pocketed a few and showed Kelly, who was shocked. "They were just mean," she said. "And rude. They were mostly sexual, like vulgar sexual comments, or 'You're a slut.' I mean, very off-color."

When Maggie allowed a glimpse into her life with Neenef, her friends were aghast—and furious and frightened. They had meetings at which they would decide, "Someone needs to say something to Maggie. Who's going to do it?" They tried talking to her directly. As Kelly recalls it, the message was clear: "Do you not see what a great and intelligent and beautiful person you are? You could do so much better! Either (a) just be by yourself, or (b) find someone else!" Maggie would laugh off their concern, dismissing it as overreaction.

But they steered clear of confronting her too often or too aggressively. Nick Duiker's memorable early warning had brought about a sudden shift in their relationship, so that for a while Maggie barely acknowledged him when they met. She was, as it turns out, not quite so good at taking the tough love and straight talk she was famous for dishing out, and she could not, or would not, bear much criticism of Neenef, probably because it opened up fissures of doubt and ambivalence. Erin, especially, opted not to alienate Maggie: "I had seen that her other friends were urging her to get out of it, and she was immediately shutting down, so I decided not to take that tack. I think I just decided to take what I could get, and just be friends with her, do what I could. And I figured that whole thing would peter out, because he was obviously so unstable, and the relationship obviously wasn't going anywhere."

Kelly was less sanguine. "I don't want to say she went into a shell," she says. "She was the same Maggie. But he just had this *spell* over her, which I don't get. Like he stole her from us."

But if she was under a spell in one realm of her life, in another Maggie was waking up. She began to think of leaving the premed curriculum behind, turning instead toward the social sciences. Erin was subversively dragging her to College Democrats meetings, which she began to enjoy. In the spring she was enrolled in a legendary Kalamazoo course, officially designated as "Community Practicum" but known far and wide as "Building Blocks." Invented by Kim Cummings, professor of sociology, it was Kalamazoo's first service-learning course, taking students out into the community years before the educational world was buzzing about such initiatives. The course is partially grant-funded, and the students must apply and be accepted. In teams of three, under the supervision of the local neighborhood organization, they undertake to organize residents on the city blocks to which they are assigned, with the goal of improving the neighborhood's safety, health, and appearance. The grant provides six thousand dollars of federal, state, and local funding to each block. For eight weeks the students canvass the neighborhood, beginning with the very intimidating step of knocking on strangers' doors—strangers who often don't look, dress, think, or talk like anyone they've known.

The course makes huge demands: significant class time, plus reading time, plus transportation to weekly block meetings, in which plans are drawn up for the allotment of the funds. These meetings tend to be delicate and stressful. The class culminates in "work weekends" during which the student-resident plans are implemented and houses are painted, roofs are repaired, and flowers are planted. On those weekends, students are on site by seven in the morning, often staying until it becomes too dark to see.

Among a stellar group of applicants that year, says Kim Cummings, "Maggie was among those in whose readiness I had the most confidence." One reason was her rootedness in her own community, as she wrote in her application:

> I grew up in a very close-knit neighborhood in which most of the children were about the same age. In our younger years, our parents depended on each other to keep track of all of us, sometimes feeding and babysitting someone else's child, and carpooling to different athletic or music practices. . . . Being able to depend on the people who lived by me was a very important part of my childhood.

Drawing on that sense of small-town interdependence she brought with her from Plainwell, Maggie plunged into a milieu quite different from any she had known. "Some of the people who attended our meetings looked intimidating," she wrote, and then added, incisively, "probably a product of living in a neighborhood where looking like that is a way to protect oneself."

Very quickly, armed with her native empathy and attentiveness, her humility, her sense of humor, and her five-hundred-watt smile, she found her way across the gulfs of race, class, and age. "Maggie always found a common ground," recalls one of her teammates, Corey Spearman. "She gave everyone the benefit of the doubt, and in return they gave her their hearts and minds." Corey saw her "blossoming into a commanding presence among our group, carefully and methodically looking for the best in each individual and utilizing these positive aspects." The residents, he recalls, bonded with her quickly and wound up adoring her. The rapport was "uncanny." Talking to them, Maggie wrote, helped her "bridge the gap between my fanciful and somewhat naive outlook on life and the realities of living in an urban neighborhood." Corey witnessed a surge in her self-confidence. On the longest work days, he remembers, if Maggie "wasn't up on a ladder painting a three-story house, she was planting flowers or playing with the children who lived on the block." Kim Cummings' favorite image of her is on that ladder—"a really *high* ladder, painting away with the serenity and self-possession so distinctly hers, and, at breaktime, of her chatting confidently" with residents.

How free she must have felt up there—how strong, how fearless, how balanced, up in the air. In acts of service alongside people very different from her, Maggie rediscovered her own integrity and capability. But Building Blocks also solidified an important shift in direction. Her written assessment of her experience at the end of the term captures this moment of evolution with striking clarity:

> This project has made me question my social responsibility in the liberal democracy into which I was born. I am no longer content to live a private life and concern myself only with affairs that I perceive to affect me. It helped me to realize how important having a public life is and showed me that the things I do in my public life *can* make a difference. I foresee

myself raising a family eventually, and I do not want to pass on to them a world which I have made no attempt to better.

Maggie was beginning to integrate the disparate influences in her life. Around this time, Rick Omilian recalled, "She wrote that her political values seemed to be a combination of those of both of her families, with her mother's liberalism and her father's conservatism in contrasting levels." Here in her Building Blocks report, the dream of domestic bliss lives, but not at the expense of a "public life," a civic existence, an exercise of agency in her world. Turning away from the science curriculum that represented her father's world and her desire to ingratiate him, Maggie realized she wanted a certain level of engagement with certain people—the kinds of people who populated Rick and Martha Omilian's professional world.

She divulged to them her new plan: she would aim toward law school—her independent Aunt Susan's path. An exciting prospect, but also a clever strategy, whether conscious or not: law school provided a good story, a respectable enough goal to satisfy the conservative wing of the family. They could imagine her as a corporate lawyer, specializing in trusts. They didn't have to know she planned on working with poor people. She and Erin began talking about summer internships in Philadelphia, where Maggie could enjoy her extended family and also continue the kind of work that, as she had discovered, set her free.

On Pentacost Sunday, Maggie took another step in self-determination when she was confirmed at St. Augustine's Cathedral in Kalamazoo. Typically, Roman Catholics are confirmed earlier in life, but the Omilians—equally typically—had left this decision to Maggie. In part, she was motivated by the chance to become godmother to Aunt Meg's youngest child, Jamie, later that summer.

Twice that spring, the hostility between Maggie's friends and Neenef came to the kindling point. In the kind of hot, gossipy communication fiasco that small campuses breed, Chris Wilson attempted to build a bridge by explaining to some of the crew that Neenef regarded them as a bad influence on Maggie—whereupon they confronted Maggie with this information, and she took it to Neenef. Suddenly Chris felt the full force of Neenef's dark side. "He could be very mean," says Chris, and he was "very upset that I went to them and 'revealed' this secret, I guess, that he didn't like her friends—which from all accounts, I thought, was very clear to everybody. I didn't think it was that big a deal." But Neenef did. He refused to speak to Chris, who then attempted a reconciliation via instant messaging. Neenef exploded, threatening to kill him if Chris ever "interfered" in his relationship again. The threat drove Chris to the Counseling Center.

Maggie, meanwhile, had been planning to room with Leza the following fall. But Leza's ability to contain her aversion to Neenef and her disapproval of the relationship had reached its limit. She told Maggie she didn't think she could share a room with her if it meant having Neenef around. A blow-up ensued, leaving the friendship in pieces. The crew reshuffled their dance cards, and Leza made plans to room with Erin in Hoben, while Maggie and J'nai Leafers decided to take a room in Trowbridge, at the top of the quad and conveniently next door to DeWaters, where Neenef would be living in a suite on the second floor. They were likely roommates, both of them thought—more studious than the others, well suited.

Perhaps Leza's line in the sand jolted Maggie into some recognition that the relationship with Neenef would have to end. Perhaps it was Building Blocks and the new clarity it had given her. Perhaps the Chris Wilson fiasco revived her awareness of what Neenef was costing her. Maybe her awareness began to formulate on one of the warm spring days when she and Erin met for an afternoon ritual. "I remember we got out of class [at] the same time spring quarter, before anyone else, including Neenef," she says, "so we would always spend that hour and a half." Maggie had an ugly old plaid quilt. "We would take it out on the quad and we would [lie] on the quad and talk or take a nap. And I loved that, because it was the one time that she and I would just hang out."

The major event of the spring term at K is the annual student dance concert known as "Frelon"—the Spanish word for "butterfly." A student-generated phenomenon, Frelon begins in the fall, with an open call for dancers. Volunteer choreographers identify their choice of music and describe their "vision" for each number, and dancers sign up. Your dance background or lack thereof is irrelevant, as is body type or rhythm or level of innate physical grace. All you have to do is want to dance. Frelon was founded by a male student who, in fact, was a trained dancer, and it snowballed. Today, Frelon is the only event on campus for which there is competition for tickets. Every one of the shows sells out the big Dalton Theater. The audience is boisterously enthusiastic. Dancing in Frelon constitutes an excuse for late papers. Frelon becomes the first act in a night of partying. Frelon is the place to be.

Not surprisingly, the dancers are mostly women. Ardent recruitment might generate a handful of men. In the spring of 1999, one of the choreographers was Neenef's buddy Frank Church. It was a couples dance, and he needed guys, so Neenef was pressed into service. He was no dancer, says Frank, but an enthusiastic, willing volunteer, and Jessica Emhoff, another dancer in the number, remembers him as getting quite good, after initially being "hesitant and uncomfortable."

There is a videotape of this dance. While the image of Neenef is none too clear, as the stage is mostly dark and the camera moves a lot, it is haunting. There he is—slight, sharp-featured, with a big watch on his right wrist. The dance itself is the genre that annoys me in every Frelon, an unimaginative reiteration of that brand of intense, sexually charged dancing that students imbibe from TV and think is edgy. Couples moving in stylized, gender-stereotypical ways, jerky and sharp, with a hint of smothered violence. Neenef does the moves as he has learned them, rigid, unsmiling, passing in and out of shadows. On a stage full of people, whether he is partnered or not, he looks utterly alone.

4

SO SCARED AND SO LOST

When exams ended in the spring of 1999 and the deep green summer settled in, Maggie's crew dispersed. She moved back to the octagon house in Plainwell. She would be working for Uncle Pete, Martha's brother, at his construction firm before the annual trip to visit her father's family in Pennsylvania and South Carolina. In Plainwell, she happily reunited with Sarah Ayres, home from Hope College in Holland, Michigan. Neenef, meanwhile, moved in with his cousin in Western Michigan University housing. Having flunked some courses, he would be taking classes at Western for the first part of the summer before flying home to Seattle for the month of August. Whether he would be returning in the fall rested with his father.

Even at a greater distance, Maggie continued to take care of Neenef. Her mother remembers Maggie writing and typing papers for him. She also recalls a pointed conversation during a trip to the mall with Maggie. "He wanted her to have his watch looked at because it was scratched," she remembers. "So he wanted her to stop at a jeweler's in the mall. And I said, 'You know what, Maggie? If he wants his watch fixed, he can bring it himself. This is just a way of him knowing that you went to the mall with your mom. You need to think about that. You know, it's a control issue.'"

The dynamics of control in the relationship were very clear to Martha and Rick, but they were gratified to see that Maggie saw them too. She seemed to be edging away from Neenef, and they chalked the relationship up to experience. In the meantime, Neenef was still welcome in Plainwell for family occasions. Once, they all visited Uncle Pete at his house in the country. Maggie's cousin from Germany was visiting—a tall, imposing eighteen-year-old. "I don't think [Neenef] liked having him around," Martha recalls. "That was part of the friction that summer, too. I don't think he ever said anything about it, but there was this other person here, who he somehow saw as a threat." A friend of Pete's had brought a muzzle-loader to the house, and they all practiced shooting it in the yard, which backs up to a big field—everyone except Neenef, who pointedly refused. He would, he vowed, never touch a gun.

Maggie was no longer as accessible to Neenef as she had been for the past six months. She lived half an hour away; she lived with her parents; she had a job; she socialized with old Plainwell friends. The situation seems to have allowed her to gain perspective and clarity, to regain her boundaries. But the circumstances also seemed perfectly designed to increase Neenef's desperation. It is at precisely this charged moment that technology, in the form of instant-messaging records, provides a window into their relationship from July through the early fall. It is an inadequate window, as IM has peculiar limitations as a medium of communication and was only one of several ways in which Maggie and Neenef interacted. But it does afford a unique glimpse into the private world of their relationship. For all of us who wonder how a relationship explodes into violence, especially if we never saw it coming, this record offers some answers.

Maggie's IM handle is "smizgirl." Neenef adapts his dangerous self-image to become "ninjoda"—a fusion of "ninja" and his father's name. The record begins with a long exchange starting at 12:56 p.m. on July 1, in the middle of a fight, with Maggie demanding that Neenef stop swearing at her—a motif in this log. Neenef expresses anxiety about her absence "in over a year," surely a reference to her junior-year Study Abroad, which to him might represent a looming chasm, teeming with demons: Maggie on her own in Europe, and him . . . who knows where? Maggie's being in Plainwell seems, for him, a foretaste of what it will be like with her on another continent. He goes on to explain the source of his premature anxiety:

Ninjoda: I'm pissed all the time cause I do'nt see you as much as I was used to since I've met you

"Pissed"—not sad, not depressed, but angry. Maggie briskly attempts to stop the downward spiral, advising that "there is no use in getting pissed about it," and tries to reset the conversation: "Neenef. . . . let's not do this right now. . . . i love you sweetie and that's all that should matter."

But there is silence from the other end.

Smizgirl: you there?

Ninjoda: yeah Maggie I'm here. I love you a lot and I don't wanna lose you . . . that's all

Smizgirl: you aren't going to so stop worrying about it

In the next twenty minutes, while he sulks and complains about their not spending enough time together, Maggie reminds him maternally to do his homework before class and twice asks if he intends to go.

A brief exchange that evening, beginning at 8:00 p.m., demonstrates how closely Neenef monitors Maggie's whereabouts. Perhaps characteristically, Maggie tries to "manage" him with levity.

Ninjoda: i just called and you weren't ther

Smizgirl: hi babe

Ninjoda: what took you so long to answer

Smizgirl: cause i was peeing

Ninjoda: oh

Smizgirl: is that ok with you? ☺

On the evening of the next day, July 2, in the middle of a somewhat suggestive conversation, Neenef suddenly reminds Maggie to erase all of her IM history, and even when she promises to do so, he persists:

Ninjoda: did you erase all of that

Smizgirl: IT'S GONE

Ninjoda: do it now so you don't forget

Smizgirl: i did it

Ninjoda: you sure it's gone

Smizgirl: yep

Ninjoda: good

Smizgirl: ☺

The IM conversations of July third and fourth are genial, teasing, and gentle. Maggie and Rob are planning on picking Neenef up on the fourth, probably for a family gathering; Neenef is helping Maggie find cheap airline fares to Savannah later in the month for her and Rob. However, something clearly went wrong on the fourth, because at 10:42 a.m. on July 5, Neenef sends the following:

Ninjoda: Maggie I'm really getting sick and tired of all this shit about me hurting you. . . . only reason I get mad at you is cause you make me feel like shit A LOT and when I feel like shit I do'nt feel like talking to anyone . . . . havn't you realized that yet

A half hour later, Maggie sends out a feeler that elicits a sullen series of monosyllables from Neenef. This time she lets him have it, and the real issue is out: Maggie spent the previous evening with Sarah instead of with him.

Smizgirl: you are so rude sometimes i can't believe that you would begrudge me time with my best friend. you spend so much time being angry with me that even when i do do something for you you don't notice. FUCK. i want to spend time with you today and you won't because you are stubborn. you think that you are hurting me by acting like this and you are right. real cool, babe.

Neenef quickly and melodramatically turns the tables:

Ninjoda: maggie listen. . . . . go spend all the time you want with your best friend that you have to call 500 times just to be able to hang out with. . . . I don't want you to take time out of your busy fucking schedule for me. . . . . so far you've come and seen me whenever it's been convenient for you. . . . have you noticed or not? it's never when I wanna hang out. . . . it's always you

Neenef then moves to the offensive:

Ninjoda: you know what fuck it. . . . what about my fucking feelings huh? just cause I don't cry to you on the phone doesn't mean I'm a cold hearted bastard you think I am. . . fuck you. . . . . I don't need you

Maggie tries to respond to Neenef's maneuvers rationally. She analogizes their relationship to that of Sarah and her boyfriend, Travis, who has just left town.

Smizgirl: i understand why [Sarah and I] had to wait til yesterday to hangout. if i was in her shoes and you were leaving i would have done the same thing

Ninjoda: ok maggie. . . . whatever you say

Smizgirl: what do you mean you don't need me. WHY ARE YOU ALWAYS TRYING TO HURT ME?

Ten minutes of silence ensues. This withdrawal is both typical Neenef behavior and an effective strategy, as it brings Maggie close to apologizing:

Smizgirl: i don't mean to make you feel like shit babe. i really don't

But when Neenef responds with an indifferent "maggie whatever," her frustration reaches its limit: "I am tired of you telling me what a bad person I am! ! ! you have your faults too. and i am trying to be better . . . . i don't like it when you put me in a position to choose one person i love over another." To this dangerously clean and accurate description of a fundamental problem in their relationship, Neenef responds, as he often does, by jerking the argument to the edge of a cliff:

Ninjoda: listen maggie . . . if you really mean it when you say I make you feel bad, break up with me. . . do it now you'd feel better and I'd feel better cause we can both move on i don't wanna have to go out and always be like this. . . . I fucking hate it too

Then he goes for high melodrama:

Ninjoda: you'll be able to spend more time with your loved ones rather than worry about me

Maggie's exasperation is palpable: "DAMMIT NEENEF! ! ! ! ! you are one of my loved ones! ! !" But he returns to cliff's edge, the dare to which she did not respond the first time:

Ninjoda: just fucking end this then. . . it would be better for you wouldn't it. . . . you can go out with all your friends like you used to and do everything you always did. . . . you'd enjoy life more

Neenef's response, rife with manipulative self-pity, also contains a recognition that he has indeed intervened between Maggie and her friends, between Maggie and a normal social life. Maggie responds by daring Neenef to jump first—"if you're not happy then you end it"—but she also gives Neenef the reassurance he craves, writing, "i don't want to end it."

Maggie then looks back in time sadly:

Smizgirl: you didn't used to be like this

Ninjoda: neither were you

Smizgirl: i remember when you were romantic and made me feel important and special. when you looked at me and I could see love in your eyes. you have changed neenef. you are so negative. all you ever tell me is how nothing is going to work out. I get tired of telling you it is. you never listen to me

Neenef eventually gets the declaration he's been fishing for, but he continues to push Maggie to break up with him. In the following exchange, we can see Maggie's place in the larger context of Neenef's sense of isolation.

Smizgirl: i don't want to break up with you Neenef. I love you.

Ninjoda: no you don't

Smizgirl: yes i do. . . . i have since that first time i talked to you.

Ninjoda: if you loved me you'd know why I look at [life] so fuckng negatively. . .

and you'd see why I wanna spend a lot of time with you. . . . it's cause right now I've got nobody. . . my whole fucking family is messed up and you don't fucking help

Smizgirl: but you aren't even positive about us, neenef!

Ninjoda: how the fuck can I be positive about anything

Smizgirl: i don't know

Ninjoda: maggie I don't wanna take this relationship any farther if this is how it's gonan be ok for your sake and mine

Maggie's responses when Neenef pushes her away range from moving closer—most likely the reaction he's seeking—to insisting that he listen to reason. Neenef continues to claim that she is making herself unavailable to him. But Maggie presents a counter-narrative:

Smizgirl: I love you. i would come over if you would let me. how many times have i wanted to see you and you wouldn't let me come over cause you were pissed at me for one reason or another you are looking for any easy way out. you never want to try and work on anything to make it good. you just tell me how bad it is.

Smizgirl: with that attitude you are never happy no matter what i do

Smizgirl: you need to enjoy the time we spend together and stop worrying about when i have to leave. what if sarah and taylor did that? they would be miserable because one of them is always leaving . . . .

Ninjoda: what the hell do you wanna do then? what the hell are you trying to accomplish by telling me all this. . . are you trying to make me feel like shit even more than I do right now

Ninjoda: why don't you just go out with taylor. . . . you love talking about them

Maggie responds to Neenef's childlike display of jealousy with an adult sense of calm—and also with a challenge. But Neenef is stuck in a swamp of jealousy, self-doubt, and suspicion of Maggie's closest friends.

Smizgirl: i am not trying to make you feel like shit, babe. we need to recognize what is going on in our relationship so we can fix it. that is, if you even want to try.

Smizgirl: I don't love taylor

Smizgirl: but i admire them because they are making it work against all odds. and they are truly happy

Ninjoda: all you do is talk about how taylor is this or taylor is that. . . . well remember

Ninjoda: when you told me you and sarah used to go out with the same guys? why don't you go for him?

Ninjoda: sorry if I do'nt make you happy maggie

Maggie repeatedly takes the bait and reassures Neenef that she loves him and wants to spend time with him. When he attempts to shut down, she returns to the root of the argument to clarify its terms, and in doing so, she begins to realize that she can't win. If Neenef can't see her on his terms, when he wishes, then she is making herself unavailable, even when she insists that she wants to spend the day with him and has set it aside specifically for that purpose. But Neenef returns to the fact that "things never work out the way they're set with you." Maggie responds,

Smizgirl: am i supposed to sit home all the time and wait for you to call me and tell me to come over? we both have lives outside our relationship and that is how it is supposed to be

She calls on the example of her parents:

Smizgirl: why can't i spend time with both of you? rick doesn't make mom choose to see either him or uncle pete

Ninjoda: maggie you're talking about siblings there

Maggie sanely looks at other, more successful couples as models and measuring sticks. Her best friend and her parents have the kind of relationships she wants. But for Neenef, the analogy fails: family trumps friendship. Maggie tries again.

Smizgirl: fine then. my mom goes out to dinner with her girlfriends and leaves rick at home. he never gets mad at her. in fact, he is happy

Ninjoda: that's cause he's married to her maggie. . . if you didn't notice

Eventually, Maggie has had it and calls Neenef on his threats:

Smizgirl: you are the one who keeps talking about breaking up. i'm not. so if you want to break up with me then do it. stop torturing me with it and lording it over my head

Neenef explains that he demands so much of her time because he is afraid of losing her. It is probably as honest as Neenef gets about what's really driving him. He'd like "to spend a night or 2 this summer sleeping together like we used to," he says, "but that obviously meant shit to you during the school year."

Maggie tries a dose of reality: "i see sarah about once a week. can't we spare one evening a week so i can spend it with my best friend?"

Ninjoda: maggie, no. . . . go spend all the time you want with sarah. . . . I don't wanna be the one in the way of you two

Smizgirl: and I loved spending the night with you at school

Smizgirl: you aren't

Ninjoda: if you did then why aren't you trying so hard to spend the night with me anymore?

Smizgirl: things are different now. i am living at home and don't have the freedom that i used to have. i will work out somethign with sarah, but it is not possible for me to spend every night with you! please understand where i am coming from

Smizgirl: and why do you have to focus on that so much. can't we spend time together during the day?

Ninjoda: I didn't say every night. . . didn't I say maybe one or 2 nights this summer?

Smizgirl: fine. i will arrange it

Ninjoda: all we do is argue during the day

Ninjoda: no forget about it

Smizgirl: well, let's work on that

Smizgirl: why forget about it?

Smizgirl: I AM TRYING AND YOU WON'T LET ME

Ninjoda: cause rememer the reason is cause you don't wanna get in trouble with

Ninjoda: mommy and daddy

Ninjoda: can you honestly say you're trying maggie?

Smizgirl: yeah, i can. i am not the one who refuses to give in at all costs.

Ninjoda: okay

Smizgirl: and right now, i am trying to save us and you're not. all you can do is be negative!

Ninjoda: SORRY. . . . . shit

Ninjoda: I'm gonna go shower now. . . . i don't feel like talking about this anymore

There isn't enough time in the world for Maggie to convince Neenef that she won't leave him, and it is exhausting to watch her working so hard and so futilely. As she pushes for continued engagement and dialogue on the subject of "trying to save us," he responds, again, by checking out. At 12:29 p.m. she says he is giving up on her. At 12:30 she tells him she loves him. Five minutes later she is in despair:

Smizgirl: you won't even respond to me. do you love me even?

Ninjoda: QUIT IT

Ninjoda: I LOVE YOU. . . is that what you wanna hear

Smizgirl: not if you don't mean it

He repeats that he wants to take a shower, and again Maggie refuses to let him go, accusing him of being tired of talking to her "as usual." Then she says, "i am trying," whereupon Neenef explodes:

Ninjoda: shut up. . . . . just shut the fuck up. . . . . God

Smizgirl: why are you swearing at me? what did i do?

Ninjoda: "i am trying" "i am trying" that's all you say . . . it's never doing, it's always tryin

After another fruitless go-round, Neenef asks suddenly if Maggie has been talking about their relationship with Sarah. Yes, she confesses, she has talked to Sarah "a bit."

Smizgirl: i told her that i felt like I was running backwards

Ninjoda: great . . . . one thing though maggie . . . . I never discuss my personal life that I have with you with anyone

Ninjoda: oh that's great . . . . . she must think I'm a good person now

Smizgirl: you don't even know what i told her. it was nothing bad. i basically told her how i was screwing up if you want to know the truth

Ninjoda: how you were screwing up and how much I love getting pissed at you right?

Smizgirl: i even lied and told her that everything is basically find with us and we were just argueing occasionally about little things

Smizgirl: NO, YOU'RE NOT RIGHT

Neenef's earlier insistence that Maggie erase her message history and his outright paranoia here about being discussed by Maggie and Sarah constitute his inordinate and alarming need to reinforce the wall of "privacy" with which he tried to encircle their relationship during the spring. He frames Maggie's transgression as a violation of their intimate, private bond. In his terms, she has been unfaithful to him, and her infidelity is the same one that she committed all year: intimacy with her girlfriends. It's noteworthy, too, that Neenef assumes that Maggie's intimacy with Sarah will result in Sarah's lowered opinion of him. For Neenef, it seems that to be known by Maggie's friends is to be loathed.

This might explain his next move, amazing even in the context of all his previous manipulations:

Ninjoda: you'd [lie] to your best friend huh?

Ninjoda: do you even know what the word "friend" means

Smizgirl: yeah, i guess i did because i didn't want to tell her how bad things really are between us

Neenef is amazingly skilled at letting Maggie know how she has failed as a person, no matter what route she chooses. She has not only violated the privacy of their relationship by talking with Sarah about it but has revealed herself as a dishonorable person by lying to Sarah about it. Later in the conversation, Maggie notes this systematic denigration, saying, "Have you ever told me that i am good at something? I don't think so. you call me stupid on a daily basis."

Neenef's need for secrecy and control is deeply alarming. His desire for Maggie to hide the details of their relationship does, however, suggest his basic understanding that he is behaving badly, that in the story of his and Maggie's relationship, he knows that he fits neither the role of the good guy nor the role of the helpless victim. The episodes during which he insists that he loves Maggie and doesn't want to lose her seem tinged with a tortured awareness of just how unacceptable his behavior has been.

Toward the ragged end of this particular IM exchange, Maggie and Neenef continue to accuse each other of lack of love, of the other person thinking he or she knows everything. Again Neenef accuses Maggie of wishing he were like Taylor, the symbolic Good Boyfriend. Then the topic shifts to what is apparently an old point of contention: how much time Neenef spends on the computer, even when she's there visiting him. She writes, "you can not expect me to come over and watch while you use the computer."

Finally, once more, Maggie tries to bring the conversation back to her primary question: "do you want to work this stuff out?" Accusations fly again, and then suddenly the air goes out of the conflict, as if they are both very tired:

Smizgirl: i wish that we could just start over

Ninjoda: me too

Smizgirl: then why don't we

Ninjoda: maggie the last thing I'd do is let go of you . . . . reason why i keep telling you to break it up is tp see if you really mean you wanna be with me. . . cause if you were to break up it would have shown to me how much this whole thing really meant to you

Smizgirl: well, is the test over?

Ninjoda: i guess

Smizgirl: fine

Ninjoda: fine what?

Smizgirl: i am glad the test is over

Ninjoda: don't fucking start talking like that already

Smizgirl: sorry

Smizgirl: i just think it was a mean test

Ninjoda: if we're gonna start over maye start by being nice

Ninjoda: it wasn't a TEST

Ninjoda: I was fucking serious

Smizgirl: ok

Ninjoda: no calling

Smizgirl: ?

Ninjoda: i don't feel like talking yet

He has to be in the right mood, he says. Maybe a shower will do it. Maggie says, "shower then / i'll talk to you later." Although her display of pique here seems minor compared to Neenef's own earlier insults and curses, it angers him:

Ninjoda: you have got the worst atitude of anyone i know . . . . 'shower then' can we be anymore rude?

At 1:29 p.m., after ninety-three minutes of conversation, they say goodbye—but Neenef has one final concern:

Ninjoda: by the way . . . . . erase all that from your history

Maggie initially responds with the query "why?" but immediately thinks better of it and types, "nevermind—i will." But she never does.

The next instant-message installment is a brief, nasty exchange on July 24, 1999, starting at 3:37 p.m. Again, it begins in the middle of an argument. Maggie questions Neenef's assumption that she will chauffeur him around on his errands, writing, "you never even asked me. you just assumed. / i will be there soon. i love you." A tug-of-war ensues. Maggie says she's coming; Neenef tells her not to, swearing that he won't come downstairs from his apartment. What is especially painful here is Maggie's aggressive insistence on giving him the help that he is now childishly, brutally refusing. It seems to be an old pattern for these two: the surest way for Neenef to keep Maggie deeply engaged is to pull away. This time the dynamic drives her to a new level of franticness:

Ninjoda: ok sorry . . . . . I'm saying NO right now . . . . don't fucking do anything for me anymore

Smizgirl: stop it ! ! ! ! ! ! ! ! ! !

Smizgirl: SEE YOU SOON

Ninjoda: i'm not fucking kidding

Ninjoda: NO

Smizgirl: neither am i . this is so unfair

Ninjoda: unfair unfair unfair . . . . . FUCK IT . . . I don't want anything

Smizgirl: i am aboiut hysterical here. EVERYTHING IS FALLING APART

Ninjoda: I won't fucking ask you for shit anymore

Smizgirl: I HATE IT WHEN YOU DO THIS TO ME.

Neenef responds by shifting the argument to the old theme: they were supposed to spend the day together, but now Maggie's backing out. Maggie reminds him that the previous night she took him food shopping and that she's had "a bad morning." She asks for some consideration. Immediately Neenef counters with a description of his own bad morning, a result of Maggie's failure to call the previous night when she said she would. "MY PHONE WAS BROKEN ! ! ! ! !" Maggie reminds him, but he is impervious to reason: "I don't care . . . . sorry for assuming you'll always be there for me."

Deep in his solipsism, Neenef seems truly unable to respond to Maggie's basic need for consideration and understanding; he instantly turns the spotlight back to his own endless misery. He gives the impression that her life, full of responsibilities and other people who love her, is unreal to him; it is a persistent inconvenience that intrudes when he wants her to himself, a competitor for her attention, evidence of the inadequacy of her love for him. A striking feature of Neenef's persona is that he depends on inflated romantic clichés in his condemnation of Maggie, such that minor negotiations get inflated into major violations of love itself.

The conversation on July 24 ends abruptly at 3:46 p.m., when Maggie apparently tries to call and Neenef says he's not picking up. That evening, just before and just after 6:00, there are three plaintive messages from Maggie that receive no reply.

Just before midnight on July 27, Neenef has an IM conversation with Rob, Maggie's brother, who is using Maggie's account. The calm rationality of this exchange stands out in sharp contrast against the

Sturm und Drang of Maggie and Neenef's sessions. Neenef tells Rob he's worried about what he will do when he has to leave his cousin's place. He says, "right now i basically have nothing," and he hopes another cousin will come through with a promise of a job and a place to stay in Chicago. Rob asks whether that means quitting school.

Ninjoda: well . . . i don't know . . . . . if my dad doesn't send me here, I don't have any money to go to school anywhere, so . . . . what's worrying me is that lately my cousin's been shaky about the deal he made with me . . . . . he thinks it would be better for me to go home to Seattle for [now]

Ninjoda: i'm really worried about it all . . . . I wish I could get some answers right now

Seattle itself is not so bad, he continues, "it's just cause I'd end up locked up in the house with nothing to do at all unless i do what my dad sayd." That summer, Neenef was looking at a giant hole where his future ought to be. His relationship with Maggie, however contentious, seemed to be the only thing keeping him afloat, and his grip on her seemed tenuous.

At this point the instant-messaging record jumps to August 6, 1999. Neenef's plans to go to Chicago have apparently fallen through, because at this point he has made plans to go home to Seattle. A long conversation between him and Maggie begins at 5:59 p.m. in a treacherous place: Maggie's car has a flat tire, and she's writing to say that she won't be able to spend the night at his apartment. Neenef announces, "we're through," and Maggie asks why.

Ninjoda: because i fucking can't stand nothing working out as planned . . . . . fucking nothgin

Maggie reminds him that plans are bound to fall through "when i don't have my own car and i live at home with my parents under their rules." Neenef then tries to rewind the summer that has brought them to this impasse of dependence, suspicion, and conflict:

Ninjoda: well from the fucking beginning you could have said to me let's take the summer off of our relationship and i wouldn't have gotten so fucking attached . . . and if we still liked each other when school started we could have continued it

The accusation suggests that in his mind, Maggie could have saved him from this misery by suspending the relationship in June—as if she controlled the relationship completely and thus could be blamed for its current state. Maggie, however, refuses the burden of responsibility, writing, "well, i didn't. and you didn't either neenef. stop blaming everything on me!" She accuses him of not loving her and then reveals her own anxiety about his leaving for Seattle:

Smizgirl: you are going home now and can have all the sex that you want. you don't want me around cramping your style do you. i feel like shit if you even care

Ninjoda: screw you man

Ninjoda: FUCK YOU

All Neenef can do with her pain is curse her. Maggie asks if he loves her, and he replies,

Ninjoda: i wanna fucking love you but how the hell am i supposed to when i can never fucking see you ha? tell me?

Smizgirl: you see me more than any of my past boyfriends neenef

Smizgirl: i talk to you on the phone at least three times a day. i see you almost every other day

Ninjoda: what about the past 2 weeks?

Smizgirl: this week i saw you [both] tuesday and wednesday. and i was supposed to see you today and tomorrow

Smizgirl: and i called you every morning except one this week

Smizgirl: i even called you last night from gillian's because i love you and miss you

Neenef's complaints seem ungrounded, and it's heartbreaking that Maggie continues to try to prove her devotion to a man who will never be satisfied with it. Maggie says she "just can't believe what is happing right now," and then, "i feel sick / brb [be right back]." Perhaps she has gone to the bathroom to vomit. While she's gone, Neenef types what seems to be a sincere apology—"sorry for everything i've put you through maggie"—and the record is silent for nine minutes. When Neenef resumes, he affirms his feelings for her in his own distinctive terms, writing, "if i didn't love you i wouldn't have gone through all this"—as if his own suffering were the ultimate measure of his love. He calls up an episode of conflict from the spring:

Ninjoda: think about how you felt during the school yr when i told you i think we should see each other less . . . . . that's how i'm feeling right now . . . . . i've gone from being used to see you every day to seeing you only when it's convenient for you

Smizgirl: i am emotionally drained and i feel terrible. i don't want to argue anymore.

Smizgirl: i love you and i am sorry that things aren't working out as planned. i wish I could see you everyday but i can't. i am sorry i am a big disappointment to you

Ninjoda: you're not a disappointment to me. . . . . can't you see how happy i get when i see you? and how i am when i'm told i'd see you and i don't? think about how i am all the time and try to think of it this way maggie

But Maggie is gone. At 9:21 p.m., Neenef tries again:

Ninjoda: sorry maggie

Ninjoda: hello?

But this time the silence is hers.

————————

There is one instant message from Maggie to Neenef on August 13, saying she'd like to talk to him. Shortly thereafter, the Omilians drove Neenef to the Kalamazoo airport for his flight to Seattle. The next message is from him, on August 15: "maggie i'm here." Maggie visits her father's family and returns home. Communication between her and Neenef while he is in Seattle is compromised because Maggie can't call him at home for fear of his father's reaction. Instead, she has her brother call and leave messages that ask Neenef to call back when he can. Neenef also disappears from the Internet for a while, to Maggie's frustration.

On August 19, he is IM-ing again, and things sound rosy. He celebrates a collection of messages from her; he writes "I LOVE YOU" forty times on her nineteenth birthday. Shortly after midnight on August 20, Maggie writes to apologize for getting him in trouble—probably by calling—and then says, "i love you and i don't want to break up no matter what. please understand how much i love you * * *." Later that afternoon he writes in more measured terms:

Ninjoda: i hope we never have to think about breaking up because you're the best person i've met in a long long time and i'll try to do what i can to make you happier. you know how i am and you know i care about you and that's why i'm the way i am

According to Neenef's reasoning, both his suffering and his difficult behavior are simply evidence of his love. He closes the session with a criticism wrapped in a warning wrapped in a promise:

Ninjoda: i love you though and i'll try to ACCEPT you loving to party hard like you so desperately wanna do. i'll talk to you later

That night he announces that their communication will be further curtailed because his brother is taking the computer back to school.

On August 22 he writes, "I've been trying to get a hold of you all weekend and i have no clue what's going on." He says he'll try to call and warns Maggie urgently not to call him at home. For the next few days the messages are sparse and confusing. In one, Neenef says he's been looking at photos of Maggie, wondering how he "got a chance" with someone so beautiful. In another, he says he's in "big fucking trouble AGAIN," and seven hours later, after 3:00 a.m., Maggie sends lines of asterisks, representing kisses. On August 26, Neenef is angry because Maggie hasn't read an important email: "i'm fucking dead serious . . . . do you care?" She tells him to "stop stressing" and says, "I think that everything is going to work out just fine." But Neenef is nervous, and Maggie's reply seems to justify his anxiety. The power dynamic of their relationship seems to have shifted.

Ninjoda: i'm not stressing . . . . i just wanna know why the hell you've been around me the way you've been. i said a lot in the email and i was hoping maybe you can respond to it, if you can ever find a time in your schedule when you're not busy. shit

Smizgirl: i sent you an e-mail. I don't know if it worked so tell me whether or not you got it

Smizgirl: good night * * *

Smizgirl: ps. stop swearing at me please

On August 27, Neenef gets to the bottom line: "do you wanna still be together? it's a yes no answer." Over three hours later, he writes,

Ninjoda: maggie sweetheart i'm sorry for those emails and messages. . . . it just doesn't seem like you care to stay in touch . . . . i really need someone like you in my life and i would like it if you could gimme another chance k? i love you

Over four hours later, Maggie responds, citing communication difficulties:

Smizgirl: Neenef, for some reason i have trouble e-mailing you—they usually come back to me with an error. i don't know why. anyways, i do love you and i want to stay in touch with you. it just makes me angry when you say things that hurt me. and then i am scared to talk to you . . . . i know that we can make things work, but you need to find inner strength so you can love yourself. until then, you can't love anyone else. i love you *****

Maggie's voice here is calm and controlled, her advice for Neenef on the mark. But Neenef translates her new boundaries into a failure to love him unconditionally. At 2:30 on the morning of August 28, he sends a forlorn and troubling monologue:

Ninjoda: just tell me one thing . . . . do you truly wanna work things out or is your way of talking to me lately trying to tell me you don't wanna be with me anymore? is the type of love you have for me . . . conditional love? maggie if you were to ask me that question do you know what i would have said? i would have said my fucking love for you has grown even more than it's ever been. not become conditional love like yours has for me . . . . have you once stopped to think how i feel . . being a human being like yourself? I just wanna fucking die every time you drive me to want to hang up cause i don't know if we're ever gonna speak again. and you are still being cold as hell towards me.

i've fucking got emotions too maggie did you know that about me? i'm trying sooo hard because i can't imagine life without you and all i'm getting is those profound lines you have to say to me. i get some credit at all for trying. i wanna fix things to the way they used to be. . . or as close as we can get them to how they used to be. if you wanna forget about me and go out and party like before just tell me cause you don't even know how shitty i'm feeling right now. my own woman telling me i'm a sore loser and wants to hang out with her friends. i'm so lost maggie

This notion—that real love must suffer everything, endure everything, and never complain, never change—will prove an especially powerful one for Neenef.

The next day, August 29, they have a phone conversation that assuages him, and he writes to thank her. She writes back in the evening, one line: "i just wanted to say hi ☺ **" He sends more effusive messages, covered with kisses; she responds, at 10:38 that night, thanking him for a poem and recounting her day at Uncle Pete's. To this breezy message, he responds, shortly after midnight:

Ninjoda: maggie that poem was exactly what i feel for you and one day God willing i'm gonna marry you cause of how much i love you and we're gonna be very happy together. i miss you hun. night

Ninjoda: God babe i love you soo much . . . . . and i miss you . . . i talked to my dad today and he asked me if i had a girlfriend . . . . and i said yes . . . . he asked if we're serious and i had to say no . . . . i think i'm playing my cards right so far though . . . . . so it's possible he'll send me over for the year. . . . . we're gonna talk again tomorrow and i gotta convince him . . . i think i will though and i'm gonna need to work extra hard when i get back to k . . . well, just wanted to tell you things are going well and that I LOVE YOU baby . . . . ****** night angel

Maggie's next IM, at 8:35 the next evening, August 30, is short and sweet: "just wanted to say hi! miss you / bye." Sometime between that morning and 11:00 p.m., they have a conversation that, based on Neenef's response, constitutes some kind of turning point. From the sound of it, time and distance have brought unprecedented clarity to Maggie. Neenef begins his long, desperate reply at 11:38 p.m.:

Ninjoda: maggie do you know how i felt when you told me you think i'm being

obsessed? I LOVE YOU . . . . . do you know what that means? i feel more connected to you than i ever did, and i thought it was natural for me to miss you
like i do, but according to you now i'm being obsessive? this is what i get for
showing you how much i love you. not once have you told me nice things since
i've left . . . . . only times taht you have have been when i suggested them . . . .
and maybe i shouldn't have. every fucking day goes by and i dread that you're
gonna end it all. and do you know why? because you've been showing how
much you love me ever since i've left. all i've been hearing is how i jsut wanna
hear what i wanna hear and how controlling i am.

Ninjoda: and how obsessive i am and whatever else you think i am. how many
bad things can you say i've said to you since i've been gone. i've fucked tried
everything i can to be nice and make things work. so now i understand how
HONESTLY you feel about me. you HONESTLY don't have anything good to
say about me do you? why? cause i don't have money?

Ninjoda: cause i don't do what you say? cause i don't go buy you things?
remember you used to say you wanted to have a man who would kinda take
action, but not be like a ruler? that's what i've tried to do for you. and now all of
a sudden you've turned into some feminist telling me this that and the other.
if this is your way of hurting me, congrats. you don't even care what this is
doing to me do you? you're probably going to message me and tell me you
couldn't sleep well last night and gonna try to blame it one me . . . . truth is you
feel good for doing this.

Ninjoda: the deal was for us to express honstly, and i thought positively, how
we feel about one another. have you had one good thing to say about me? do
you care that this is killing the self esteem that you've left me with.

Ninjoda: check back on your history . . . . have you said you love me on your
messages when i wasn't there? now tell me . . . . . do you honstly love me
maggie?

Three minutes pass and he writes again: "tell me now so i know what
to do." Another ten minutes, and he tries again, casting her in a mythic
role in the tragic drama of his life:

you know how highly i used to think of you maggie? I seriously used to think,
and have told everyone i know, that you're a god sent angel. that i couldn't
be any happier in life. that this was it for me. that finally something good happened in my life that was gonna show me that life is worth living despite what
i used to think.

Three minutes pass, and he reflects on a previous conversation:

am I seriously scaring you? and wait . . . . . you said you might be afraid to get too close? maggie you know my life inside out . . . . . . you've just opened me up like no other human being has EVER . . . . . and now you're afraid of getting too close. . . . don't you think this is being selfish? and don't tell me i'm talking irrationally. . . . . don't i have the right to feel like this. . . . like you just don't care anymore after having brought me this far?

At 12:07 a.m., Maggie responds:

Smizgirl: i am used to being miles away from people that i love . . . you just don't want to understand anything. you say things that scare me and when i tell you, you get pissed. i thought that we were going to be honest with each other. you don't want a relationship! you just wnat to tell me how it is and for me to just tell you what you want to hear! I love you and i have always shown that i do. because i don't do it how you want me to i am evil that's not fair. i thought that everything was going better. i thought that we werer sarting things out and then you have to launch in to 'fuck this, fuck that, fuck you.' that's not dealing with anything. can't you see that? you are just losing your temper and not giving me a chance to explain myself. i do miss you neenef, but you want to believe that i don't for some reason. i love you . night **

Ninjoda: i am so scared and so lost. i was willing to give anything up for you, and i tried to change my whole attitude just so my girlfriend maggie would like me more and coudl tell people nice things about me and mean them. please don't do this to me. please tell me something nice for god's sake. tell me that all i'm trying isn't going no where I LOVE YOU . . . . please look deep inside yourself to understand how i mean it

Maggie's messages during these last days of August suggest that she hoped she and Neenef could move forward together, that their relationship could mature. But Neenef clearly can't hear her, most likely because he has few if any models of mature relationships in his life. How would he even recognize one, much less participate in it? Maggie's advice that he love himself is probably as foreign an idea to him as women driving cars once was. She is subsumed by his worst fear: that she will simply pull away and leave him behind.

Maggie picks up the argument again that afternoon, August 31, and they circle the same issues once more. It is unclear whether they have broken up by this point. It's possible that for Maggie, who is conspicuously silent, the relationship has ended, while Neenef insists on continuing to negotiate.

Ninjoda: You know what i'm gonna do for you maggie to make you happy? i'm not gonna message, email, or call you anymore. if i do come back to k and you decide you wanna work on our relationship, i'll give it one last try. if not, fine. i'll understand what type of person you are.

At 3:38 that afternoon, in spite of his threats to the contrary, Neenef seizes the thread again:

Ninjoda: and havn't you once thought of how many people i've lost in my life due to my family moving from one place to another? do you understand why i miss you so much and why i'm so afraid that i might lose you? i'm not worried about you meeting someone else . . . i'm worried about losing you completely whether i stay here or come back. try to understand maggie

At 5:06 p.m., he writes in a gentler tone, imploring Maggie to "look at me the same way" that he looks at her, and noting that she hasn't said she loves him. Just before 8:00, Maggie answers, in a voice that couldn't be more different from the frustrated, panicky, imploring voice of July:

Smizgirl: Neenef—i do miss you. But i don't like it when you say "fuck you, etc." and please stop bringing up the "you don't want to get too close" thing. that is something you took out of context and now you want to use it against me constantly! I do want you to call me but I am not going to beg anymore. it just makes me feel worse. I miss you and want to talk to you! jesus. don't make things harder than they already are. love, maggie

On September 1, there is a brief, carefully impersonal exchange about a shelf Neenef is building for his mother, preceding what seems to be an upbeat phone call. At 1:08 the next morning, Neenef writes to thank Maggie for the conversation.

Ninjoda: . . . for the first time In a long time, i didn't worry about anything after hanging up the phone; i actually felt good about myself this time . . . . normally i've always said good bye and hung up and just sat thinking to myself i wished i were different . . . . . but without you even trying today, you made me feel as if i don't have to change my whole being to be with you

Another exchange of kind messages on September 3 is followed by a return to the swamp on September 4. Apparently they have had a bad discussion about sex, and Neenef has "promised" to leave Maggie alone, because "of course i'm wrong again." The new Maggie breezily bids him good night, and comments that he's "acting petulant." He asks, "wut does petulant mean," and she explains, "whiny," whereupon he tells her to go to hell.

Then on September 8, at 2:03 a.m., Neenef writes with big news:

Ninjoda: baby guess what? i'm comin bck . . . . i had a long talk with my dad tonight and things worked out. He does have GREAT intentions in mind for us, but he's just confused on showing it. BIG TIME. He made me tell him that i'm not gonna be seeing any girls so, we're gonna have to be secretive when it comes to him. But it's all good. Please, please, don't take things in a bad way.

Ninjoda: I'm trying to do what's gonna be good for me and for us. You know i love you and i always will and now taht things with him are solved FINALLY, i'm feeling better about us. Meaning, my problems with him have been relieved a lot and now all i have to think about is coming back to school and doing well and fixing our relationship up, because those are my two top priorities. So don't take what i said to him about you personal.

Maggie doesn't respond. At 2:12 a.m., he writes again to say he's left a message on Maggie's phone. At 5:15 a.m. on September 9, a howl into cyberspace: "Margaret Lynn Wardle . . . . where in God's name are you?"

Maggie, by this time, is back on campus, practicing with the golf team. Erin Rome, who has been working in Harbor Springs, Michigan, over the summer and has been out of phone contact, returns home, and the two of them are able to debrief. "You're going to be really happy," Maggie tells her. "It's totally over with me and Neenef."

If Neenef has not heard or perhaps cannot accept this message, he certainly knows that the relationship is in serious jeopardy. He tells Maggie he's coming back to Kalamazoo early so that they can spend time together before school starts. On September 9, at 3:23 p.m., he apologizes for an argument and asserts, in the face of his greatest fear, his simplistic brand of romantic faith: "From what i understand, if you love someone enough you'd be willing to work things out."

But apparently Maggie, who in the past has used the same line herself, has grown to understand that the rules aren't that simple. Her messages to Neenef during this time show that she's established in her own mind a distinction between loving someone and pursuing a relationship with him. Neenef's responses reflect his unwillingness to give up.

Ninjoda: maggie, by you saying love can't solve our problems, you're saying love isn't a BIG thing . . . . and i don't agree with that. Love, from what youv'e shown me, is enough to make anything work.

At 4:05 p.m., Neenef writes, "please don't hate me." He sends unanswered messages that evening, and on the next day, September 10, at 1:51 p.m., he apologizes for writing so much and imagines being with her again, holding her, kissing her. He implores her to give him another chance. Early in the morning of September 11, Maggie finally responds, in a way that cannot have comforted him:

Smizgirl: Neenef—I'm sorry i didn't get to talk to you today but i had a match and then we had the 'golf party.' i am just getting home now. i'll talk to you later.

Neenef's reply comes the next afternoon at 12:24, grimly eloquent:

Ninjoda: don't matta

It is easy, reading this record, to feel claustrophobic, caught in the endless circles of accusation, defense, self-pity, and self-dramatization. It is easy to see the patterns in Maggie and Neenef's arguments and the way they accuse each other of the same transgressions at times, as partners often do.

In some ways, their relationship isn't all that different from many relationships that devolve into mutual dependency, blame, and helplessness. At times the two of them sound like average college students trying to figure out how to fight, tripping over each other, tying themselves in knots. What is distinct—what glows neon-red with danger—is the power dynamic created by Neenef's extremism: his disproportional responses to Maggie's social life; his resentment of her time with her best friend; his wild accusations and condemnations.

To read this exchange is often to feel frightened—by Neenef's obsessive rage and drive for secrecy and control, by Maggie's naive insistence on trying to defend herself against his absurd accusations, her attempts to salvage a working relationship with a person with whom that is impossible. Above all, to read their exchanges is to feel the chilly shadow of the future.

What held Neenef and Maggie together throughout July and August of 1999? It's easier to discern Neenef's reasoning: He invested Maggie with a large portion of his self-esteem, his hope, his life's meaning. It's much harder to understand Maggie's tenacity in the relationship, but it seems due to a combination of factors, including her memories of how good their relationship had felt in the beginning; her empathetic understanding of his genuine pain; her desire to heal the wounds and preserve the relationship. She may have been reluctant, as so many women are, to be the one to cut the cord. She may have hoped that Neenef's absence in August would allow them to separate more easily. It's even possible that she hoped he wouldn't come back to K in the fall.

Neenef's struggle seems in some ways more complex. Fighting to hang onto Maggie only reinforced how "attached" he'd become. A classic contradiction in socialized masculinity: a man is supposed to fight for "his woman," but a man is not supposed to be dependent, especially on a woman. This was a young man who had trouble riding in a car with a woman driver. How was he to deal with depending on Maggie not only for transportation to do his basic errands—food, haircuts, watch repairs—but, as he felt, for his very existence? How could he be sufficiently sure of an American woman, one raised with all the freedom women were given and claimed for themselves in his adopted country?

There is a clear disparity in Neenef and Maggie's maturity levels—a topic about which Maggie would sigh to her mother. While in their IM exchanges they both often speak from that tumultuous place between childishness and adult understanding, Maggie demonstrates an ability to assimilate knowledge and learn from it, to progress. In contrast, Neenef's rhetoric is unwaveringly simplistic and dualistic: you either love absolutely and eternally, or you don't really love; Maggie will either make the effort to repair the relationship, or he "will know what kind of person" she is; Maggie says only "bad" things to him (using "bad" words like "obsessive"), never "good" things. Maggie herself is alternately "a god sent angel" or the antonym of an angel: "some kind of feminist." In fact, Neenef seems to live in a Manichean universe—not unknown to adolescence—where there is no middle ground between romantic redemption and utter perdition. In such a universe, if Maggie is not there ("Margaret Lynn Wardle . . . . where in God's name are you?"), then there is no firm ground upon which to stand.

Finally, an eavesdropper on Maggie and Neenef's instant-message exchange during July and August might be struck palpably by two very different energies. Neenef's is centrifugal, inward and downward, a maelstrom pulling him down into the dark; psychologically, he is in quicksand. Maggie's energy, even when she is struggling, is centripetal, outward and upward, mobile, changeful. She is interacting with an array of people. She looks for hope, for health, for normalcy, for solutions to problems, for happiness. By summer's end, she has extricated herself. She is getting on with her life.

Whether there was a single moment when the relationship ended is anyone's guess. Given the way these things usually work, probably not. The ends of relationships are often incoherent, inconclusive. They tend to be ragged and drawn out. But Maggie's closest friends believe—and the IM evidence supports the theory—that the breakup occurred while Neenef was in Seattle, just before Maggie returned to school for golf practice in early September.

"We all cared too much about what men thought, and needed a good shot of self-respect," says Heidi Fahrenbacher. "I think Maggie was starting to tune into her own self-respect when she broke up with Neenef."

KALAMAZOO COLLEGE

To: Kalamazoo College Students
From: Danny E. Sledge
          Dean of Students
Date: September 22, 1999

"To enhance our community,
we accept responsibility for its social well-being.
We commit ourselves to treat with respect those with whom we differ,
to recognize the rights held by others,
and to resolve conflicts."

This statement is a part of the *Respecting Others* section of the Honor System. I remind you all, as students, of this statement that shapes our community and provides expectations of our interactions with one another. I share this because of a very real concern related to some disquieting realities present in our broader society. Specifically, the apparent increase in violent behavior demands that we take a more proactive stance. Although we are committed to providing a safe environment, we cannot assume that any place is immune to such violent behavior.

Therefore, because of the increase in violent behavior in our society and the frequency with which weapons are involved in that violence, we are assuming a zero tolerance for weapons on campus. By College policy, you may not have weapons (including game, sport, martial arts and theatrical equipment such as guns powered by compressed gas, laser guns, hunting knives, throwing knives, swords, darts, etc.) in your campus rooms, and they may not be used on campus. Beginning this quarter, violation of this policy will result in immediate suspension from the College.

If you have unknowingly brought some item that meets the above definition of a weapon to campus by mistake, you may call to request that a security officer come to your room to get the weapon. It will be kept until the next time you can take it home. If you must practice with some type of weapon, you will have to find an off-campus site or be under the supervision of a faculty or staff member.

This action is being taken for the well being of the entire Kalamazoo Campus community. Please be aware that there will be no warning. If a weapon is found in your room or you are using one on campus, you will be suspended immediately.

Maggie Wardle
self-portrait, age 7.
(Courtesy Rick and
Martha Omilian)

Millennium Girl:
Maggie at 17.
(Courtesy Rick and
Martha Omilian)

Neenef Odah (*right*) at Kalamazoo College. The brand name on his shirt, "Wilson," is also his father's first name and his own middle name. (Courtesy LaVange Barth)

Maggie (*right*) and Neenef (*center*) on the quad, "Spring Fling," May 1999. (Courtesy Kirsten Paulson)

Nick Duiker and Maggie (*at center*) at the Homecoming Dance. This is the last photo ever taken of Maggie. (Courtesy Niklaus Duiker)

Looking west up the quad to Stetson Chapel. (Courtesy Office of Communications, Kalamazoo College)

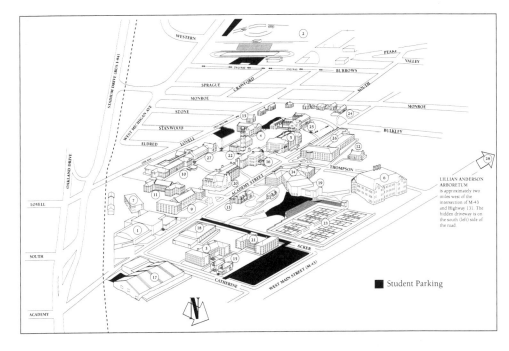

The Campus Map

1. Anderson Athletic Center
2. Athletic Complex
   ·Angell Football Field/
     Calder Fieldhouse
   ·MacKenzie Soccer Field
   ·Softball Field
   ·Woodworth Baseball Field
3. Crissey Residence Hall
4. DeWaters Residence Hall
5. Dewing Hall
   ·Career Development Center
   ·Center for International
     Programs
   ·Registrar's Office
6. Dow Science Center
7. Facilities Management
8. Faculty Residences
9. Harmon Residence Hall

10. Hicks Center
    ·Bookstore
    ·Counseling Center
    ·Gilmore Parlor/
      Dining Room
    ·Richardson Room
    ·Security Office
    ·Student Health Center
    ·Student Dining Hall
    ·Student Organizations
11. Hoben Residence Hall
12. Hodge House
    (President's residence)
13. Humphrey House
14. Light Fine Arts Building
    ·Dalton Theatre
    ·Dungeon Theatre
    ·Connable Recital Hall
15. Living/Learning Houses

16. Mandelle Hall
    ·Admission
    ·Business Office
    ·Financial Aid
    ·Human Resources
    ·Office of Alumni Relations
    ·Office for College
      Advancement
    ·Office of College
      Communication
    ·Olmsted Room
    ·President's Office
    ·Provost's Office
17. Markin Racquet Center
18. Natatorium
19. Nelda K. Balch Playhouse
20. Olds·Upton Science Hall
21. Severn Residence Hall
22. Stetson Chapel

23. Stowe Tennis Stadium
24. Stryker Center
25. Trowbridge Residence Hall
26. Upjohn Library Commons
    ·Information Services
27. Welles Hall
    ·Stone Room
    ·Studetnt Dining Hall

Campus map of Kalamazoo College. (Courtesy Office of Communications, Kalamazoo College)

5

HOMECOMING

1

The convocation that opens each academic year at Kalamazoo College invariably takes place under the same perfect sky: brilliant blue, lit by sharp mid-September sunlight. It's like a natural law, ridiculously predictable in a place like Michigan, a peninsula where the proximity of vast bodies of water usually spells tumultuous weather. Opening Day 1999 was no exception. I was in my second-row seat on the north side of the quad, sweltering in my polyester academic robe. My foremost thought was about meeting my first-year seminar students and their parents after the ceremony ended. I was starting my twenty-second year at K. I was the senior member of my department (by several lengths). I was also entering my twentieth—and, as it turned out, my final— year coordinating the women's studies program, which I had helped to launch as a young upstart in 1980. I was the faculty advisor to the student-operated Women's Resource Center, and I was organizing a new committee to support teaching excellence. It would be a busy year. But the first priority was to pull myself into this moment and look into the eyes of the terrified eighteen-year-olds whose roads had converged with my own.

We entered that fall term already diminished, as the first issue of that year's campus *Index* demonstrates. It mentioned the death of Charles Tully, a sophomore, a gifted theater design student, who succumbed in July to the leukemia he had battled for most of his life. It announced a memorial service for Jessica Lowery, a senior, who had died in August in a car accident. But its lead story featured the stunning death of Ben Davies, a thirty-two-year-old physics professor who collapsed on the tennis court at noon on September 27, with classes barely underway. The doctors said his heart had probably stopped by the time he hit the clay. Some of us noted that, over the years, when the dark angel swept down over the college, it usually took more than one.

Martha and Rick Omilian sent Maggie back down the road to Kalamazoo with satisfied minds. She seemed, they thought, much more at peace than she had been during her first year. Personally, philosophically, academically she had turned a corner. She told them she planned to join the Campus Democrats, completing the left turn she had gradually made the preceding year. She had decided to jump the premed track and now spoke of law school as her academic goal. As her relationship with Neenef disintegrated over the summer, Martha and Rick said to each other, "Well, that was a learning phase; we're not going to get involved; she's grown up." Martha elaborates: "We didn't want to interfere too much, because she figured it out."

That year's golf team, in those days before the other students returned, cohered even more quickly than its previous incarnation. It had gained a member in Emily Ford, a new transfer student. On Emily's first day on campus, she was carrying her golf bag up the sidewalk on Academy Street and looked up to see Maggie flashing "one of her smirks," lugging her own bag downhill. Emily asked how she liked the team, and Maggie responded enthusiastically and reassuringly. "I felt very at ease my first day on campus and each day following because of her."

The Omilians remember Maggie taking a new, more relaxed attitude toward golf back to campus with her, as if she was no longer in it to please anyone but herself. In fact, Emily remembers a bad shot upsetting her and Maggie telling her, "Emily, just have fun; it's only golf practice." Teammate Sara Church remembers a match later on that fall in which

Maggie had "a frankly crappy round, including several shots straight into the same water hazard," but Maggie "was laughing about it the whole way home." From that day came a team slogan: "Twenty shots in the water and still smiling!"

Maggie was golden, striding into her second year of college at once energized and relaxed. Katherine Chamberlain, a friend of Kelly Schulte's who had moved into Maggie's circle at the end of the previous spring, remembers Maggie having "an incredible ease about her. Everything appeared to come really easily to her."

Before Neenef flew back from Seattle, he contacted Erin Rome, the one member of Maggie's group who was always friendliest to him. He wanted to start again, he said. He wanted them all to be friends. He wanted to be friends with Maggie. Could they hang out when they all got back?

To that end, he was there to help Erin move into the room in DeWaters Hall that she would share with Kelly Schulte. Erin's mother remembers Erin's agitation at having him around. He made similar overtures to Chris Wilson, but Chris was still smarting from last spring's conflict, during which Neenef had threatened to kill him for discussing with Maggie's friends the fact that Neenef didn't like them.

> I wouldn't say I was angry, but it was still affecting me. I learned my lesson. "I'll be civil, but I won't try to be his friend again, like we were before." I wasn't going to put myself through that again. So if I see him around, "Hello," and keep walking.
>
> I'd heard that he and Maggie had broken up, and I just suspected that he would be upset about it. And so the few times I would see him, he'd look at me with the puppy dog eyes, like he was looking for a friend. It was a total 180 from the last time I'd really spoken to him, when he was very upset and angry with me. Very supplicating, almost. "Ohmygosh, it's so good to see you, Chris! How've you been? How are things?" I'm like, "Fine. Good. Bye."

Neenef seemed to understand the morass he had created during the preceding year, and he apparently returned with a determination to make amends. He might have thought of it as a way to get Maggie back, too.

That fall he was living in DeWaters 201, a double room connected to 203 by a common bathroom. The room was directly above Erin and Kelly's. If you entered the dorm from Lovell Street, you went up one flight to Neenef's floor, and his room was the first one on the left. If you entered on the opposite side, the quad side, you were already on the second floor and had only to walk to the end of the hall. DeWaters, a small building, was a highly social place that fall. As Neenef's friend Kirsten Fritsch remembers it,

> Most everyone who lived there that year knew each other, so we made a point of always having our doors open when we were in. Part of living in that building was being social with your neighbors, and so my friends and I made a point of trying to get to know everyone, especially people who were a little quieter than most. Neenef was definitely one of the quiet ones, but he went along with the open-door policy and was almost always sitting at his desk, facing the hallway, when I would come in from class. We never had a deep or serious discussion, but he was always friendly.

Neenef's roommate was Eric Page, a fellow computer science major and member of the football team. Across the bathroom were Brian Newman and Navin Anthony, both premeds. Navin had met Neenef two years before and was among his closer friends, though he describes the nature of the friendship in classic masculine terms: "If you needed something, he was there for you. We would go out and play sports— play basketball or throw a football around. He enjoyed playing soccer; I wasn't that big of a soccer guy." Navin was well acquainted with Neenef's family pressures, and he quickly got up to speed on the Maggie situation. Beyond Neenef's overt friendliness, Navin saw a closed door, an unwillingness, or perhaps inability, to use words to alleviate his suffering.

The instant-message record between Ninjoda and Smizgirl early that fall is intermittent. Neenef's messages are frustrated, troubled, or accusatory; Maggie's, mostly terse. It is clear from these messages that he is not reconciled to their split. In a September 16 message, the familiar self-pitying persona appears:

Ninjoda: did you ever once think of writing me a nice email? tell me how much you loved me?

Ninjoda: or how much i meant to you? no you didn't

Ninjoda: God i can't believe things got this bad. . . .

On September 18, they argue about whether she has blocked his messages or not. On the nineteenth, he confronts her:

Ninjoda: maggie why are you ignoring me so badly

Ninjoda: it hurts like hell

When she responds, curtly, that she's just busy, he returns to the supposed agreement that they would try to be friendly once they were back on campus:

Ninjoda: you've remembered all your freiends but me

Ninjoda: what you've got another boyfriend or something?

She denies it, but he persists.

Ninjoda: i'm really glad it took you a second to get over me

Ninjoda: why can't you see how much this is killing me . . . . why can't we spend time as friends at all?

Ninjoda: like you said you hacn't called, messaged me, or anything at all . . . . i feel like i keep pushing fro nothing

Maggie protests, and an old pattern reappears:

Smizgirl: erin just got here today neenef . . . i haven't seen her in 3 months

Ninjoda: everyone gets to see you . . . and i'm last on your list

Ninjoda: i'm not even on your fucking list

Ninjoda: so this was 8 months of nothing to you right?

Ninjoda: man you've fucking killed me . . . i can't even go up to a girl and talk to her

Ninjoda: i can't fucking talk to anyone anymore

Ninjoda: and i bet you're gonna close icq soon to ignore me and not talk to me anymore . . . isn't that right?

Smizgirl: No

Ninjoda: you are just as bad as those new stuck up freshman girls . . . . your friends have given me a second chance . . . look at you

Ninjoda: the fucking girl i loved is killing me

Maggie doesn't respond, at least not via instant message. The next day, September 20, he writes to wish her a good first day of classes, as if none of this had transpired.

Nandini Sonnad remembers that Neenef would repeatedly draw Maggie into contact that fall, ostensibly about something else, and then press the relationship. This pattern is borne out by his last instant message of any length, on September 22:

Ninjoda: just think about how much time i'm constantly thinking about things . . . i want a chance with you as a friend . . . to sit and talk . . . . to forget the bad things in the past and remember the good times we had . . . . . to try to put the past behind and let's try to start new please. if i still didn't care about you i wouldn't be spending this much time in thought about all that's been going on . . . .

Ninjoda: i understand that you want some space, and if that's what it takes then ok . . . . . take all the time you need but please don't lost track of what we had cause you've been the most special person i've ever known . . . . take things easy maggie . . . . . i'm not going to judge anything you do from now on, so if you ever wanted to talk about anything i'm here, as nothing but a friend ok

Ninjoda: this was all i wanted to say to you today maggie . . . i didn't wanna talk on the phone to fight . . . take care

Neenef flails to get a grip on the relationship. The overture of simple friendship blurs with "start[ing] new," his old fantasy of revising history, erasing "the bad" and opting to see only "the good times."

When Nancy El-Shamaa first saw Neenef on campus after having only sparse communication with him over the summer, she asked how things were with Maggie. "And he said, 'We broke up.' He didn't want to talk about it; he just said, 'It's over.' Maybe he called her a bitch a couple times." Nancy saw that he was very depressed. A few weeks later Neenef filled her in more fully: "Basically, it's done, and she cheated on me over the summer, and I never want to have anything to do with her again."

The cheating story was circulated widely and accepted by his friends. Nancy tried to encourage Neenef's final sentiment—that he wanted nothing more to do with Maggie. She told him, "That's healthy, Neenef. I don't want the same thing to happen as last year, where you got really mad at that girl"—probably a reference to Stephanie Miller and Neenef putting his hand through a window. This time when she and Neenef talked, Nancy didn't see the signs of depression. "I thought Neenef was back again," she says. "I thought he was fine."

The antagonism between Maggie and fellow golfer Leza Frederickson had evaporated with the summer haze. With Neenef out of the picture, Maggie and Leza were able to spend a lot of time together. Leza saw a new awareness in Maggie, noting that she seemed to understand the negative dynamic that existed in her and Neenef's relationship. She was also aware that Maggie was dating other people.

Maggie and J'nai Leafers were living in a corner room in the section of Trowbridge known as Pebble Beach—because it looks out onto a roof covered in stones on which you can sit on towels in the sun if you're so inclined. Their room became a popular stopping point as Maggie's crew made their way around campus of an evening. They often found Maggie at her computer, playing games, with her headphones on, listening to the *Jurassic Park* sound track. The phone rang into the small hours, with Maggie constantly "on call" for counseling. No one understood how she got her work done, but she did. And when the weekend rolled around, she was ready to rock. The cocktail of choice was vodka—Popov, the cheap one—mixed with the Gatorade that J'nai, a runner, always had around. Off campus, Maggie "knew every bouncer in the greater Kalamazoo area." Her only continual source of worry was her brother, whose struggles often landed him in trouble and weighed on her parents.

That fall Maggie was enrolled in social science courses, notably David Barclay's survey of twentieth-century European history, which she took with Kelly Schulte. Barclay's specialty and great passion is German history, whose modern phase, of course, presents compelling material for those galvanized by the ways in which the past haunts the present.

Barclay's recollections of Maggie afford a valuable glimpse of her as a student. "She had a seat by the window, so it was to my left," he recalls. "It became obvious to me after about two days in the class that Maggie was picking up on stuff that nobody else was picking up on, with the exception of one of the exchange students from Bonn," Almuth Wietholtz. In Maggie's comments and questions in class and in his office, he spotted something extraordinary. He says, "She was one of those students that we dream of, who show up in the office actually wanting to talk about *history*, and not just talk about 'what I have to do to get a certain grade' and that kind of thing. That happened in the first week, and it amazed and astounded me."

Barclay made two sets of supplementary readings available to the students, one in German, one in English, both comprised of primary source material. Students were required to report to the class on some subject in the readings, educating each other. "Maggie signed up for the very first one," Barclay recalls, "which involved a reading of the 'Futurist Manifesto' by Filippo Tommaso Marinetti. So first of all she came to my office to sort of talk about that stuff and tell me about her grandmother who was born in Germany. She had a special interest in European history because of her grandmother." It was the epiphanic moment when the professor finds his student—and vice versa. Barclay recommended a book for her research. "It was immediately very evident that she was one of these students who takes up the ball and runs with it," he recalls. "She actually went off and read the book." The results, a few weeks later, were even more exciting.

She put together an intimidatingly good PowerPoint presentation. If I were some of the other, more "slackish" students in that class, I would have been scared as hell, thinking that I was going to have to try to somehow live up to the standard that she set with that first presentation—particularly given the fact that those were fairly early days for PowerPoint and that sort of thing. She had dredged up photographs that I had never seen of Marinetti and incorporated some of the artwork [from Marinetti's anarchist circle]. She did a really, really fine presentation. . . . I think I've maybe given half a dozen A-pluses for anything in thirty-four years, and this was one of them.

So she discovered she was really, really interested in history and had this special interest in Germany and decided she wanted to be a history major, with a particular interest in Germany. So you can imagine how delirious I was, that a bright student was actually interested in doing this. Oh, my God—this doesn't come along every day!

He learned that Maggie had been to Germany with her mother six years before to meet her relatives there and that she was excited about returning. Now, she said, she "wanted to talk to them in a somewhat different context, in a more adult context," about their experience of being German in the twentieth century. The earlier trip, along with her intimacy with her grandmother Doris and the ethnically diverse brood of her Aunt Megan and Uncle Mike, gave Maggie a personal stake in the intercultural education central to K's mission. "She was one of these people interested in reaching out culturally," Barclay says. She had already committed to the college's program in Erlangen, the more demanding of K's two German sites, for her junior-year Study Abroad.

When Barclay asked about her post-baccalaureate plans, she told him about law school. "I had already developed, of course, my sinister strategy to convince her of the incorrectness of that, and that she should get a PhD in history," he recalls, "but that was going to be in the future."

Beneath the strong current of Maggie's sophomore fall—academic excitement, social freedom and experimentation, athletic competition, tight friendships—Neenef's ominous persistence runs like some kind of muddy undertow. His recognition that the relationship was over, like his promise not to judge Maggie's behavior, was short-lived. He began to abuse her over the phone and to her face, calling her a whore and a slut, leaving her in tears. DeWaters residents heard him yelling at her on the phone.

As ever, Neenef's rage tended toward physical violence. In October, he accused his roommate, Eric Page, of having said something negative about him, and Eric thought he was in for a fistfight. Another DeWaters acquaintance, Vaughn Preston, said that Neenef tried to fight him during that same period. Navin Anthony recalled that when Maggie left Neenef's room after a particular argument, Neenef proceeded to punch out one of the closet doors: "When I went in to see him, I was like, 'What's this all about?' I was pointing to the closet door. He was like, 'I don't know, man, I just got angry.' I was like, 'What's going on?' And he explained to me how he and Maggie had got into a fight and things weren't going very well."

Navin noted that something in Neenef could not, or would not, communicate the heart of the trouble. "He was very—he would try to verbalize what was going on between them, but he would try to internalize it, too," Navin says. Navin, meanwhile, saw the struggle in fairly simple terms: "In Neenef's mind, it was like 'we're still kind of working on things.' I'm not sure what Maggie was thinking about; Maggie was probably thinking, 'This is done.' I know that they had many conversations together, or at least a few, and every time they had a conversation, it usually ended up becoming a fight. She's doing something else, and he's still harping on the relationship. And she's moved on."

Neenef's inability to swallow that hard fact locked him into obsession. He would lure Maggie into meetings on the pretext of friendship and then pressure her; he would track her; he would verbally harass and attack her. Above all, he seems to have been crucified on one of his own rigid, romantically naive rules: you don't love someone and then stop.

Katherine Chamberlain says that Maggie kept her continuing contact with Neenef somewhat secret, as she had kept other aspects of their relationship to herself the year before. Those friends who found out were understandably exasperated by her willingness to engage with Neenef on any level at all. Erin Rome deployed her usual tactic for staying close to Maggie: compartmentalizing. When she discovered that Maggie was still in communication with him, she said, "If you're going to be talking to Neenef, I don't want to hear about it. I've had enough of your weird relationship." Golf teammate Heidi Fahrenbacher, on the other hand, who believes that some of Maggie's other friends took too much from the men in their lives, got right in her old friend's face when she heard about the verbal abuse. She says, "I was always the person who was like, 'Once you break up, don't talk.' . . . I told her, 'Listen, you need to not see him anymore—like, don't even talk to him.'"

Maybe Maggie was too kind a person to cut Neenef off completely at a time when he felt "so lost and so alone." Maybe her willingness to talk with him had to do with her long history of caretaking and tending damaged relationships. Maybe she genuinely hoped they could pull a civil relationship out of the ruins of their romance. Maybe for Maggie it was less trouble to talk with Neenef than to risk his hysterical, verbally violent reactions to her silence and distance—the path of least resistance.

Why couldn't Neenef find his way through heartbreak and anger to acceptance and recovery the way most of us do—with a little help from our friends? He was surrounded by devoted peers who were working overtime to help him digest the breakup and move on. His advisor, Alyce Brady, after initially seeing him as a classic loner, discovered that "he had really quite a network of friends." They spoke of him, in fact, as the peacemaker, "the one to smooth things over and get people to talk to each other"—a remarkable role for someone with a hair-trigger temper who is infamous for threatening others. Perhaps the only sense that can be made of this seeming contradiction is that Neenef was adroit at peacemaking among others and hopeless at making peace with himself.

This contradiction is itself part of a larger one: the contrast between Neenef the young man with the network of friends and Neenef the lonely outsider. Navin Anthony may have found the key to this puzzle. "He really trusted Maggie," Navin says, "and I think maybe they connected in a way that he was able to tell her a lot of things. And when that whole relationship wasn't working out—I think he knew he had friends, but he didn't have a friend as close as Maggie." He wasn't simply losing his girlfriend; he was losing his best friend, his only truly intimate friend. She had broken through his shell of hurt and fear and pretense as no one ever had done before. He confided in many people, supported and was supported by many people, but his deepest, most intimate connection was with Maggie.

As Kelly Schulte saw it, Neenef's lack of intimate friendships gave him no personal resources to face either the family pressure or the breakup. He had no basis for comparison that would have told him that other people felt as angry and isolated as he did, that he wasn't alone, that breakups and family pressure are endemic to youth, and that there were options and help available. "I think he was so alone," Navin continues, "and I think he felt —obviously—that there was no answer or outlet. He was a failure."

93

Perhaps it was the sense of utter failure, more than simply the loss of love, that consumed Neenef as September turned to October. Kelly's interpretation is probably as close as we can come to the truth of Neenef's situation, as he saw it. It was obvious, she says, that he was desperate "to please his father and to make his parents proud—and he was failing. And he failed at this relationship. And I think that pushed him over the edge."

Sometime early that fall, Neenef told his roommate Eric Page that while he was home in Seattle he had attempted to buy a gun, with the intention of killing himself. He had given a friend money—Eric was unsure whether it was 150 or 250 dollars—to make the purchase, and the friend had given Neenef some drugs to hold as collateral. The friend had never returned. Neenef repeated a version of this story to his new friend Heather Barnes, a first-year DeWaters resident, but in this version, he recounted taking 250 dollars in cash from his bank account and planning to tell his father that he needed the money for computer parts. He did not tell Heather what he actually planned to buy, and when she tried to clarify the point with Eric, he said, "You don't want to know." Later, Eric would tell the police that Neenef confessed to having been suicidal after he and Maggie broke up—perhaps referring to the same incident. Was the Seattle gun story another tall tale like the man left for dead in the Chicago alley? Even if it were, it was a classic cry for help, the clearest of Neenef's garbled messages to the world, announcing that his situation was critical.

On the morning of Friday, October 8, probably in a borrowed car, Neenef got himself to a gun store called On Target, out on M-43 past the city limits, as it heads west to the Lake Michigan shore. He told the clerk, Chet Dillenbeck, that he was going up north with some friends on his first hunting trip and wanted a shotgun. He was insistent that the gun have a camouflage finish. According to Michigan firearms law, he was required to wait twenty-four hours to pick up the weapon. That night, he asked Eric Page if he could use his car on Saturday. Eric had a football game that day and left his car keys behind in their room when he left at 9:00 a.m. Neenef returned to On Target and, at 1:32 p.m., purchased a Mossberg model 695 twelve-gauge shotgun, along with scopes and ammunition for a total of $347.62, charged to a Visa card.

If Neenef had tried to buy a handgun, Michigan law would have mandated a background check. His out-of-state driver's license would have meant contacting Seattle sources. For a shotgun, all he needed was the willingness to wait twenty-four hours.

At the Lovell Street entrance to DeWaters there is a small student parking area. It's most likely that, after buying the shotgun, Neenef parked Eric's car there, slipped inside the building, and ran up the flight of stairs to his room. In the week that followed, Eric's father paid a visit to take measurements for a loft they wanted to build for Neenef. Later, Eric would remember how nervous Neenef seemed whenever Eric's father got anywhere near his bed.

One October night, a group gathered on the roof called Pebble Beach: Maggie, J'nai, Katherine, and their buddy Jeff Hopcian, who'd gone to high school with Katherine. Probably some Popov and Gatorade were involved. It would be one of the last nights warm enough to hang around outdoors for any length of time. Katherine remembers Maggie warbling "Somewhere Out There," the song of separation and yearning from *An American Tail*, the Disney epic with which they had all grown up. Says Katherine, "She was probably the most alive out of all our friends."

2

In the early hours of Thursday morning, October 14, Neenef e-mailed Stacy Lantz, a friend in DeWaters who had apparently made overtures to him that he had resisted. She had asked if he was angry with her.

> na i'm not upset. it's just that i got screwed by a girl i was with for 8 months too so i do hate girls and think they're all B's. what she did to me was something noone deserves. You can't steal someone's heart and all of a sudden stomp on it and let it sit there for no freakin reason at all. and i told you i liked you because i thought you were cool and because heather told me you liked me. one more thing, try to understand that a relationship is the last thing i want right now from anyone. i can't put myself through the last 8 months again to have it end up getting hurt.

anyways, it's a bit too late for me to be still up so i'm gonna go get some shut eye. I'll talk to you lata

neenef

Thursday is the day of the week that now marks the beginning of the weekend on campuses across the country. It was probably on October 14, the Thursday of the fourth week of classes and the week preceding Homecoming weekend, that Maggie attended a party off-campus. There she found herself talking to Nick Duiker—sane, protective, trustworthy Nick, who had been the first one to warn her about Neenef. She made sure he wasn't seeing anyone, and he made sure that Neenef was out of the picture. He had heard from Nick Porada, he said, that Neenef was very angry and wanted Maggie back. She assured him that that chapter was closed. Around 3:00 a.m., he walked her back to Trowbridge. She was talking about the golf tournament coming up that weekend and about Homecoming. "Do you want to go to the dance with me?" she asked. But Nick had to work at his job at Ponderosa that night until 10:00. "Maybe I'll meet you after my shift," he suggested.

That week, David Barclay had handed back the first in-class exams in the Twentieth-Century Europe course. To his astonishment, Maggie had received a B-something. She had apparently also done less than spectacularly on an exam in Professor Jerry Mayer's political science course, for which she was also working on a research paper on gun violence in schools. On Friday, October 15, she visited both profs, telling them that she had been distracted all week: her brother, Rob, was in bad trouble. David Barclay reassured her about the grade—"not to worry about it; one understands these things; I was confident, etc., etc., etc." They then discussed David's becoming Maggie's academic advisor, making plans to start the paperwork soon.

On Homecoming Saturday, October 16, the Kalamazoo women's golf team ended its season at Defiance College in Ohio. Maggie shot her best round of the season. Her coach, Lyn Maurer, says that the team had become "exceptionally close" that fall. She remembers Maggie's satisfied smile that afternoon, the sunny grin everyone seems to associate with her. Before leaving Defiance for the van trip home, they stopped at Burger King. Maggie and Emily Ford sat on the ground and painted their toenails in preparation for the dance. The two of them, along with Heidi Fahrenbacher, piled into the back seat of the van, where they bounced to the beat of the music, says Lyn, "constantly pleading with me to turn [it] up louder," though it was already "so loud that Henry Williams, our assistant coach, and I could hardly hear ourselves think in the front seat." When they reached the campus and Maggie jumped out of the van, she turned to Lyn. "Well, Coach, will you miss us now that the season is over?"

Lyn replied, "Maggie, all I have to do is turn the music up really, really [loud], and I'll think you're still there."

Back in her room, Maggie got a call from Nick Duiker: he had gotten out of work early; did she still want to go to the dance? She said she would meet him at the student center.

The golf team met for a preparty at the off-campus home of their senior captain, Gillian Hooker. "Maggie seemed so happy," Sara Church recalled, "all gussied up in her dress. I remember taking a picture [of the team] with various liquor bottles in hand, laughing at how Coach would get a kick out of that." The women split up before heading to Hicks Center for the dance.

When Nick got there from his apartment off campus, Maggie was standing outside, waiting for him. "She jumped in my arms and gave me a kiss and said, 'I had one of the best tournaments, and it's all because of you—I was really excited to see you.'" Nick didn't have a ticket to the dance, which was sold out, so some sleight-of-hand was perpetrated at the entrance: a friend of Maggie's distracted the gatekeeper while they nabbed a ticket for Nick. He and Maggie went up the stairs to the room known as Old Welles, the former dining hall, a cavernous, echoing space used for just such occasions. "We just kind of danced and talked a lot of the night," Nick recalls. "We danced almost the whole time."

Someone took two photos of the couple dancing, the last pictures taken of Maggie. Both are crowd shots, Nick and Maggie wedged into a mass of bodies. One is shot from behind, so that all you see is her long, shiny ponytail and the back of a strapless dress. The other is taken from the side. They lean into each other, making themselves heard. Maggie is smiling gently, her mouth open, speaking. The look on her face is hopeful, anticipatory. Her skin glistens. Nick's dark hair is shaved up over his ears and brushed up in the front, and his lips part slightly. He looks slightly drunk—as, in fact, he was. They might be about to kiss. The students around them seem to be moving and talking in a million directions. You can feel, hear, smell the frenetic energy in the room. But it is as if Maggie and Nick are in the quiet eye of a hurricane, completely oblivious.

Partier though he was not, Neenef showed up at the dance. Soon after he arrived, he danced with Kirsten Fritsch, who lived upstairs from him in DeWaters. "He didn't seem angry. He didn't seem sad. . . . His shirt was cool and smooth under my hands, the coolest thing in that room full of energetic and perspiring people." Brian Newman, Neenef's suitemate across the bathroom, saw him smiling and apparently enjoying himself. "Everything seemed fine." But within a matter of minutes, Neenef spotted Maggie and Nick on the dance floor. When he saw Brian again, the weather had changed radically. Neenef "said it was the worst day ever," and began to make the rounds, recounting his betrayal to his friends. He told fellow computer science major Nate Cooper that Maggie and Nick "were sucking face." Nate later told police that he thought he had heard something about Neenef saying, "I should kill that guy," but he wondered if he was imagining it. Given Neenef's previous threats against other men, Nate's memory could be accurate.

Nancy El-Shamaa is haunted by her last effort to help her friend put his relationship with Maggie in the past that night.

I saw him sulking in a corner somewhere, and I was dancing with my friend. I beat myself up a lot over this, but in the end, it's done, and I can't bring that night back. I saw him sulking and I said, "Neenef, what's going on?" and he said, "She's dancing with some guy; she's a whore," and he probably called her a couple other names, I don't remember. And he was like, "How can she be shoving it in my face like that when we were talking about getting back together? She's just shoving it in my face; she's dancing with another guy." I said, "Neenef, we told you that you deserved better. I thought you were getting over her. She cheated on you once; don't worry about it! *Let* her date another guy. You deserve better than that. You might get back together and she might cheat on you again. Move on."

The conversation lasted maybe half an hour. Nancy finally said, "'Let's talk about this later. If you're so upset, call me tomorrow.' And I went back to my friends. It's something . . . I don't know if I can ever feel fine about, you know?"

Near the end of the dance, Nick Duiker looked over to the edge of the ballroom to see Neenef standing on a chair, staring at him. Maggie said, "Oh, just ignore him." But Nick was annoyed. "I guess my past instincts, and my adrenaline . . . I don't really like to be stared at. He's a little guy, I don't know why he's so aggressive." Direct eye contact functioned exactly as it does between male dogs. "He just stared at me. I said, 'I'm going to go talk to him, because I don't really like it.'" Nick's masculine response collided with Maggie's feminine training. "No, no," she said; she insisted that he stay put. She would be the peacemaker.

The conversation was loud and volatile, although buried by the music and the noise of the crowd. Neenef insisted that Maggie not go home with Nick, and she finally agreed, probably only "to pacify him," in Nick's view. "Whatever," he thought, "just leave us alone." He didn't see Neenef again. What if he had overruled Maggie? Nick wonders. What if he had taken Neenef on, punched him out? Would that have been the end of it?

Later, drunk and exhausted from dancing, Nick and Maggie walked to his house, several blocks off campus. They sat and drank water, trying to rehydrate themselves. And they talked.

> We talked about her life, what she did this summer, how upset she was about Rob; we talked about a lot that night. I had a similar situation: my brother and I weren't getting along that well either; we were kind of fighting. But we just talked about our families. I guess my real attraction was that she was so quick-witted. She was able to keep up with me. My humor is very zingy, and she zinged me right back. And it's the first time I'd ever been with someone that fun loving. I'm very fun loving, and I like to joust back and forth, and we did a lot of that. We talked about her working in construction with her uncle. She showed me her arm [muscle] and I said [sarcastically], "Wow, that's really big." She hit me. It was almost like we were together for a lot longer than we were, really. And we just kind of went to bed. It was pretty late, and I had to work in the morning.

Back in DeWaters after the dance, Nate Cooper tried to get Neenef to hang out in his room, but Neenef said he was too upset. Stacy Lantz eventually talked him into coming to her room for a while, where she undoubtedly heard the story. Neenef finally went off to bed, according to Nate, around 6:00 a.m. But earlier in the evening, Ninjoda sent Smizgirl two final messages—attempts to continue punishing her for her behavior at the dance, but also, of course, to check on her whereabouts.

1:12 a.m. maggie you fucking amaze me

2:21 a.m. maggie you there?

Around 9:00 Sunday morning, Nick drove Maggie back to campus, stopping on Academy Street in front of Trowbridge. "OK," he said, "I'll give you a call Monday. I have to work, and I have a paper to write." Before she got out of the car, Maggie said, "I really want this to be more." Again he assured her he'd call.

Maggie ran up the steps to the front door of Trow, and Nick drove off to Ponderosa, hungover. "That was the last time I saw her."

Maggie's posse had a tradition of Sunday brunch together in the cafeteria. They all grilled Maggie about what happened with Nick, but according to Erin, she deflected their questions. "Oh, nothing . . ." Then, when they left, she spun around to Erin: "OK, now I can tell you what really happened!" Maggie was in the throes of new-romance excitement.

She had plans that night with Heidi Fahrenbacher to go to the Zoo, one of two local gay bars. Maggie, who had never been there, was curious, and Heidi, who knew the place, was happy to show her around. But Heidi, who had been drinking enough the night before to get herself ejected from the Homecoming dance, woke too hungover to contemplate an evening out, and she canceled.

Around 1:00 p.m., Maggie, J'nai, and Emily Ford showed up at Erin and Leza's room on the bottom floor of DeWaters to make plans for congregating that night around ten to watch *When Harry Met Sally*. When they arrived, Erin was messaging an old friend. Preoccupied, she found their intrusion annoying. She remembers Maggie pressing her nose against the window screen outside, insisting on her attention. Maggie told her, at some point, that she had agreed to go to Neenef's room that night, but she didn't say why. Erin's impression was that he had asked for a few minutes to get some closure on the relationship. According to J'nai, Maggie spent the rest of the afternoon at the library at Western Michigan University, studying for a Spanish test.

Navin Anthony had gone home that weekend. Arriving back on campus Sunday afternoon, he crossed the bathroom to say hi to Neenef, who was typing at his computer. Navin asked how the weekend had gone. "Terrible," Neenef said and recounted the story of the dance, where he said Maggie had been "acting slutty." Navin says, "He was really pissed off, *really* pissed off about the whole thing. I remember him saying that so many times—he had brought up the whole Maggie situation so many times . . . I was kind of like, 'I think you really have to let this go, man. I mean, she's definitely moved on. It's time for you to let this go and try to move on, too.' He kind of agreed to that, but you could tell that there was more to that whole thing."

Neenef's agreement was indeed perfunctory; the fresh air of Navin's good counsel could not permeate the miasma that Neenef was now breathing. Neenef told him that Maggie was coming over later and said he might drop in to say goodnight to Navin after she left.

Neenef went to dinner at the cafeteria that night, and several friends said he seemed fine. Around 6:00, he told Nate Cooper that Maggie was coming over later. At 6:30 Brian Newman— Navin's roommate across the bathroom in 203—and another friend, Dan Wegner, visited Neenef's room, finding him "upbeat and normal." At 7:42, Neenef sent an ominous e-mail to Stacy Lantz. Beginning and ending with reassurances, he pushes her kindly away again. But this time he describes himself as lethal, like an unexploded bomb.

> stacy,
>
> it's all good. . . . it would be a lot better for now and for a while to kinda stay away from me and to not get too close. I've had nothing but 20 years of fucked up shit. wherever i go, and whatever i do my life seems to be centered around trouble [so] i'm telling you now it's a good idea to kind of back off. i don't know how long i'm gonna continue living this kind of life, but i hope not for too much longer cause i can't handle it. a person

can only take so much before he loses it. anyways, this doesn't mean we can't chill every once in a while so. well i'm gonna get going now. lata

neenef

Around the same time, Nick Duiker finished a paper and picked up the phone to call Maggie. He says, "And I thought, 'No, I'll just call her on Monday.' Why, I don't know. I did. 'Maybe I'll just let it be.'"

Somewhere between 8:30 and 9:00 that night, Neenef's new friend Heather Barnes dropped by DeWaters 201. Heather had begun calling Neenef her "adopted brother." But tonight Neenef seemed cold, focused on something he was typing into his computer, clearly not wanting to chat.

Around 11:00 p.m., Eric Page left the room to help a friend with a ceramics project across campus in the Fine Arts Building. Neenef told him that Maggie was coming over, and they agreed on their usual signal: if Eric was not to enter, the model of a football helmet on the door, bearing the number 6, would be turned around so that the number read as a 9.

Next door in Trowbridge, in Maggie and J'nai's room, Maggie, J'nai, and Emily had decided to skip *When Harry Met Sally* in favor of homework. Maggie was on her bed, studying. J'nai was at the computer, writing two papers simultaneously. Around 11:15, an instant message popped up on the screen from Neenef, looking for Maggie. His roommate, he wrote, had left; she could come over now. J'nai identified herself but didn't call Maggie to the computer. Neenef wrote again, and again J'nai said, in effect, "It's me, not Maggie." She told Maggie he'd written, and Maggie called him back. When she hung up, she said Neenef wanted her to come over to "read something," but would not say what it was.

Emily and J'nai, worried about Neenef's continuing pull on Maggie, both urged her not to go. "It'll only be twenty minutes," Maggie said, donning her blue sweatshirt for the short jaunt from Trow to DeWaters. J'nai warned her, "I'm going to call if you're not back in twenty minutes."

After Eric left DeWaters 201, Heather Barnes returned; this time she was with Stacy Lantz. They found Neenef still preoccupied and distant. He told them that Maggie was coming over. They wished him luck. Heather hugged him and told him to come and get her after Maggie was gone, and the two women left. On their way down the hall, they passed Maggie coming in.

THIS ENDLESS NIGHT

1

At about 11:20 p.m., something prompted Navin Anthony to check on his neighbor. Not realizing that Maggie was already there, he went through the bathroom, knocked on the door, opened it, and stuck his head in. Neenef rose from his computer and came to the door, and Navin took a step into the room. Maggie was sitting on a couch in the room, facing the bathroom door. Her face was red. "I could see that she was crying. I saw her look at me. She definitely looked at me." Neenef said, "Yeah, we're kind of talking right now," and promised again to stop by later. "And immediately I just closed the door and went back to my room." He was the last person to see either of them alive.

Downstairs in DeWaters 110, Erin and Leza were in their room watching *When Harry Met Sally* with their buddy Jeff Hopcian. Around midnight, they heard a loud sound overhead, "a sound like a dresser falling over." They were startled, but, as Jeff put it, "One doesn't find these types of noises unusual after a few years of college dorm life."

At that moment, Brandon Chuchran, who lived directly upstairs from Neenef in 302, was walking down the second-floor hallway toward the back stairs, headed outside for a smoke. He was about fifty feet from Neenef's room when he heard loud screaming that, to him, sounded like a wounded dog. He also heard loud banging, like something being knocked over or thrown against the wall. But neither sound alarmed him enough for him to stop, and he continued outside.

Directly across the hall from Neenef's room, in 202, Aaron Beckwitz, Mark Brooks, and John Evans also heard the eruption of sound, which Aaron described as being "like pots or pans or dishes hitting the wall." He and Mark also heard a woman yelling. John leaned out into the hall to see what was going on, but saw nothing.

In the room adjoining theirs, 204, Eric Snyder heard yelling and what he thought were objects being thrown around, as well as a female voice saying something like, "I'm sorry, Neenef!"

Neenef's "little sister" Heather Barnes was on her way outside with Mike Calhoun, who lived in 206, and Will Burkhill, from 304, for the popular midnight smoke break. Mike heard screaming and two loud bangs, and froze. Heather heard something like, "Neenef, no!" and the loud noises. She pictured Neenef sweeping everything off his desk, computer and all. After pausing in the stairwell, they continued downstairs and outside.

Back in 205, Heather's roommate, Alisha Serras, was typing on her computer when three loud bangs—two close together, the third after a short pause—shook the walls of the room. Across the hall in 206, Kathleen Mitchell, who was visiting Vaughn Preston and Mike Calhoun, heard a muddle of loud noises and a female voice: "No, Neenef, no!" Her roommate, Elizabeth Weakland, was on the phone in their room, 207, with the door open, when the three loud bangs sounded.

In 208, Anthony Pagorek thought that someone was nailing something into the wall. His roommate, Mark Pietka, thought someone was probably kicking a soccer ball around the corridor, as Neenef was known to do. Annoyed, Anthony looked out but only saw John Evans, doing the same.

Back in 203, Navin heard the screams, and the words, "Neenef, don't do that!" followed by the loud bangs. Like everyone else, he reached into the realm of the known to make sense of the sound:

It was kind of like he was taking a bat and hitting it against the wall, you know? I had no idea what was going on. I didn't understand what was happening. I know he had a bat in the room, I remember seeing a bat in the room, I thought he was hitting it against the wall, that's what it sounded like. No clue what was going on. It just kept going, and all of a sudden there was nothing. It was just, like, silence.

And then I just kind of smelled some smoke. I was so naive—I had never even smelled gunsmoke before—I didn't understand what it was.

Navin went out into the hall, where people had started to gather. He banged on Neenef's door and heard only more silence. Spotting Heather Barnes, he told her what he'd heard. They went into Navin's room to approach Neenef's room through the bathroom.

When they opened the bathroom door, Heather saw blood and something "like chicken" seeping under the closed door from 201. Trying to domesticate this surreal image, she decided it might have spilled from the refrigerator that Neenef had knocked over during the fight. Navin simply couldn't process what he was seeing: "There was blood and it seemed like some brain matter on the ground—so when you opened the door, the bathroom floor, there was blood there and pieces of flesh on the ground. I didn't know what to make of it, I still couldn't connect until later. I didn't even try opening the [far] door. I thought maybe he had tried hurting himself or even hurting her. But everything was just silent. It was just very, very strange. It was a strange silence." Quietly, he closed the door.

In a state of what can only be called severe cognitive dissonance, he met Jeff, Leza, and Erin in the hall. "Something's wrong," he said. "Neenef and Maggie are having a really bad fight." He said he thought they were even throwing things at each other because there was something—something that looked to him like raw meat—all over the bathroom. Neenef's roommate Eric Page was a hunter, Navin reasoned; maybe he had stocked the mini-fridge with meat. Navin led Jeff through his room to the bathroom. "Inside, the room was literally covered in blood and bits of flesh," Jeff says. "Maggie. I can still see it. . . . The air was heavy and warm with a smell. I recognized gunpowder—which later, in retrospect, seems strange because I can't remember having encountered the smell of gunpowder before this. Time was moving slowly. I turned around (did I speak?) and went to my friends, outside waiting for me."

"Did you talk to Maggie?" they asked.

He said, "I think we need to call the police."

Someone told him that College Security had been called. Now terri-fied, Erin and Leza banged on Neenef's door, Erin yelling, "Get Maggie out! Just get Maggie out!" Unable to imagine the worst, she, like the others, wrote her own scenario: Neenef had knocked Maggie uncon-scious, jumped out the window, and was on his way to kill Nick Duiker. It was the other men, after all, that he was always threatening to kill. Jeff stood by, dazed.

> I knew what had really happened, or at least part of it. I knew someone had been shot. I knew that person was dead. . . . Did anyone else know? I'm not sure. They all seemed to think Maggie and Neenef were sitting there having a private conversation, failing to answer our loud knocks and calls because they wanted to ignore us. I didn't say anything. . . . I didn't want to. I didn't want to say it and make it true. What if somehow I was wrong?

Navin had gone for the resident assistant on duty, Brad Zielaskowski, who lived on the top floor, in 410. Brad ran down, tried the hallway door to 201, and then ducked into Navin's room to go through the bath-room. When he opened the bathroom door, he looked for a moment, then backed out and closed the door. "Oh my God," he said. "That's gunsmoke." He called College Security. Other RAs showed up, banged on Neenef's door, and then, like Brad, tried the bathroom access.

By now a crowd had assembled in the hallway, everyone wanting to know what had happened. When the security guard arrived, Erin found herself herding everyone down the hall, away from the door, toward the lounge. The guard, Brian Napkie, was a twenty-two-year-old rookie, drawn, as the guards often were, from the graduate student popula-tion at Western Michigan University, where he was a business student. He keyed into 201, opened the door, and began to step inside. "Oh, my God!" he cried, and backed out. "He opened the door and closed it mere seconds later," Jeff Hopcian recalls. "His hand never left the knob."

Brian called the Kalamazoo Department of Public Safety on his ra-dio. It was around 12:10 a.m. Then he and the RAs ordered all the students back into their rooms.

Down campus, in a college house that served that year as a cooperative living-learning unit for students in the arts, Heidi Fahrenbacher was up late, finishing a paper. Her housemates were all out; she was alone in the house. Just after midnight, before going to bed, she went to the bathroom. Suddenly she heard someone calling her name, a female voice. She paused for a moment and then shook it off as imagination. And then she heard it again. It must be Suzanne, her housemate, she thought; maybe she'd come in and Heidi hadn't heard her. She turned the light off, opened the door, and called, "Suzanne?" But the house was silent.

2

The police cars arrived at the Lovell Street entrance to the campus drive without lights or sirens, in the hope of saving lives. Public Safety Officer Kelley was first on the scene, followed soon by Officer Hendricks and Sergeant Johncock, who would be the scene commander, and then by Officers Crouse, Kozal, Hemengway, and Doerr. They spoke quickly with Brian Napkie, the security guard, and Brad Zielaskowski, the RA. And then Kelley and Johncock went down the hall and opened the now-unlocked door of 201. "I was behind Sgt. Johncock," Kelley wrote in his report, "and saw a female [lying] face down on the floor on the west side of the room. I also saw a male slumped over in the south west corner of the room. I was unable to see either of them clearly but was advised that both were obviously dead, and Sgt. Johncock and I backed out of the room and I began to take witness statements." Johncock assigned Hendricks to secure rooms 201 and 203, as well as the exit across the hall from 201. Hendricks then guarded the door to 201. Crouse had been dispatched to the Lovell Street entrance to the campus, to help the ambulance find DeWaters, but in his own bleak words, "Moments later it was confirmed that two bodies had been located and Life would not be needed."

Crouse then guarded the immediate entrance to the dorm, while Doerr, Kelley, and Kozal were directed to various floors of the dorm to interview students, who were all ordered to go to their rooms. The building was secured.

Jeff Hopcian found Erin Rome. "Is Maggie dead?" she asked, and he said yes.

———————

Will Burkhill, who lived in DeWaters 304, came back in from his smoke break and told his friends on the third floor that something was up. They included third-floor resident Kirsten Fritsch and her boyfriend. Kirsten had danced with Neenef at Homecoming.

> Very quickly after that we saw the flashing of ambulance lights as the vehicles pulled up to the back door of DeWaters (visible from our shared hallway window), and remarks were made that "whatever was going on couldn't be that bad . . . there were no sirens after all . . . no one was rushing away to the hospital." Then the RAs came through the building, asking everyone to stay in their rooms. Then police officers came through the building, asking us all in turn if we had seen or heard anything unusual that night. Shortly after this, [the two guys] ventured out again and were stopped in the hallway and told to grab whatever they needed for the night and to evacuate the building. An RA, I believe it was Brad Z[ielaskowski], then told them what had happened to Neenef and Maggie. The guys came back up and broke the news.

Kirsten dropped to the floor, "right there in the hallway, speechless. I just couldn't believe that Neenef could have done something like that." Her mind went to the dance the night before—that cool, smooth shirt.

———————

Gail Simpson, in her tenth year as assistant director of Security, was at home that night, shortly before midnight, when Brian Napkie called to tell her that the guard due to replace him at midnight had called in sick. Gail asked if Brian could stay for a few more hours, promising to come in early herself the next morning. He agreed. Fifteen minutes later, her phone rang again. Brian said, "I need you *now*." As Gail recalls, "I asked him if he had called the police, and he said yes. I didn't even know exactly what it was. It was just his voice . . . just in the tone of his voice, I knew that something had happened really bad, you know, so I got dressed and came in to work. Half way here, I called to see where he was, because I realized that I didn't even know that."

The drive in from Gail's home in Bloomingdale, west of Kalamazoo, usually took thirty-five minutes; this time it took twenty. "By the time I got here, the building was filled with police officers, there were students standing outside crying, and then I knew something horrid had happened. I'd gotten into DeWaters and Brian was sitting in the lobby with his head in his hands. I walked over and asked him what happened, and he says 'Gail, there was just a bloody mess.'"

A police officer walked over to shoo Gail out of the building, but when she identified herself, he filled her in. Gail, who made it her business to know the students, had an idea who Maggie and Neenef were. Brian told her that when he was called, nobody mentioned blood or loud bangs, so he had keyed into the room in ignorance, walking into billowing gunsmoke and a nightmare of carnage. "What if [Neenef had] been sitting there, you know, waiting for the next person to come in?" he asked.

Brian had also called Glenn Nevelle, Gail's boss, who was on vacation that week. A big ex-cop who looked like a marine drill sergeant, Glenn had been hired to head College Security ten years before, after two sexual assaults in one of the dorms prompted the college to move to twenty-four-hour security. Brian's composure during this call, in striking contrast to his call to Gail, impressed Glenn: "He was so cool. He said, 'Well, we've got a murder-suicide.'"

After a pause, Glenn said, "What did you say?"

"We've got a murder-suicide. I called the police."

"A murder? *And* a suicide?"

"Yeah."

"I'll be right there."

He quickly dressed and began the fifty-minute drive from his home in Caledonia.

The head resident in DeWaters called Vaughn Maatman, associate dean of students for Residence Life. Living near the campus, Vaughn was the first college official on the scene, and he would not leave it for days to come. It was either Vaughn or Glenn who called Marilyn LaPlante, vice president for Experiential Education, who lived five miles west of town.

At once formidable and gentle, a rare amalgam of "company man" and independent woman, Marilyn came as close as anyone on campus to being held in universal respect. I had been mentally referring certain kinds of questions to her, asking myself what she would do in a given situation, for several years when I discovered that others did the same. From then on, "What Would Marilyn Do?" became an in-joke.

An Iowan, Marilyn had come to K in 1979 as associate provost. In those days women candidates for anything other than clerical staff were so few and far between that their itinerary was organized to include a meeting with other women faculty and administrators. In fact, that meeting had been a high point of my own interview two years before Marilyn arrived. In Marilyn's meeting with us, some of us asked her pointed questions about her principles and loyalties where the status of women was concerned. "Let me put it this way," she said at last. "I will be an ally. But I won't be an advocate." Her honesty planted a respect in me that continually blossomed and grew over the next twenty years, during which time I had occasion to consult with her and to work with her on any number of projects and problems.

As associate provost, Marilyn did valuable institutional research, met with chagrined students, and handled the overload in the academic affairs area. But the minor and major convulsions of the eighties and nineties revealed and polished her inordinate skill at solving problems, putting out fires, conciliating fierce personalities, rising to whatever occasion presented itself. And at a small and radically understaffed college, occasions always do present themselves. She could always be relied upon to take the Institutional View of things, but she got a reputation for wisdom as well (the two seem frequently opposed in academe).

After several years as associate provost, she found herself dean of students and then vice president for Experiential Education, a hat designed specifically for her under the presidency of James F. Jones Jr. The institutional power chart was rearranged to accommodate her in that new role: both the dean of students and the director of the Career Development Center reported to her, and she also oversaw various programs in service learning. But her most important role became the one not listed in her job description: she counseled the president. In fact, she rapidly became his Number One. Jimmy came to rely on her judgment almost totally, and she rapidly emerged as the one person who could tell him to his face when he was wrong or that he should shut up—an absolute necessity for a president. The 1999–2000 school year was supposed to be Marilyn's last before retirement.

As she sped down M-43 toward the campus at 1:00 a.m. on October 18, she called the president's house. She told Jimmy what had happened and then, before signing off, confessed that she was driving about sixty-five miles per hour and hoped she wouldn't get pulled over. He told her to be careful.

Jimmy had come to K College three years earlier to whip us into shape. He arrived in the midst of financial straits, after two presidencies in a row imploded, faculty got cut for the first time in living memory, and the atmosphere became toxic. After years in St. Louis and Dallas, he yearned to return to the east coast, and he assumed the faculty at K was also leaning lustfully in that direction. That is, he wanted administrators, faculty, and students to aim for Amherst, for Williams. To pursue an alternate legacy—say, the distinctive tradition of the midwestern liberal arts college—was not on the agenda.

The Jones presidency was marked by a linguistic shift at K. Most notably, what we always called "the cafeteria" or "the caf" or just "Hicks"—the name of the student center in which the dining hall is housed—was now "the refectory." The fall ceremony we had previously referred to as "Convocation" or simply "Opening Day," became "Matriculation Day." Jimmy, a scholar of eighteenth-century French literature, brought with him a Eurocentric academic ideal. The ancient universities of Paris and Bologna were invoked on most public occasions. Latinate locutions proliferated.

President Jones's vocabulary was not, however, the first thing we noticed about his presidency. We first noticed how good it looked. James F. Jones Jr. could play the part of the president of the United States in a movie. Tall, trim, with rosy skin and well-cut, wavy dark hair silvered at the temples, he is always immaculately dressed. His suits and white shirts would unravel in shame before they would show a particle of dust or a wrinkle. As a kid I never knew what it meant when my elders spoke of someone as looking "like he just stepped out of a bandbox," but that's how Jimmy looks.

Southern by birth, Jimmy speaks of everybody as his dear old friend, including the famous and powerful. He loves to tease and, even more, to be teased. His characteristic mode is hyperbole. He has a supply of expensive cigars, and he never fails to bring a fifth of good bourbon to an elderly woman who has a lot of money she might want to give to the college. Military by training—he signs e-mails "Semper Fi"—he has a backbone like steel, well-set shoulders (both of which features make his blue suits show even more impressively) and the administrative style to go with them. He works like an engine—answering e-mail daily for several hours before going for his early morning jog—and expects as much of everyone else.

On October 18, 1999, Jimmy Jones had experienced only one other student death in his career. While he was dean of arts and sciences at Southern Methodist University, two drunk boys fell while "elevator surfing"—that is, riding on top of side-by-side elevators and jumping back and forth. One died; the other was permanently disabled. But Jimmy knew that, grisly as that incident had been, this was different. There was nothing accidental about it. He pulled on some clothes and ran down the block to Academy Street and then up behind the chapel to DeWaters. By the time he got there, Marilyn had arrived. It was around 1:20 a.m. when they walked into the DeWaters lobby. "Police were everywhere," Jimmy said, "and the students were just sitting in the lounge looking like survivors from a war zone, which of course they were."

Vaughn Maatman had also called dean of students Danny Sledge. Danny was raised in Benton Harbor, the largely African American city situated next to the very white St. Joe, Stephanie Miller's town. Danny and his wife, a K alumna, had raised two sons in Kalamazoo, one now off at college. He came to K as associate dean for Multicultural Affairs and had recently become dean of students, on July 1. Danny is a warm, approachable man and a renowned hugger with remarkable patience for students' sometimes prolonged and wavering developmental arcs. His decidedly unbureaucratic outfits, including colorful shoes that match his tie or his shirt, were famous on campus. Danny also has a lovely Irish tenor, which won him the dubious honor of leading us all in our painful rendering of the Alma Mater each fall on Matriculation Day.

As Danny drove in, it all felt very surreal. His clear, longstanding career objective had been to become a dean of students. Now, only a little more than three months into the job, the unimaginable had happened. "This is the stuff you read about or watch on TV," he thought. As he approached the campus, he thought about his own son at the University of Michigan, imagined getting the call. He made "a conscious effort to put my personal emotions in check" and get into professional mode. He wasn't the only one to say later that the sense of immediate, compelling professional responsibility helped him keep it together.

Another one of the earliest people notified was Tom Ponto, vice president for Business. A twenty-year veteran of the college, Tom had a reputation for airtight management and the kind of unswerving fidelity to the bottom line that successive presidents loved (hence his longevity) but that is often called "bean counting" by those with more laissez-faire financial philosophies. A more businesslike, procedure-oriented, tight-lipped administrator would be hard to find. He was deputed to call the rest of the senior administration, plus other college personnel whose presence was critical. That would include his sister, Pat Ponto, the director of the college Counseling Center, whom he called around 1:00 a.m. "There's been a homicide-suicide at the college," he explained, "and you have to come." He told her to bring her young son, Luke, to his house, where his wife, Sue, was also awake. On her way to the campus, Pat called her assistant director, Alan Hill, and as many of the interns working in the Counseling Center that fall as she could reach. She prayed the shooter wouldn't turn out to be a student client. "Whenever there's an emergency, I think, 'Did we miss somebody? Did *I* miss somebody? Did we not take good enough care?'"

When Pat arrived, she had a hard time getting near DeWaters. The Lovell Street side of the building was banked in swirling police lights; the north side, facing the quad, was clotted with weeping, frightened students. Pat finally made it into the lounge immediately inside the quad entrance, where the residents were now huddled, a trauma scene jacked up by anxiety and frustration as the police refused to let anyone leave. "And nobody could call home, call their families—the kids were just frantic about that," Pat says. Until the police notified Maggie and Neenef's parents, neither their names nor what had happened in 201 could be made public. "All these kids were upset, and . . . we couldn't tell them exactly what happened, we couldn't tell them to whom it had happened, so we had a lot of frenzy."

Navin Anthony says, "I remember it seeming like an eternity. I still thought that maybe he'd hurt her, or he'd hurt himself, but that was it, and I thought maybe someone was still alive in that room."

Soon thereafter, Kalamazoo Public Safety was advised to contact the Seattle Police Department so that officers could be dispatched to the

Odahs' home. Captain Jerome Bryant and Officer James Doerr began the drive to Plainwell, to knock on the Omilians' door.

It was associate dean Vaughn Maatman who, after conferring with police and being permitted to look inside Room 201, told the students congregated in DeWaters what had happened. Afterward, when he came out of DeWaters and walked toward his colleagues, Danny Sledge thought, "I do not want to hear this."

The immediate issue was the DeWaters residents. The police were insisting that they all remain in the dorm. Jimmy began to argue. "My first concern was to get the students on the [second] floor out of that hellish place as soon as possible. Marilyn, Pat, and I stayed with the students in the lounge until I could prevail upon the police to let them go. This entailed having the police interview the students, which they did en masse, before we moved them to the Chapel. We eventually moved them to Trowbridge."

The DeWaters students were released around 2:00 a.m. With DeWaters in police custody, as it were, Trowbridge, next door, became the heart of the crisis that now began to spread across the campus. And beyond: the shootings had been broadcast on police radio and picked up by the media. The press began to arrive and congregate outside of DeWaters.

Marilyn LaPlante called a meeting of the Crisis Management Team for 3:00 a.m.

3

When J'nai Leafers heard a knock on her door in Trowbridge and opened it, a first-year male student who lived across the hall was standing there, refusing to look at her. "Something's happened in DeWaters," he said. "You should go over there." J'nai went over but was prohibited from entering, so she returned to her room, not worried, only confused.

Chris Wilson was on his way out of Trowbridge and wondered, "What's all the commotion?" People told him there were ambulances outside, and someone mentioned that they'd pulled up without sirens. He wondered why. Word began to spread outside DeWaters: something bad had happened involving Neenef and Maggie. No one was saying what exactly it was. When Chris heard the rumor, he immediately recalled what Neenef had said about wanting to shoot his professor.

Neenef's friend Caitlin Gilmet and her roommate were at their desks in Trowbridge, "finishing homework (her) and procrastinating (me)." One of them got a message from a friend in DeWaters, saying that there were police cars outside. "We went to the window to look and saw that there were a bunch of cars in the lot. We wrote back to [our friend], who said that Maggie and Neenef had disappeared. I remember not being too worried—I mean, college students go away for the weekend all the time, and I hadn't really talked to either of them much since the new school year began."

J'nai and Nandini met outside Trow and sat, waiting for news. Maggie and Neenef had had a fight, they heard, and Maggie was in the hospital. Marilyn LaPlante walked up to them and asked them to come inside. "It doesn't look good," she said. The two of them, plus Chris, were ushered into the head resident's apartment in Trowbridge, where counselors Pat Ponto and Alan Hill had established themselves to deal with people named by other students as closest to Maggie and Neenef.

J'nai doesn't remember being frightened. But she also doesn't remember Pat Ponto telling her that Maggie was dead. Pat recalls "saying to her—and she was still thinking Maggie might be alive—'She didn't make it.' And I remember thinking, 'I don't think she really understood that.'"

A police officer came to take J'nai's statement. "I'll never forget the look on his face," J'nai says. When they finished, he asked if there was anything else she wanted to know.

"Is she going to be OK?"

The officer glanced at Marilyn LaPlante and then turned back to J'nai. "She's dead. She's been murdered."

In many ways the story of this night is about what the mind cannot grasp. Memory is a trickster in any case; in such a case as this, memory shattered by trauma struggles to piece together a logical story and often comes up with conflicting narratives. For example, Nandini and Chris remember the events in the head resident's apartment in Trowbridge very differently from J'nai. Nandini recalls the room as charged with the unspoken. "I could tell," she says, "somebody knew something in that room." The three students asked to know what was going on. At that point, President Jones came in. According to Chris's account, he "started giving a little mini-speech, and at the end of it, he seems kind of flustered, but he says, in a very dry manner, 'and I just don't know how to tell a person that their child has died. I don't know how to tell Maggie's parents that their child is dead.'

"It hit, like, five seconds later: 'Oh. She's dead.'"

Nandini says that this is how she and J'nai found out. They began to cry. "For some reason I held it in," says Chris. "I was definitely bewildered and shocked. And I remember walking out there in this trance, not knowing what was going on, and walking out there and realizing that everyone else has heard what we've heard before, and people just sobbing on the sidewalks."

As snatches of information swirled through the building, Caitlin Gilmet found her way down to the crowded lounge. She recalls seeing Jimmy Jones. She says, "I remember thinking that something very bad had happened to make this confident, even inflated character seem so drawn and human." Word spread in Trowbridge—from the police, from Marilyn LaPlante, from Pat Ponto, and from other students. Eventually they all heard the brief, terrible truth.

Kelly Schulte was off campus, at a friend's house, watching a movie, when she was suddenly, completely overtaken by an anxiety that surged up from nowhere. "It was the weirdest—I've never had this feeling before in my life. . . . I said, 'I have to go right now. I have this weird feeling; I don't know what it is.' I just had to leave. I remember that I was driving [into the campus drive at] the back of DeWaters and I saw all the police cars. I pulled up in front of Hoben and illegally parked."

She called Katherine Chamberlain, who was up writing an English paper in her room in Harmon, adjacent to Hoben, and asked her to join her for a smoke. They were sitting on the Hoben steps when they spotted their buddy Jeff Basta walking toward them. Katherine says, "I remember looking at him and thinking, like, his face had gone blank. He just looked very disturbed. His eyes were really blue. I couldn't stop staring at his eyes."

Kelly asked about the police cars. "Do you know what's going on?"

Jeff stammered, "Something happened to Maggie. I can't tell you." But the two women demanded to know.

"It was just like he saw a ghost," says Kelly, "and I knew that she was dead." When Jeff confirmed it, she had, at once, no doubt who had killed her. "And we kind of stood there. Later we tried to find out what happened, but in that moment, time stood still." Katherine remembers "freezing."

They moved to Kelly's room in Hoben, then to Katherine's in Harmon, where they told the news to her roommate, Carrie Heist, also a good friend of Maggie's. In the meanwhile, Vaughn Maatman, whose mission was to track down the people named as Maggie's closest friends, arrived at Harmon in search of Katherine. He told her to sit down, and then he confirmed what had happened. "Very sweet. Very kind. I remember him hugging me." Kelly remained standing, frozen and expressionless.

Before heading to Trowbridge to find J'nai, Nandini, and Erin, Katherine called home, crying, and the enormity of what had happened sank to another level of knowing: "I realized something really bad had happened by hearing the shock in my parents' voices."

Dan Poskey, one of Maggie's crowd, had been working on a paper in the computer lab in Olds-Upton, at the foot of the quad. Around one o'clock, as he was leaving the lab with his roommate, they saw the police cars moving through the campus. Dan asked an officer where they were going, and he pointed up to DeWaters. "I didn't think any more of it," says Dan. They went back to their off-campus apartment and went to bed. Suddenly his roommate was knocking on his bedroom door, saying that the head of Residence Life was on the phone. Two of their friends were dead, she said, and they needed to come to Trowbridge immediately.

I was half asleep, which probably left me more confused than anything, but nonetheless, I was in complete disbelief. I spent the ten-minute drive to campus literally counting off my friends and trying to figure out who it was, trying to figure out who had died (not just one, but two friends) and how it had happened. It was the worst ten minutes of my life.

When we arrived at the Trowbridge lounge, I started looking at faces—accounting for my friends and adding them back to the "alive" category. At that point there weren't many people who knew—it was very late, and they had only been contacting Maggie's friends. Then Katherine Chamberlain came up to me, crying, and told me that Neenef had shot Maggie. At first I was confused, because I kept thinking "two." Then someone else confirmed what had happened, and I understood.

The president of the Student Commission that year was Simone Lutz, a senior political science major. An outgoing, gregarious type, she knew practically everyone on campus, though she knew Maggie and Neenef only slightly. She was in the Student Commission office that night, working on a paper for her senior seminar. She didn't so much finish it as give up on it, some time after 1:00 a.m. "I was incredibly tired, and I said, 'I'm done. Dr. Elman's getting what she's getting.'" She got into her car with a friend to drive to her apartment off campus. They headed down the campus drive in front of Hoben, when she saw Nick Porada, Neenef's second-year roommate, and his girlfriend, Renae Placinski, who was crying. "I stopped the car, and I remember rolling down the passenger window and saying, 'Nick, what'd you do now?'"

Nick shook his head. "No, no, no, it wasn't me." Renae, sobbing, told her what had happened.

Simone was shocked and incredulous. "I was positive she was wrong. Just complete and utter disbelief." She told her friend, "I'll call you in a little while. I'm going to go up to DeWaters."

Marigene Arnold, the professor of anthropology who had taught and counseled Neenef Odah, was asleep when her phone rang just before 2:00 a.m. on October 18. It was K's vice president for Business, Tom Ponto.

"Marilyn wants you to come to the college."

"Why?"

"We've had a murder-suicide."

Marigene had come to Kalamazoo College with a new PhD from the University of Florida in 1973 as a one-year hire in the Department of Sociology and Anthropology. The college hired her for another year and then another and then moved her to the tenure track. For over thirty years, she had lived and breathed Kalamazoo College. She knew everyone, served on every standing and ad hoc committee, advised and taught and counseled thousands of students. She was passionate about football, attending every home game and a good number of away games, too. A dedicated feminist, she also had what seemed like infinite patience with and compassion for the inarticulate, masked, awkward male students, often jocks, who drive many women faculty crazy. Neenef would sit in her office, "it seemed like for hours," ostensibly getting help in her course but more likely seeking temporary sanctuary with a caring adult. In 1999 she was Marilyn LaPlante's closest friend and advisor.

She was up, dressed, and halfway to the campus before realizing she didn't have either her glasses or her contacts, so she returned home.

> I didn't even ask who it was! I didn't even think to ask who it was, you know, I just came. And when I got there, there were kids out front, and they were already burning candles, vigil candles, big candles in glasses. There were maybe two candles there at that point, but pretty soon there were lots and lots of candles. Marilyn came right away and walked me down toward Mandelle [the administration building], to sort of tell me what she wanted me to do.

Stationed in Trowbridge lounge, to the left of the front door, Marigene was to send Maggie's friends to see counselor Pat Ponto, who was operating out of the head resident's apartment, and Neenef's friends to see counselor Alan Hill, located in a side room. But she expanded her mission: "I went and sought out people who were sitting by themselves. Because the other people were talking to other people and I thought they were OK, so I would go up to anybody I saw sitting alone and say, 'Do you need to be alone, or do you want to talk?' So it wound up that I talked to all males. There were no women that were by themselves. I had good conversations with them."

All the young men she spoke with were Maggie's friends, and in these discussions, Marigene discovered a distinctively masculine pattern. She says, "They felt—I'd say to a man—they felt somehow that they had failed because they hadn't protected Maggie. It was kind of an interesting response: 'Maggie was my friend; I should have protected her; I should have taken care of her.'"

At some point one of Marigene's advisees showed up, a student who was in a uniquely painful position: she was on the golf team with Maggie, but she was also a close friend of Neenef's; in fact, she had asked him to come home with her for Thanksgiving the following month. Marigene immediately took her back to Pat Ponto. By now the room was full of weeping women students. The young woman began to cry then, "and she said something like, 'Oh, Neenef, Maggie didn't deserve that.'"

Trowbridge took on the atmosphere of an emergency room or a triage station. Alan Hill remembers the night as chaos, a blur. "I just remember being all over the place, sometimes even in the outer reaches of Trow, when . . . people would say, 'Over here!'" calling him to deal with a particularly distraught student. "There were some people who were crying, some that were just stunned, and once in a while you would hear somebody just break down," as if suddenly stricken by "awareness that there was a great loss here." Pat Ponto was likewise operating moment to moment: "People would come up and say, 'You need to talk to a roommate, do this'; even police officers saying, 'Somebody over here is really upset.' So I think we went sort of from person to person to try to check." Most often Pat and Alan saw shock and denial—not a refusal to believe but an inability to integrate this terrifying knowledge.

Maggie's crew—Kelly Schulte, Erin Rome, Nandini Sonnad, J'nai Leafers, Katherine Chamberlain, Carrie Heist, and Leza Frederickson—dodged the media and converged outside of Trowbridge on a bench and a flight of steps. Katherine remembers Marilyn LaPlante and Vaughn Maatman asking, "What do you need? What do you want?" and getting them coffee and cigarettes. Katherine recalls sitting on the bench with Erin and Leza, holding hands. "It was just silent. It was so quiet. We were all in such despair and complete shock." No one could imagine what to do next or how life might possibly continue.

After "numerous quote-unquote adults" telling her to go home and get some sleep, Student Commission president Simone Lutz found her way to the steps where attention was focused on Maggie's closest friends. "To this day, I can still see all of their faces," Simone says. "I'm just sitting there for hours, on the stairs, sometimes silent, sometimes talking. . . . I know that Jimmy came back and forth; I know that Marilyn came back and forth to the steps where that core group of friends were. I don't remember any of Neenef's friends being there. I only remember Maggie's friends. I'll never forget their faces."

Nancy El-Shamaa was a resident assistant that year, living down campus in Severn. "At about two o'clock my roommates woke me up. I guess they talked amongst themselves before they talked to me. They didn't know he was involved. They woke me up and said, 'There was a shooting in DeWaters.'" Nancy ran next door to Crissey, where her sister Mariam was an area coordinator. Mariam had the full story. "I honestly don't remember the next couple of hours. I remember walking around the DeWaters-Trowbridge area in a haze, comforting people, being comforted. I don't remember the rest of that night, really."

In his apartment several blocks off campus, Nick Duiker couldn't sleep. After resisting the impulse to call Maggie that evening, he now couldn't think of anything else. He says, "I just kept tossing and turning, replaying the whole night, how much fun I had." At about two o'clock, the phone rang. He wondered who would be calling at that hour.

Some minutes later, two of his housemates came into his room, saying they needed to talk to him. "Larry said, 'I need to tell you that Maggie's been shot.'"

"What hospital's she in?" Nick demanded, jumping out of bed to get ready to go.

His friends looked at him steadily. "No, she's dead."

Nick dropped back down onto his bed.

When he was able to move, he took off on foot for campus, half-jogging. Outside DeWaters, he was directed by someone to Trowbridge, where, he was told, counselors were available. "I just went there and sat in the corner. I don't know why I was there, I just felt like I had to go there. I just sat in the corner." Alan Hill spotted him and began to talk to him, assuming he was a friend of Neenef's. "And I said, 'No, I just started dating Maggie.' And he looked at me with utter shock. . . . I don't think I even talked, I just sat there crying."

4

At 3:00 a.m., the Crisis Management Team convened in the Olmsted Room, the long, high-ceilinged, wood-paneled space where faculty meetings, lectures, and readings generally take place. They sat around long rectangular tables pulled into a square. The team included the president, Marilyn LaPlante, Tom Ponto, Danny Sledge, Vaughn Maatman, Pat Ponto, Alan Hill, provost Greg Mahler, associate provost Carolyn Newton, dean of Information Services Lisa Palchick, Security director Glenn Nevelle, and Paul Manstrom, the head of Facilities Management. Ordinarily the secretary for the group would have been the director of Communications, Jim Van Sweden, but that weekend he was camping, unreachable by phone. All had been advised to bring their crisis management notebooks.

From the first, there was no doubt as to who was in charge. As Jimmy Jones remembers it, Marilyn "began our meeting by quietly but firmly stating, 'Please turn to tab four.'"

Some years earlier, Pat Ponto had heard from a close friend, a guidance counselor, who had just dealt with a student suicide. The friend told her, "Pat, you can't think [when this happens]. You have to have a plan." At that point, Pat and Marilyn began to develop a specific plan for dealing with student deaths. Having gone through many revisions, it was ultimately lodged at tab four in the crisis management notebook.

Most of the people around the table had never had occasion even to peruse these notebooks. Now, here, in the middle of the night, most of them still trying to believe what had happened themselves, all of them horrified and confused, their minds racing in multiple directions, they discovered that there was a tab four, which opened to a clear, organized list of steps to be taken and constituencies to be considered in the event of a death on campus. There was also Marilyn, composed, focused, and in charge. And so they began.

As they discussed their various responsibilities, Jimmy Jones remembers very clearly feeling a grateful relief, looking around the table and thinking to himself, "If I have to go through this living hell on earth, I would rather have these folks at my side than anyone I could possibly think of."

Provost Greg Mahler's thoughts were different. Although the provost's job is to execute the president's academic agenda, Greg was in many ways the anti-Jimmy: soft-spoken, unassuming, unpresuming, self-effacing, given to Jerry Garcia ties and sport coats. He was a political scientist educated at Oberlin, among other places, so that midwestern liberal arts colleges were congenial for him. And as the discussion turned to how the college would interact with Maggie's family, "the face that I saw," Greg remembers, "was Neenef's dad." Greg had met Neenef and his father walking on campus on Neenef's first day. "I hadn't met his mother, I had met his father. The thing that periodically went through my mind was, you know, 'How would you feel if you were his father?'"

The team met for over ninety minutes. Toward the end, Tom Ponto advised people who had parked on the street to bring him the tickets they would inevitably receive. Only Tom would have had the presence of mind to consider such a practical detail.

Shortly after 2:30 a.m., two forensic lab specialists, Karianne Thomas and Tyler Fall, arrived and were briefed by Sergeant Johncock of the Kalamazoo Department of Public Safety, who told them that a search warrant was being drafted. Tyler Fall noted in his official report, "I was also advised that some of the blood and body matter had traveled under two doors and into room number 203." Informed that the resident had granted access, Fall now entered Navin's room. The impact of what he saw resounds behind the clinical, detached language of the report: "I . . . observed blood and body matter on the floor near the door that goes into a shared bathroom between room 203 and 201. When I looked into the bathroom from room 203 I observed a large amount of blood and body matter on the floor and walls."

The search warrant appeared and was read at 3:10 a.m. by Captain Bryant. Fall and Thomas could now enter 201. In her report, Karianne Thomas described the scene:

> I observed a subject (later identified as Margaret WARDLE) lying on her stomach, feet toward the south. Wardle was wearing a gray sweatshirt, blue jeans and black shoes. Her legs were crossed at the ankles. There appeared to be an entry wound in her back. Approximately 2/3 of Wardle's head was missing. There was blood and brain matter surrounding Wardle's body. A green shotgun casing was near Wardle's right hip.
>
> I also observed another subject (later identified as Neenef ODAH) just to the south of Wardle. Odah was in a fetal position with his knees up and head down. Odah's face was not visible. Between Odah's legs, in his left hand was a camouflage colored shotgun. The barrel was pointing toward Odah. Odah was wearing a black shirt, jeans, and white socks.

The back of Odah's head was gone and there was blood pooled around his legs and the gun.

Thomas would later say that it was one of the worst crime scenes she ever witnessed.

When Caitlin Gilmet went back to her room in Trowbridge, she called Stephanie Miller, whose brief string of dates with Neenef had turned so strange and ended with his fist through a window. Caitlin says, "I don't remember what I said, but I remember her breathing in as she processed what had happened." Stephanie was living in Kalamazoo now, with LaVange Barth, whom Neenef called "cousin." LaVange recalls, "[Stephanie] burst into my room early in the morning wailing, 'Neenef and Maggie are dead! Neenef killed Maggie and then killed himself!' I'd never heard a voice go to the place that Stephanie's was. . . . I can't quite describe it. Raw? Pure despair. Horrifying."

Caitlin doesn't remember crying herself until she finally called her parents in Minneapolis. The following weekend they would drive the twelve hours to Kalamazoo to be with her—"an act of love that still amazes me," she says, "and makes me wonder how scared I sounded on the phone." When her three suitemates in Trowbridge woke and heard the news, one of them loaded up her car with blankets and drove them all out beyond the city.

> She said a few years ago that she didn't know what else to do with our grief but to get us away from campus. We finally stopped at a parking lot, where we [lay] down to look at the sky in silence. It sounds like a cliché, but all four of us saw a perfect shooting star streak long across the sky. We packed up the car and headed back to campus.
>
> I met up with some friends—Nancy [El Shamaa], Renae [Placinski], Nick Porada, Mark Stern, others—in Crissey Hall. We were worried about our friends from Neenef's class who'd known them and were on study abroad, so we spent a few hours trying to find a phone card that would allow us to call people in China or Australia. I think it was good to have a distraction.
>
> I spent the rest of the night outside, where students had lit candles.

In the morning, I walked into the lounge, where Marigene Arnold had stood watch over the students . . . all night. I didn't know her well, but I'll never forget the way she made me feel protected and cared for just by being there for us.

The night was filled with walkers, drifting around the campus like ghosts. Nick Duiker eventually left Trowbridge and wandered until 5:00 a.m., when he called his parents. A group of Navin Anthony's friends showed up and took him for a walk. "I remember them asking me questions," he says, "but they didn't ask me too many questions, because I was pretty—I just wasn't really with it. I was definitely in shock, and I couldn't really put things together. I just remember not being able to think straight."

J'nai Leafers and Nandini Sonnad left the steps and wandered the campus, and people came out of offices and offered them coffee. At about 6:00 a.m., J'nai called her parents from the area coordinator's apartment in Hoben. Then she went to Nandini's room, where she curled up on the floor next to Emily Ford.

Nancy El-Shamaa had been up all night. In the early morning she wandered back to Severn. "The reporters had started showing up when I was walking back to Severn," she remembers, "and I was like, 'Please get out of my face.' Finally got in bed, and I couldn't really sleep." A friend arrived, lay down beside her, and stroked her head.

Whenever there was a space of time to spare, Jimmy and Marilyn walked. Danny Sledge remembers Jimmy's saying he needed to do this because Marilyn "centered him." Jimmy recalls, "Marilyn and I moved through the entire residential system, building by building, all through the night."

"I did a couple laps with Marilyn, too," Greg Mahler says. "Marilyn was just being everywhere, and keeping track always, and being available." Danny Sledge recalls Marilyn's outward calm, betrayed only by her tight lips. "I knew she was in that 'dean mode.'" As Danny took his own laps around the campus, he kept thinking, "'This cannot be happening.' But it was."

After the Crisis Team meeting, Jimmy Jones called Phil McKenzie, the head of Dining Services, and asked him to get urns of hot chocolate into every residence hall as quickly as possible. Around 5:00 a.m., he reached for the telephone to make the three calls he dreaded, the most difficult of his life, to Seattle, Plainwell, and Pennsylvania.

———

Three hours after they started taking evidence, lab specialists Thomas and Fall finished their work. They had made photo, video, and sketch records, and they had collected the rifle itself, plus casings; wadding; a paper bag containing two boxes of shells, gun lock, and gun manuals; and vials of blood, which would reveal the presence of no alcohol or drugs in either body. Medical examiner Jim Kinney called Mall City Ambulance, and as the air began to grow gray with the coming morning, the bodies of Maggie Wardle and Neenef Odah were carried out and taken downtown. As Neenef's body was lifted, Karianne Thomas saw the entry wound over his left eye.

Assistant director of College Security Gail Simpson was allowed into the room to retrieve a course notebook belonging to Eric Page, who had asked if someone could get it for him. Officer Hendrick, making sure that the doors to 201 and 203 were secure, turned the scene over to Gail, who took up her post at the end of the second-floor hallway.

———

Before light, Heidi Fahrenbacher's mother woke to a radio voice saying that there had been a fatal shooting on K's campus. No names were yet given. Terrified, she called and woke her daughter.

Without missing a beat, Heidi said, "It's probably Maggie."

"Don't say that!" her mother protested.

"No, no," Heidi insisted. "It was Maggie." It felt like something she already knew.

Subject: Urgent Message from the President
Date: Mon, 18 Oct 1999 08:13:48–0400 (EDT)
From: Important Notice *bulletin@kzoo.edu*

October 18, 1999

Dear Members of the College Community:

It is with profound sadness that I must announce the deaths of two students following a late-night argument on Sunday, October 17th. Neenef W. Odah, a junior from Seattle, Washington, and Margaret ("Maggie") L. Wardle, a sophomore from Plainwell, Michigan, were found dead from an apparent murder-suicide when Kalamazoo City police arrived at DeWaters Residence Hall after being contacted by a Kalamazoo College security officer. The case is being investigated by the police at this time.

The principal officers of the College administration arrived on campus within thirty minutes of the deaths and spent the early morning hours attending to our students. Trained counselors and staff are located in the residence halls, Chapel and the President's Lounge in Hicks Center to help students cope with this tragedy. These resource people will be available in those locations all day.

All students, faculty, and staff are being notified of the deaths by this e-mail. Staff in the Center for International Programs are contacting our centers abroad to develop support systems for students far away from family and friends.

Because of the terrible nature of this event, all Monday classes and LAC events will be cancelled. Assignments that had been due today will be due at the next scheduled class time. Students who have questions about classes should contact their instructors. Athletic practices today are optional at the discretion of the student.

At noon, we will all gather as a community on the quadrangle to share our grief and support for one another. Throughout the day we will be encouraging our students to be together in comfortable places on campus, and we will come together again at 7:30 PM in the Chapel.

Students, faculty, and staff are reminded that they are under no obligation to speak to members of the media who might approach them with questions. Inquiries may be directed to the Office of College Communications at extension 7304.

Yours sincerely,
James F. Jones, Jr.
President

7

HOLD FAST

1. Monday

Jimmy Jones had canceled classes for the day, but the Crisis Management Team knew that students who awoke unaware of what had happened wouldn't necessarily find out before heading to class. Part of the team's plan was to station selected faculty and administrators in all the residence halls early on Monday morning, so that students would have both reliable information and support. Calls and messages went out to employees with any counseling or social agency background and faculty seen as "student-friendly" who, in Pat Ponto's words, could also be relied upon "to take care of themselves." Around 6:30 a.m. these people convened in the Olmsted Room. They included Marigene Arnold, who had been up all night without even the benefit of caffeine (a counseling intern had been sent out for coffee and returned to Trowbridge with quarts of decaf). The group was divided into teams of two, each team assigned to one of the six residence halls, the central lounge in Hicks Center, and the chapel. At the start of the meeting, Pat recalls people asking, "What are we going to do?" and looking at her. She remembers thinking, "We're gonna try."

At 6:30 a.m. on Monday, October 18, Sara Church's alarm went off in the double she shared with Maureen Kelly at the south end of the second floor of Trowbridge, looking straight at DeWaters. She had an 8:00 class. Sara noticed a Post-it note on her computer. In the dark she snatched it and started to move toward the hallway so she could read it without turning on the light and waking Maureen. But before she could make out the message, the phone rang—a weird occurrence at that hour. "Weirder still," Sara says, "was the fact that it was my mom asking if I was OK." It turned out that Sara's father "had heard on the radio that morning that a female K student had been killed and had immediately called my mom." As Sara spoke to her mother, Maureen woke. Sara told her mother she didn't know what had happened and said goodbye.

Maureen, a night owl, had been up later than Sara, studying. She'd seen the commotion outside DeWaters and spotted her friends Kelly Jones and Nisse Olsen—who along with Sara and Maureen were on the golf team—crying. She got the word that someone had died in DeWaters, but she decided not to wake Sara and instead left the Post-it. Now she and Sara got online and within minutes discovered Maggie's name in an early news article.

Golf coach Lyn Maurer reached Sara shortly thereafter, in a series of calls to her team. For Sara, who was not personally close to Maggie, the sisterhood of the links was important. "It was a great group, and Maggie was a central part of that gang," she recalls. She replayed her memories of the final match of the season and the Homecoming pre-party at Gillian's. "And now Maggie was gone? The one laughing in the backseat after an entire round in chilly wind and rain?"

At 7:00 a.m. provost Greg Mahler, who had dashed home to shower and change clothes for what he knew would be a long day, was back in his office, launching a calling tree to let the faculty know as quickly as possible what had happened and to advise us that classes were canceled. It was a clear, golden fall day.

Across the quad in the Student Commission offices in Hicks Center, Simone Lutz was initiating another calling tree, this one designed to get the word out to seniors, the primary off-campus population, so that they would show up for the meeting on the quad scheduled by the president for noon. "It was very hard, because a lot of seniors didn't know [Maggie or Neenef]. But at the end of the day that didn't matter." Friends helped her get the word out. The Commission office functioned for the rest of the day as one of many gathering points. "People were in there all day," Simone says, "just grieving and crying and questioning and talking, and we were making phone calls to get people on campus, and we just had an open door, basically."

At 7:00 a.m. Jimmy Jones, having also run home to clean up, met the local media. He first read them the statement that would be sent out to the campus community via e-mail an hour later and posted on the college's Web site. Factual as this first public announcement was, it is startling to listen to the recording of Jimmy delivering it. His ordinarily strong, mellifluous, Georgia-inflected baritone is thin and tired. After the opening five words—"It is with profound sadness"—he stops for a long moment to compose himself as his voice threatens to break. Then he continues, wearily. After he finishes, he adds, his voice thinning and wavering again, "This is every parent's worst nightmare, and certainly every educator's worst nightmare, and we are struggling, all of us, as best we can, and have been since 12:15 this morning."

He takes three questions: How long did it take the security guard to get to DeWaters? ("A minute and a half?" he guesses.) Does the college have a weapons policy? (A question for which he has clearly prepped.) And finally, the most difficult question: could this have been prevented? He goes straight to the big, abstract issue, the "plague of violence" in the United States. As he was dressing, he says, he told his wife that he wished every elected official who had voted against gun control could have walked the campus this night and spoken to "my wonderful students." Those last words are almost a whisper.

By 7:30 a.m. on Monday, history professor David Barclay was up, with the radio on. "I think it was WKZO or one of those local stations," he recalls, "and that's kind of unusual, because usually I would turn on some stupid breakfast TV show. But I turned on local radio that morning, and they said there'd been a shooting at Kalamazoo College, and a nineteen-year-old student named Margaret Wardle . . .

"I'll never forget this till the day I die," says Barclay. "I'll never forget the sense of almost electric shock that went through me when I heard that news."

Around the same time, director of the Computer Science Program Alyce Brady was getting herself and her daughter ready for the day when she got a call from Eric Nordmoe, the chair of the Math/Computer Science Department. He told her she'd better sit down. "You know Neenef Odah, right?" he asked. Alyce said she was his advisor, and Eric delivered the news.

"And so at that point I said to my husband, 'You're taking Lauren, because I'm going straight in.'" Alyce went immediately into high professional gear. "We do a lot of group work in computer science, so I knew that Neenef was working on a project with another student, so I immediately think, 'What's the impact on him?'" She also knew that Neenef's roommate, Eric Page, was a computer science student. "I mean, I would have been worried about his roommate regardless, but this way, I did know who I was worried about. She also thought of Nate Cooper, who she knew was tight with Neenef.

When she got to campus she learned that Trowbridge was Information Central, so she wandered up. "I sort of said who I was, and said, 'If you know of any kids who are in computer science or something, I'm just gonna be around all day.'" She eventually found some of the kids she was looking for, and some of them found her.

Karyn Boatwright had joined the Psychology Department only the previous fall. As she was driving to Kalamazoo early Monday morning from her home in Marshall, forty minutes east, she heard about the shootings on the radio. When she reached her office in Olds-Upton Hall, she got the full report. Someone told her faculty were needed in Hoben Hall, next door, where she took up her station with Lanny Potts, a young member of the Theater Department. The first student who came in was J'nai Leafers. Karyn, whose specialization is counseling psychology, had a career as a therapist before entering the academic world. She and J'nai had a long conversation. J'nai "was shaking, mostly crying, mostly unable to articulate her deep feelings. . . . She didn't spend all that time talking about Maggie. She spent some of her time just talking about how it was hard to talk about things and just how in shock she was and how she needed some things from her dorm room and she was afraid to go up to her room."

Karyn's counseling training told her that it was important for J'nai not to develop an entrenched phobia about the room she and Maggie had shared. "I said, 'J'nai, I could accompany you up there to get your books or to get some clothes or whatever you need, supplies.' . . . I thought if I could go up there with her and make it a real comfortable—well, as comfortable as we could—maybe she would not dread going back." Together they walked up the quad to Trowbridge. Inside the room, "what you could see was Maggie's bed, a little messed up; she hadn't been back to sleep in it but she had been [lying] on it and the book that she was reading was placed on the bed. It looked like she had just gotten up."

Kirsten Fritsch had spent the night in some friends' room in Trowbridge, along with her boyfriend and some others. They had tried to find Navin and failed. "Some of us slept," she recalls. "Most of us didn't. We didn't talk much either." Early in the morning they looked out the window to see camera crews set up outside DeWaters, along with police tape blocking the front door. Kirsten remembers,

> Someone turned on the TV, and we watched as the events of the previous night were recapped on the early morning news. It is surreal and

disorienting to see your home being described as the scene of a murder. To watch out the window and know that the people standing just yards away with the microphones are talking about a place that made you feel safe, and a person that you would see every day, smiling and waving as you passed his room to head upstairs to your own.

Later that day, after calling her parents, Kirsten walked the two blocks to St. Thomas More Catholic Church, a student parish, and let herself into their basement lounge. "I don't know how long I was there, but I do know that I prayed and slept. I didn't cry. I didn't cry for nearly six months."

———————

For Nick Duiker, "That day is sort of a blur. I didn't sleep all that night. I lived with nine people, and we all went out to breakfast. Why, I have no clue." At the restaurant, he left the table. "I just went in the bathroom and cried. I just didn't want to be around people at all. I'd never really dealt with death."

———————

Two blocks away from campus, Maggie's childhood friend and fellow K student Brooke Nobis was preparing to go to class. She was sharing a house this year with some friends, and like many off-campus students, they hadn't heard that classes were canceled. In Plainwell, Brooke's mother heard the news, now with Maggie's name attached. She called Brooke, weeping. "I didn't know what she was talking about, and I was really, really confused, and I was really blurry," Brooke says. The dissociation would go on, for Brooke as for others, all day. "And I remember taking a shower, ready to go up on campus. And two people had already sent me baskets of flowers." Not until she got to campus, saw people gathering on the quad, and met up with Emily Ford did Brooke really understand what her mother had said, or hear how it was that Maggie had died. "I kept seeing, like, her hair," the hair Brooke remembered Maggie taking such pains to keep soft and shiny in high school. "I don't know why I kept thinking about . . . I was just envisioning her with her beautiful hair, really soft, and then someone . . ." Brooke trails off into silence, shaking her head.

After the bodies had been removed, Paul Manstrom, the soft-spoken, highly professional head of Facilities Management, entered 201 DeWaters. It would be his task to get it clean. He immediately realized that this job would be far beyond what his custodians could manage. "I was shocked but not to the point where it affected me physically," he remembers. "I didn't start to shake (which has happened to me before in auto accidents) or become nauseated or anything like that. I think the fact that the college was counting on me to handle this cleanup helped me maintain a 'safe' level of detachment from what I was seeing."

As a result of what he saw in DeWaters, Paul came to a "stark realization of just how fragile the human body is and how quickly and unexpectedly life can end." Then, like many college officials that night and day, he thought about his own children, invoking a wave of sadness for Maggie and Neenef's parents. Finally, he "thought about what a selfish act suicide can be and how it was absolute selfishness to take another life with yours." When that long day was over, Paul says, "I really needed to talk to someone about what I had seen, so I pretty much unloaded on my wife. It would have been really inappropriate for me to talk about this on campus."

Paul couldn't find a Kalamazoo firm that could handle the job. Director of College Security Glenn Nevelle gave him a contact number at the Department of Public Safety, where Paul learned about Aftermath, a Chicago firm experienced in cleaning crime scenes. They could be there the next day. But already Paul was carrying the memory he would never shake: "the smell of death in that DeWaters room that lingered even after the cleanup was complete."

At some point that day, Jimmy and Marilyn went into 201 as well. "Something from the ninth level of Dante might approximate the physical horror," said Jimmy. Ever afterward, he regretted allowing Marilyn to accompany him.

Sometime early that morning I got word that classes had been canceled and that the president would be addressing the community at noon on the quad. I arrived on campus around ten and went to my office. Things were very quiet; none of the students I might have expected to show up appeared, including the one who had called me in the middle of the night.

As morning moved toward noon, the quad began to fill with people: faculty, students, administrators, media, and counselors and clergy from all over town who had been summoned to help. The idea of the president's addressing the campus on the quad at midday was a flash of inspiration—at the very heart of the campus, a ritual gathering, one that would serve to inaugurate the process of reweaving the fabric of our collective life, which had been violently torn. The common language that day and in the days immediately following was mostly physical: you saw someone you knew, you opened your arms and held each other, often wordlessly.

At noon, Jimmy emerged from Mandelle administrative building onto the quad, with Marilyn at his side. She stood solidly next to the podium as he spoke. As is his wont, he began with a quotation, this one from Robert Louis Stevenson's "Aes Triplex," on the power of death. And then he went for his theme, obviously one that Pat Ponto had urged: "We want to know if we could have foreseen something going hideously amiss, if we did not catch a comment in a classroom, dorm room, on the golf course with the Women's Team, some indication that Neenef was going to take his own life, and with his life Maggie's as well." No such indication was to be found, he said. "We are indeed our brothers' and sisters' keepers, but in an instance such as this, we cannot claim foreknowledge or take blame for what demons may be lurking in someone else's mind at a fragile moment." And now he reached the heart of his message:

I ask you, therefore, on this serene quad on this October day, not to second-guess yourselves, not to imagine what you might have done to have protected Neenef and Maggie, and all of us here at the college, from this event most unserene. Philosophers since the beginning of time have tried to find explanations for tragedies of similar magnitude. Not one has ever succeeded. And we shall not succeed today to make any sense of this endless night and of their deaths. When faced with the unforgivable and unspeakable, all we can do is to hold fast to each other.

Jimmy then asked for commitment to end "the plague of violence that has somehow descended on American life at the end of the twentieth century," and by repeating his fantasy of anti–gun control legislators walking the campus on this terrible Monday morning. And then, at the last, he urged once more, "Let us all hold fast to each other in the hours and days to come." After concluding his statement, Jimmy briefed the press and, as the local paper put it, "his patience slipped—showing the toll of the previous 12 hours, when he was asked what, if any, new information he had. 'We don't know any more than we knew this morning,' he said curtly. 'We have two dead students and a grieving campus.'"

I remember walking up to Jimmy, telling him he'd said just the right things. His normally bright, rosy complexion was waxy and pale. He looked intently into my eyes and said, "You think so?" I said yes; no other word could have been spoken to the man at that point. But already I had some questions, as did other people. Jimmy had said that Neenef and Maggie "died in Neenef's room in DeWaters around midnight, apparently of a murder-suicide," using the same vocabulary and sentence construction he had used in his early-morning e-mail to the campus community. It was as if a "murder-suicide" were something that could just "happen" to two victims. The e-mail had announced "the deaths of two students following a late-night argument," as if an argument had caused their deaths, rather than a person with a gun. Some faculty and students were disturbed that the perpetrator had not been differentiated from the victim. Similarly, the foregrounding of gun control seemed very strange, as if, again, there hadn't been a finger on the trigger, a decision made to pull it. At this moment the struggle began over how this story would be told.

Ministers, priests, rabbis from all over the area moved among the students, along with counselors and social workers Pat and Alan had managed to recruit from their networks. College officials chased the press away from students. I remember approaching Danny Sledge as he spoke to a small frightened knot of African American students. One of them, whose home neighborhood was beset with violence, spoke angrily: "This is what I came here to get *away* from!"

And I remember Stephanie Schrift, Maggie's first-year calculus study buddy, this year a resident of the Women's Resource Center. Stephanie had seen the lights from the police cars the night before, but when she and some housemates went outside, they were told to go back in. So it was not until Monday morning, when she arrived at her work-study job in the Admission office, that she found out what had happened.

Did Stephanie and the other WRC residents approach me, or did I find them? Either is possible. As director of the Women's Studies Program and their advisor, I had it on my mind to check in with them, and I think I was walking up toward the WRC when I saw Stephanie. What I do remember vividly is her face—wide eyes full of one and only one question. It was the same question Pat Ponto had heard earlier that morning, but with a different implication. *What are we going to do?*

It was a question the WRC women had been asking each other ever since they'd heard the news, and its context was very specific: their organization existed to address women's needs on campus and to educate the campus about the impact of male dominance on women's lives. A woman student had now been murdered by a former boyfriend, who had then killed himself. What, indeed, were we going to do? I had been pondering the question all morning myself. The option of doing nothing did not occur to any of us. We quickly agreed that I would round up some concerned faculty and we would meet at the WRC in the early afternoon.

The president had spoken of a "plague of violence." He had also, twice, addressed the murder-suicide as a gun-control issue. Depression—Neenef's—was starting to emerge as a factor. But so far, no one had spoken of Maggie Wardle's death as a case of violence against women.

Yet when I had received my wake-up call that morning around three, that was my first thought, especially since it wasn't the first time this kind of violence had erupted on campus. On a November Friday in 1978, my second year at the college, Daniel Travis, the disturbed ex-boyfriend of a secretary in the Food Services office named Virginia Hinkleman, had arrived at Hicks Center and abducted her at gunpoint. Her boss, Gordon Beaumont, tried to intervene, and the gunman shot him dead outside his office. He drove away with Virginia, whom he shot twice before killing himself. She lingered for two days and then died. I couldn't get over the uncanny, sickening parallel.

That afternoon, we convened at the WRC: eight or nine young women, mostly sophomores, plus a roughly equal number of faculty. All women, except for a new member of the Department of Sociology and Anthropology, who'd asked to join us. Stephanie recalls a philosophical discussion. She says, "I remember, I think, [political science professor] Amy Elman saying, 'This is violence against women.' We were talking about how do we proceed with this, and what is our message to the community? And I think the question was 'Are we going to be political about this? Are we just supportive, are we just educational, or are we going to be political?' And I think we decided there's no way around being political."

For my part, I don't remember anyone raising the question of whether or not to "be political." The gendered dimension of the two deaths seemed so obvious as to be assumed, without much discussion. And to talk about gender was, inescapably, to "be political." We ultimately decided on a kind of teach-in, a panel of speakers with expertise on the issue of violence against women. I was entrusted with the task of inviting Barbara Mills, the long-time director of the Domestic Assault Shelter at the Kalamazoo YWCA—the first such shelter in the state. After dividing tasks, we dispersed.

Back in my office, I decided that priority one was to reach Barbara. When she answered and I identified myself, she said, in her throaty alto, "I was wondering when I'd hear from you."

Director of Security Glenn Nevelle had urged his assistant director, Gail Simpson, to go home. But she was scheduled to be on duty at 8:00 a.m., anyway, so she stuck around, walking the campus. Remembering that Brian Napkie had told her he had a test that day at Western, she called his professor, securing a reprieve for him. At noon, as Jimmy began to speak on the quad, Gail took up her post at the end of the second-floor corridor in DeWaters. Until 6:00 p.m. she stood there—sometimes sitting on the floor, as no one had bothered to find her a chair.

In her eighteen years at K, Gail often heard from students things they wouldn't tell faculty or counselors or their parents. She was always very popular among students; she took pains to know who they were, and she was able to combine the authority and reassurance of a security guard with approachability and compassion. During her six-hour vigil, she found herself playing a remarkable role—part therapist, part confessor—as student after student came into DeWaters and sat down with her to tell their stories of what Jimmy had called the "endless night."

She heard about what the RA had seen coming under the bathroom door. She listened to Navin Anthony as he sifted through his confusion when he heard the shots. Students told her of hearing the voices, hearing the shots and deciding it was "just a boyfriend and a girlfriend having a fight" and that they should mind their own business. They told Gail about going back and forth in front of 201 five times, six times, troubled by the yelling, "but they never thought to talk to the RA until the first bang." Students repeatedly said that they hadn't understood what the shots were. "I think that was such a surprise to so many of the students," says Gail, "that something like that would happen in their haven. It's a horrific thing to have happen amongst teens, and that's really what they are, they're teens. They're older teens, but they're still teens." On a campus swarming with professional counselors that day, some of the kids sought instead a person who had answered their questions when they were new on campus, let them into their dorms when they'd lost their keys, and made them feel safe at K. With her they made their first attempts to turn the preceding night into a story that could be told. With her they first began to struggle with guilt and regret.

On Monday afternoon, Detective Alofs of Kalamazoo Public Safety called Neenef's father to arrange for Neenef's body to be transported home. Wilson Odah offered the name of a family friend and distant relation, a professor at Western, who could serve as contact person in making these arrangements. He also agreed that in the interim, Langeland's Funeral Home could serve as the local agent to care for Neenef's body. Detective Alofs asked Odah if his son had been a hunter, and Odah said he never knew his son to hunt or to express interest in doing so.

Wilson Odah had one question for Detective Alofs: Was there any way they could tell who had shot whom? Detective Alofs said that it was apparent that Neenef had pulled the trigger. With that, denied the straw at which he was desperately grasping, Wilson Odah disappears from this story. Associate dean Vaughn Maatman, designated by the Crisis Team as the college's contact person with the Odahs, worked with the local contacts and had Neenef's remains, along with his belongings, returned to his family.

There were those who were shocked that the Odahs didn't come to Kalamazoo to retrieve their son's body, or that their only direct contact with the college was the single call from the president. For others of us, their silence held the kind of unearthly wail of grief and shame that is beyond normal hearing. Their invisibility was surely the turning of their faces to the wall. Along with God only knows what else, their American dream ended here.

That night, at 7:30, eight hundred students, faculty, administrators, and staff crowded into Stetson Chapel, which seats less than seven hundred. For the next hour, there were no words, only music. Barry Ross, senior member of the Music Department and Concertmaster of the Kalamazoo Symphony Orchestra, had spent his day arranging for the KSO string quartet to play Samuel Barber's "Adagio for Strings." Leslie Tung, the department chair, a pianist, joined with student violinist Joanna Steinhauser to play the ancient Jewish melody "Kol Nidre." Barry and Les together performed the "Meditation" from Jules Massenet's opera *Thaïs*.

It was restorative to sit quietly and listen, breathing and allowing the furiously tangled mind to unravel a bit. I remember realizing how much had gone on all over the campus on this day: my Music Department friends had obviously spent it scrambling to get this program together in so short an interval and under such conditions. Other than music, the only sounds were weeping and sniffling. Marigene Arnold remembers seeing Eric Page "falling apart; he was just sobbing." Computer science professor Alyce Brady sought him out where he was standing with his parents. She and her colleague Ray McDowell "both just kind of stood near him, whether we wanted to talk or just be there, so that he knew there were some people nearby." Afterward, we all stood around the chapel steps silently, holding white candles. Then, in teams of two, some of us faculty were dispatched again to the residence halls, to be available to students. I went to Severn, Marigene to Harmon. Nobody came to us. I think I went home around ten o'clock.

2. Tuesday

For the next two or three days, at least four people—dean of students Danny Sledge, assistant dean for Resident Life Vaughn Maatman, director of the Counseling Center Pat Ponto, and assistant director of the Counseling Center Alan Hill—got very little sleep. Some, like Vaughn, stayed around the clock for the first two days; some went home briefly to care for children or to shower and change clothes. Danny took a nap on a sofa in the Black Student Organization room to get him through the long hours. Otherwise, he says, "It was a performance—I had to stay in a certain mode for everybody else." That "everybody else" included Maggie's family, who had congregated in the Student Development offices Monday afternoon when they first arrived on campus. On his first "real" trip home, Danny dropped down into a chair and wept.

On Tuesday night, Pat Ponto convened a group of Neenef's friends. She was particularly concerned about this population, whose grief would be complicated in painful ways by his violence. Alyce Brady, who was also dealing directly with his friends, puts it this way: "All these kids who knew him and liked him were dealing with a sense of betrayal" and, in fact, of guilt. What was wrong with *them* if they chose a friend who turned out to be a murderer? The group that met with Pat voiced a primary concern: the representation of Neenef in the local press. Brian Newman, Navin's roommate, complained to a reporter about a TV report he had seen. "I was in disgust," he is quoted as saying. "They portrayed him as a psycho and a person who intended to harm people. . . . That was completely the opposite. He was a wonderful guy, a great guy, somebody personable that you could talk to. . . . It wasn't like he was into satanic stuff or anything. No tattoos. . . . I just don't have a clue why."

Nancy El-Shamaa had a similar reaction to the media coverage. "His face," she said, "the picture they put on all those newspapers and stuff—made him look like a psychopath. Maybe that's the easiest way for people to deal with stuff like this, is just to be like, 'Oh, it's one of those crazy people.'" What the friends who met with Pat that night wanted most to communicate was that Neenef wasn't a monster. He was one of them. Pat drafted, on behalf of the group, a letter to the editor of the local newspaper that offered their version. It's a valuable record of how Neenef's friends began to construct their version of who he was and of what he had done:

> To them, Neenef was the very friendly student at the end of the hall whose door was always open and who greeted everyone who passed by with "Hey, what's happening?"
>
> He was a playful young man who frequently dribbled a soccer ball down the hallway—getting in trouble with staff, who said—"Do that outside, Neenef."
>
> He was the guy who often gathered friends to play basketball, soccer, and Frisbee.
>
> He was the Frelon dancer who goofed around at rehearsals and then performed beautifully.
>
> He was the upperclassman who was very welcoming to first year students—and was "officially adopted" as a big brother by one just last week.
>
> He was a strikingly polite and well-mannered young man.
>
> He was a friend they knew was having a hard time letting go of the girl he loved—as so many of their friends do.
>
> He was a friend they saw and talked to on Sunday—in the hall, at dinner, on IM, and he seemed "normal" to them.
>
> He was a friend who made a tragic and "awful mistake" that they can't imagine him doing, will never understand, and so deeply regret for him, for Maggie, for the parents about whom they're very concerned, for Maggie's friends, and for themselves.

This story—of a perfectly normal, lovable Neenef who made one huge mistake—was crucial to his friends as they attempted to integrate what he had done. In one sense, there is wisdom in this narrative. Neenef *was* one of them, and one of us; to turn him into a monster becomes an easy way to put him beyond the pale and explain him away by labeling him Inexplicable. In another sense, though, this version of events isolates and compartmentalizes the murder so that a clean, innocent version of Neenef can be maintained. It represents an understandable, even necessary means to negotiate the terrible complexity in which these kids now found themselves: unable to tell the good guys from the bad; having loved someone who was capable of hideous violence. This version of the murder-suicide as a single, unaccountable deviation from the real Neenef was a way to excise the violence like a tumor, so the rest of Neenef, the part his friends knew, could remain intact.

While Neenef's friends gathered with Pat Ponto, another story was being told. The Women's Resource Center sponsored a vigil specifically dedicated to Maggie's memory. It was a chilly, wet night. Perhaps fifty people showed up outside the WRC on Trowbridge's ground floor, including Jimmy Jones, Greg Mahler, and several members of Maggie's family. Greg walked over to me and asked, "How are *you* doing?" I remember being moved that he would ask. I put the same question to him, and he told me that he—the academic vice president of the college—had been in DeWaters with Vaughn Maatman, moving furniture. A student too stricken to speak asked me to read a poem that she handed me, and I did that—poorly, having forgotten my glasses and operating by candlelight.

Rick Omilian spoke for Maggie's family that night, as he would often do in the months and years to come. A particular concern was a chalking they had seen on the sidewalk that afternoon. Chalking is an honored K tradition. To announce a special event or to comment on a particular occurrence, students chalk the walkways. Sometimes the content is merely advertising; sometimes it's celebratory or affirmative; sometimes it's subversive; sometimes all three. The sidewalks had filled with messages in the past twenty-four hours, most deploring Maggie's death or expressing grief. But one of them said something like "Neenef and Maggie, together forever." As Rick described it to the congregants at the vigil, there was an intake of breath, certainly including mine. As Marigene Arnold recognized, this "Romeo-and-Juliet interpretation" of the two deaths "was sick and puzzling, but kind of understandable" among certain students as a form of denial—"trying to make it into something it wasn't." Rick stressed to the assemblage that Maggie's murder had nothing to do with "romance" and must be seen as an act of violence. Listening, I recognized that what we had here, as well as a tragedy, was an imperative "teachable moment."

As we stood, holding our candles and each other, the rain increased.

Some of the WRC residents approached me. There was hot chocolate and tea inside; did I think Maggie's family might want to come in? I checked with Jimmy and then approached Martha Omilian. Almost before I could introduce myself she put her arms around me—or, more accurately, she collapsed into my arms. She was doing this with almost everyone, as if her only means of moving through time at this point was connection with anyone even distantly connected with her lost girl. It was the first time I laid eyes on her. I have seen her several times since, but the image of her I carry is the one I saw in that cold darkness: a Greek mask of helpless, bottomless grief.

3. "Return to Normalcy"

Late on Tuesday, Aftermath arrived from Chicago to begin cleaning De-Waters 201. By Wednesday evening they had done what they could do. In the process, they discovered that what Facilities director Paul Manstrom calls "a good amount of brain and bone material" was embedded in the ceiling. The ceiling texture treatments, however, contained asbestos—harmless unless disturbed. Paul hired a local company to abate the ceiling, a process that was not completed until later the next week. In the meantime, all the residents of DeWaters' second floor had found alternate housing, either on their own or with the college's help.

On Wednesday, October 20, an e-mail went out to all faculty and staff, titled "Campus Crisis and a Return to Normalcy." The staff memo, which would have gone to student workers' supervisors, came under Jimmy's signature, the faculty version under Greg's, but the memo was probably drafted by Marilyn LaPlante, with advice from Pat Ponto. First came a paragraph of thanks for everyone's efforts. The second paragraph identified a "crash point" for students:

> I think that most of our students will make it through the first few days on pure adrenaline or simple momentum. The real challenge for us is going to be to help our students continue their progress toward adjustment over the next few weeks. For many of our students, even though they think they have totally comprehended the significance of this event, the fact of the matter is that they have not yet done so, and over coming days and weeks they are going to face continuing challenges.

The third paragraph gave us a directive: "I am told that the best way for students to handle crises such as this one is to 'return to normalcy' as quickly as possible. That is, we should encourage them to return to classes, homework, written assignments, and exams [the staff version listed 'jobs'] just as if the nightmare had never taken place."

However, we were then warned, normalcy would not come for some students, and we should be on the watch for signs of continuing trauma. We were encouraged to keep the Counseling Center and the Dean of Students' office informed.

The staff memo included this line: "Students may need to be excused from their jobs or responsibilities with you because they simply cannot bring focus to their normal activities. Please give them some slack, even as you press them to return to normal." The memo to faculty contained no corresponding advice to excuse students from assignments or to extend deadlines.

I think most of us on the faculty wrote in the missing lines. Many of us taught out the rest of the term, and indeed the rest of the year, in a permanently flexible, reactive mode. We watched students' behavior, listened to what they said, and made arrangements on an individual basis. Some of them certainly did crave a return to normalcy—for good and bad reasons. Some couldn't have returned to any semblance of normalcy if their very lives had depended on it.

For Alyce Brady, the immediate question before her class reconvened on Wednesday was one of physical space. Neenef always sat in the same spot in her close, intimate computer lab. "After the murder-suicide, I thought, 'I can't go in that classroom. There are empty chairs. I mean, it's so obvious.' So I called the Registrar's office and said, 'I need to switch rooms.'" Alyce then met the class on Wednesday in the new location and introduced Counseling Center associate director Alan Hill.

> He talked to the class for half an hour or so. Then, when he left, I told the class that anyone who wanted to go with Alan was welcome to go, or anyone who wanted to just walk around the quad or something, because you know, we had been talking about heavy stuff here. This was a good time to go walking around the quad or whatever was right for them to

do. [I said] that I was going to stay there, and anyone [who] wanted to stay there was going to stay, and we were going to pretend to do data structures; maybe we'd get somewhere with it. And I don't remember if Alan had used this phrase with that group in that half hour or just talking to me and other people earlier in the week, but there was a phrase that Alan used that I've gone back to many times that quarter: "We'll fake it until we make it." And whether he'd just used the phrase or not, that was certainly what I was telling the students. So, we'll go through the motions, because the motions are kind of useful, and pretend to do it, and it will help us eventually do it. So one student left, and the rest stayed, and as I said, we sort of did data structures half-heartedly, only because that's as much heart as we had, and we met there for the rest of the quarter.

<hr />

When the European history course reconvened on Wednesday, David Barclay began to read from a five-page document. It is characteristic of Barclay both that he would directly address Maggie's death and that he would do so in carefully shaped prose. But his reliance on the Bible is less characteristic. He began,

> I've been getting up in front of classes like this for a quarter of a century, but this is surely the toughest and most difficult of these occasions. And I know too how difficult these last days have been for each of you, including this morning. Nothing can possibly prepare us for what happened last Sunday night. We have lost a member of this class, a friend, a fellow student. Confronted by something like this, people like me, who make a living from words, feel painfully the inadequacy of those words to express our feelings.

He went on to remind the students that each of them was "at once *both* an individual, precious life, *and* the future of all of us." He quoted from the Twenty-second Psalm ("My God, my God, why has thou forsaken me?"), from the book of Job, and from Ecclesiastes, calling their authors "fragile, confused, flawed human beings like us, [who] would thus surely understand our own feelings of anger, loss, grief, despair at this time." And he concluded in full historian mode:

At the end of this century, and at the dawn of a new millennium, the events of the past hundred years in the rest of the world, and of the past hundred hours on our little hill, should remind us, as Voltaire would say, to cultivate our garden however we can, with the means that are most appropriate to us, remembering our common humanity, and how fragile we are. At the same time that, at a college like this and in a course like this, we look at the so-called big picture, our loss reminds us of our daily necessity to love our neighbor as ourselves, to listen to them, to hear them, to talk to them, to appreciate them, to remember that we are all sinners and fallen short of the glory of God, and to do our very best to do the good.

Until the end of my days, I shall never forget Maggie; and I hope that you too will keep her in your own memories for decades to come. She loved to study the past, and I'm sure would want us to keep on with it ourselves. She was a competitor, after all, and always wanted to do her own best. So let us dedicate the rest of this quarter, of this course, and the rest of your college years to her and to her memory.

As he finished, Almuth Wietholtz, the student from Bonn, got up and fled the room. Excusing himself, Barclay followed her down the hall to a lounge, where she sat sobbing. As they sat together, she spoke of being German—"about how she had come from a culture and from a history that was drenched in violence, and didn't want to deal with that. Even though she's obviously too young to remember anything [of German history] but prosperity, she is very sensitive to the past and its consequences." Barclay had put Maggie's death in an historical context where, for Almuth, it suddenly joined the deaths of millions.

Navin Anthony and Brian Newman had moved into another room in DeWaters. When the asbestos abatement in 201 was complete, Navin went back to the room with Eric Page, both to retrieve some of his own things and to help Eric move some of his. Navin was uneasy: "Oh, man, I don't know if I want to be here." When he walked in, he saw that a portion of the ceiling was missing. "I guess they couldn't really clean it," he concluded. As the days went by, Navin kept himself surrounded by friends. "I didn't like being alone for a while. I couldn't sit in my room alone. I needed someone to be with me."

Nancy El-Shamaa found herself going through cycles, numb and then suddenly emotionally raw. One night during that first week, she was at a table in the cafeteria with friends. "I was just sitting, trying to eat one of my first real meals in the cafeteria," she recalls, "and I just started crying, and the whole table, without [saying] a thing, just came around me, hugging me, holding my hair, four or five different people, without saying a word."

For those first days, Jimmy Jones describes himself as "almost bipolar: . . . part of my brain was trying to respond as the president of the college while the other part of my brain was trying to grasp what this meant to me as the father of three children. One of the worst fears that any parent has is to outlive one's child, for this goes against life's patterns completely." Indeed, in several interviews at the time, he framed the deaths as "every parent's worst nightmare."

Until the police officially closed the case, Maggie's family was denied access to her room, even though Gail Simpson offered to escort them: "I told Glenn I would be willing to go up there and stand and make sure they didn't take anything, you know, just to [allow them to] look at their daughter's stuff." But the police said no; they were still searching her computer and other effects. When they issued the all-clear, Gail took the family there and waited while they packed it up. "The uncle," she recalled, "any time he picked something up, he'd start to cry. The mom would just pat him on the back and would say, 'Everything is going to be OK,' and would take some stuff [out to the hall], and I am sure that the minute she walked out of the door she started crying, because you could see the red eyes and she'd be wiping her face all the time."

4. Managing

In the constant meetings during those first weeks, Danny Sledge observed how faithfully the college's leadership cleaved to their individual roles. Glenn Nevelle "kept the situation anchored as a *crime*." Pat Ponto kept the focus on the reality of two dead students, emphasizing that Neenef's friends were among the walking wounded. Tom Ponto kept his unblinking eye on the institution's legal position. His aim, in Danny's words, was to "manage the situation to decrease the college's liability." If it were discovered, for instance, that someone in the college's employ—Counseling Center, RA, faculty member—had known that Neenef was a serious risk, the college could be liable for a wrongful death lawsuit. Danny had a clear sense of his own boundaries as well: "I decided that it was other people's responsibility to manage the situation. It was my responsibility to lead those who were dealing with students." College liability was not his issue. "I was convinced if we did the right thing, it would work itself out."

One hand orchestrated everything. As Glenn Nevelle put it, "Anything Marilyn said was what we did." He and Marilyn had discussed at length what was certainly a major issue before the president: the possibility of a full-scale in-house investigation of the deaths. "I was sort of against it," Glenn recalls. "You know, to drag these kids in here and then go over everything that the police had already done. I know that [option] still lingered in Marilyn's mind," probably as a way to make sure the college was in the clear. Ultimately, however, she took his advice.

A horror story always breeds. From the statements given to police by students, two secondary tales emerged to travel the campus and do their damage. Both emerge from student statements taken later in the week after the deaths by Detective Alofs from the Kalamazoo Department of Public Safety. One story came from the unwitting Navin Anthony, who, in his initial conversation with Officer Kelley on the night of the deaths, "said he seems to remember Odah showing him a gun at one time but could not remember when or any specifics about the gun. Anthony also said he knows Odah had a bad temper and has seen him punch holes in closet doors when he got mad."

On October 22, Alofs recorded his follow-up conversation with Navin: "Anthony said that he is not sure if he is just making this up or not but he seemed to recall that earlier in the year, Odah may have shown Anthony something in Odah's drawer that Anthony thought may have been a small gun but this item was never taken out of the drawer and Anthony is not even sure if it was a gun or if he is just imagining this because of what happened. Anthony said the gun was definitely not a long gun if it was a gun he saw in the drawer and he did not know Odah had a shotgun and had no indication that Odah would do something like this." This story merged with the widespread assumption that Eric Page, living in such close quarters with Neenef, must have known about the shotgun. Alyce Brady recalls Eric's despair. "I can remember him saying to me, 'It doesn't matter what I say, they absolutely think I must've known he had a gun in the room.'" People would actually say it to his face.

The second story comes from Nate Cooper's statement to Detective Alofs on October 21: "Cooper mentioned the fact that Odah had apparently tried to overdose last year while at Kalamazoo College and that Odah's advisor at the time knew about this and this advisor's name is Alyce Brady." Alyce quickly found herself summoned to the provost's conference room in Mandelle to talk to the college's lawyer. The rumor was rapidly dismissed; in fact, this story, like the other, seems to be a confluence of two streams: the NoDoz episode and the story Neenef had told about the attempted gun purchase in Seattle. The lawyer asked Alyce if Neenef had ever said anything about being suicidal, and Alyce said he hadn't. The advising relationship was probed: had Alyce ever done "personal counseling" with Neenef? No, they had only talked about classes and about his notion of transferring to Western.

Already, for Alyce, the guilt was kicking in. "I have to say," she told the lawyer, "that I keep wondering even to myself if I should've seen something." He replied, "I say this in my professional life all the time: responsible people tend to feel responsible." His wise proverb became one of Alyce's mantras. That day she discovered what would be another important support. "Thank goodness Marilyn LaPlante was in there with me," she said. Marilyn would be "in there" with her all year.

On November 8, both the rogue tales would be scotched in a letter from Tom Ponto to Public Safety chief Gary Hetrick. The letter's foremost purpose was legal: to document the outcomes of a meeting with Chief Hetrick and Captain Bryant on November 2, where the investigation of the murder was thoroughly explained. First, Tom writes that the college had decided against an internal investigation because of the thoroughness of the police's research. He then reports that Alyce has been questioned:

She clarified that she first heard about the previous suicide attempt *after* the murder-suicide. We inquired as to whether you thought it was necessary for one of your officers to interview her. You indicated that you did not think that was necessary as you had closed the file and felt certain of your conclusions.

Those conclusions were that Mr. Odah acted alone and that there was nothing about his conduct that would have alerted other people, including his roommate, the college, or others, to the impending disaster. Apparently, the gun had been carefully concealed and there was no indication of the impending tragedy.

Having thus carefully covered his legal ground, Tom then reiterates the college's decision to withdraw a request for the visual records of the crime scene, which would have been available after five years. "We all agreed," he wrote, "that because of the disturbing nature of the photographs and video, the more limited distribution the better." The college also asks that the police refuse similar requests from others, at their discretion.

Finally Tom addresses the second rumor: "I learned late last week that as college staff were preparing to ship Mr. Odah's personal belongings to his parents they came across a paint pellet gun. . . . While we can't say for sure, we think the paint gun may have been the gun that Mr. Odah showed to the other student."

In the aftermath of the tragedy, it became apparent that some faculty members—perhaps the more traditional academic types—were less comfortable in the emotional realm than others. It's possible that some of them got only as far in the provost's memo as "return to normalcy" before hitting "delete." At a loss as to how to function professionally on a completely traumatized campus, perhaps some faculty clung gratefully to the reassurance and stability of Business As Usual where they could play their customary roles.

In any case, Chris Wilson had a quiz coming up on Friday in a class that conflicted with Maggie's funeral. He and some fellow students raised the issue, asking if people who wished to attend the funeral could take the quiz at another time. The professor refused. "But it's the same time as the funeral of this girl who just died, who's a friend of ours!" The professor affirmed the importance of sticking to the schedule. Chris avers that the prof eventually said, in effect, "You need to get over it," which may be a student's resentful shorthand of an unsympathetic professor's message, but may also be a clumsy professorial translation of "return to normalcy." As Chris says, "I mean, this was a week after it happened!" He and the others went to the funeral and took an honorable F on the quiz.

Jeanne Hess was assistant chaplain at K that year, in addition to her roles as teacher, coach, and director of Women's Athletics. Late that week she kept an appointment with her massage therapist. "I've scheduled an extra half hour for you," she said when Jeanne arrived. "I knew you'd need it."

During the last half hour, the therapist simply held Jeanne's feet. Anyone who's had massage or reflexology knows what powerful transmitters the feet prove to be. Soon, Jeanne "went away," as she puts it. "Went somewhere else." She saw a figure approaching, robed in dark red. She identified him as Christ. Under each of his arms he carried a lifeless form. As he came closer, Jeanne saw that they were Maggie and Neenef. "Both of them were with him," she recalls.

Maggie's body had been cared for by the funeral home in Plainwell owned by the father of her best friend, Sarah Ayres. From the small service there, David Barclay remembers two poignant details. The first is Maggie's golf shoes, placed next to her coffin. The second is the presence of the entire women's golf team from our near neighbor and frequent opponent, Albion College.

The funeral mass for Maggie on Friday took place at St. Augustine's Cathedral, several blocks from campus, where Maggie had been confirmed in August. The sanctuary was packed, and the scene was deeply emotional. Alyce Brady remembers spotting some of the football team standing together around Eric Page. Not all of them knew Neenef or Maggie, but they knew they had "this traumatized person in their midst. . . . They were just kind of standing around awkwardly . . . and I went up to them and just started giving big hugs."

For some of Maggie's friends, the day was only surreal and exhausting. Katherine Chamberlain recalls frustration with the crowds in the cathedral and at Maggie's gravesite at Cooper Cemetery, halfway between Kalamazoo and Plainwell. She wanted to be alone with her friends, mourning Maggie together. The shock that had enveloped Dan Poskey all week finally broke as Emily Ford drove him to the interment. "It hit me like a truck," he remembers, "and I sat in the passenger seat of Emily's car and lost it."

That weekend, most of them, along with many other students, went home.

Subject: Message from the Counseling Center
Date: Thu, 21 Oct 1999 15:1200-0400 (EDT)
From: Important Notice *bulletin@kzoo.edu*

Dear Faculty and Staff,

I've been wanting to write to you to give you our Counseling Center perspective on helping the students through this terrible tragedy. For many students, this is their first experience with death, and they have little context for understanding it and no sense of the process of grieving. The complexity of this situation, compounded by the recent deaths and memorial services for Jessica, Charles, and Ben, is overwhelming to them—especially for those students who started college just 6 weeks ago. They are feeling their way through and, as is developmentally appropriate, doing so mainly with their peers. I think "older" adults (we, their parents), however, provide a very important sense of stability in their badly shaken sense of their world. As time passes, they will rely on us more to help them come to terms with their experience.

In contrast, the students who have experienced earlier major losses seem to be suffering in a somewhat different way. For a few, their previous experience gives them perspective that enables them to come to terms with this loss more readily. For the majority, this experience stirs up the earlier losses and whatever is unresolved about them. I am more concerned about these students—I think we have seen them earlier and will see them longer. I believe they will also struggle more with their academic work.

Our experience with the students in general is that they are sad, angry, confused, and overwhelmed. Many look forward to resuming their routines and know that doing so will help them recover. Others are overwhelmed and can't focus, can't concentrate, or can't see the relevance of academics in the face of such a tragedy. We have advised those who are having difficulty working for any of these reasons to contact you and are hopeful that you will give them extensions at least for this week. We have also asked them to see us if their focus, concentration, and motivation do not return by the beginning of next week.

Our final concern is related to the complicated nature of the murder/suicide—some students (mainly Neenef's friends) are telling us how hard it is to be placed in discussions in and out of class where he is regarded as a "monster." We are worried for them because this is not their experience of Neenef and, in my view, it is not in their best interest psychologically to be in situations where they feel they have to defend him or listen to views of him that hurt them. If you are aware of such situations, may I ask you to make it clear that students can leave such discussions if they find them upsetting?

We will contact you if we have concerns about particular students of yours. Please call or e-mail us if you have concerns or questions.

Thank you very much for your support of these wonderful kids as they try to come to terms with this most difficult experience of their young lives.

Pat Ponto

8

FAULT LINES

1

In her role as student government president, Simone Lutz had spoken at the vigil outside the chapel on the night of October 18. She remembers saying, "'This is a time for hugging and crying and mourning.' Because at the end of the day, two people had lost their lives, and both of them had friends and family who cared very much about them."

There is no arguing with this truth. But in its subsuming embrace, other truths were temporarily lost or elided. More complex truths and more troubling responses erupted almost immediately. The force of collective, unifying shock and grief could not efface the fissures appearing across the campus. Necessary comfort had to make terms with equally necessary discomfort.

Like other small college communities, Kalamazoo College folks talk incessantly about community. When such colleges were staffed by married, middle-class white American men and attended by middle- and upper-class white American children, community probably wasn't discussed so often; it didn't need to be. Homogeneity makes it relatively easy to form and sustain community. Nowadays at K, we tend to hold it up as an elusive ideal and talk about it as if it equates to harmony—as if community were an end rather than an informing principle, static rather than dynamic. The months after Maggie's murder and Neenef's death challenged this notion of community and forced us to at least consider that it might be more useful to view community as a living, evolving organism, one in which struggle and conflict are the norm rather than violations of the code. There were some, perhaps many, who just wanted it all to go away—wanted to "put it behind us," as they say, in keeping with the touted "return to normalcy." Others yearned for the simple grief that would allow mourning without anger, clarity instead of confusion. But for most of us, I think, belonging to the Kalamazoo College community that year spelled out a much tougher story.

The fissures across the quad traced to two insistent underlying questions. The first was about gender: Was gender relevant to what happened on October 18? Did Maggie's death belong under the heading of so-called "domestic" violence or violence against women? The second question was about the perpetrator: Who was Neenef, and how were we going to talk—or not talk—about him?

But those two questions seemed inevitably to bleed into each other. You couldn't approach one without eventually getting to the other. In retrospect it's clear that those two questions were actually one, and it was about Neenef.

2

Caitlin Gilmet calls Amy Elman, then associate professor of political science, "an icon: venerable, fascinating, intelligent, and fearsome." At least outwardly incapable of being intimidated, she has one of those diamond-sharp intellects that have no patience for ambivalence. An East-Coast emigreé, she is uninterested in that timeless midwestern tradition, making nice, and she is not noted for taking care of others' feelings, including those of her students. She is a formidable and transformative teacher, but her reputation does not rest on "supportiveness." Students who admire her hold her in that reverence that is one degree away from terror, which lies one degree shy of loathing, especially in the case of a woman, so she is also often demonized.

On the evening of Tuesday, October 19—the Day After—she met her senior political science seminar, the one for which Simone had been up writing the paper on Sunday night. Along with four or five of the women in the seminar, Elman took on Maggie's death as femicide, the extreme point on the spectrum of male violence against women. When confronted with the assertion that two people died, not just one, she concurred: both had died from male violence. In other words, the issue was not only the gender of the victim; it was the gender of the perpetrator.

A volatile discussion ensued. Simone remembers it as centering on the pervasive fear of male violence that circumscribes women's lives. "It was too much anger," says Simone. "And it was too much hate. And I remember going at it with her. I think I held my tongue for as long as I could, which was not common in her class because most of the time I opened my mouth quite freely."

This classroom discussion would recur across the campus in the weeks to come. At issue, immediately, was how, as a community, we would talk about what had happened. Those who tried to make Maggie's death meaningful within a context of violence against women were generally accused of "too much hate"; indeed, it became difficult to clarify and maintain the difference between anger and hate, or even between analysis and hate. But Elman's seminar raised another question as well: Was it even possible to bring these two deaths into the classroom? Some of us couldn't imagine not trying. Others felt that a clear boundary between School and Life would protect all of us—would, in fact, keep us all going. Still others felt that some events were beyond intellectual analysis, at least until they had firmly become Past. Simone was one of them. In her seminar, the conflict between empathy and the detachment of academic discussion became unbearable. To frame what had happened as violence against women, with Neenef as Perpetrator and Maggie as Victim, seemed to make a concrete, immediate disaster into a cold, depersonalized abstraction. Simone says, "I remember people who were seniors and were so far removed from knowing the two of them, and it was a very scary, detached conversation. And I remember saying, 'You weren't there that night. You don't know what her friends are going through. And you don't know what her family is going through. So until you experience loss like this, keep your mouth shut. Have some respect, and just consider the magnitude of what's happened—not from a detached academic perspective.'"

Caitlin, a sophomore English major, was in Elman's other class, a lower-level course on feminism and politics in which all the students were female. Famous for her rigid no-cut policy, Elman e-mailed the class on Monday morning, October 18: Even with classes canceled, she said, she wanted to meet to discuss what had happened but would understand if individuals didn't feel able to attend. "As a friend of Neenef's," Caitlin recalls, "I was already beginning to understand the precariousness of mourning him as well as Maggie, and I was definitely not prepared to sit through a class while my vociferously feminist-identified classmates tore him to shreds. I don't think any of the women in my class had known Maggie, either, and I wasn't interested in learning what symbol they'd turn her life into." She wrote Professor Elman to say that she wouldn't be in class, and Elman wrote back, agreeing to permit her to skip as long as she would meet with her privately later in the week. That meeting brought Caitlin into sharp confrontation with the dilemma of her own grief:

> I don't remember everything about our meeting clearly. Dr. Elman was polite, and certainly compassionate about the loss we'd experienced. I appreciated her caring and concern. She wanted to know about Neenef, specifically about his [Iraqi] heritage and his relationship with his family. I assured her that he loved the women in his family, and he'd loved his female friends, but she asserted that he couldn't have loved women, because he'd just killed a woman.
>
> If only it were that simple, you know? I'd just hate his guts, and we'd all move on.
>
> I was exhausted and scrappy enough to take on the most-feared professor at K that morning, so I argued that she didn't know a thing about him. We went a few respectful but tense rounds, with her championing some academic argument about the tautology of power dynamics and me rolling my eyes, before I left her office. . . .
>
> I wanted change in the world, knew I'd work for change in the world, and knew acutely that feminist rhetoric had failed to address what I'd just experienced. . . . I'm not sure what Dr. Elman wanted me to learn from that exchange, but it was far too soon to start sorting out my feelings about Neenef the murderer and Maggie the victim.

In her meeting with Elman, Caitlin experienced the same collisions that brought Simone out of her seat in Elman's seminar: abstraction ran up against experience, head against heart, academe against real life, political against personal (for all our feminist insistence that they are indistinguishable)—and all of it too abrupt or too absolute or just too soon to generate anything worthwhile.

3

Members of K's upper administration met many times during the week after Maggie and Neenef's deaths. As tensions manifested between certain groups on campus, Jimmy and his various teams forged their official stance. The notekeeper at meetings of the Crisis Management Team was Jim Van Sweden, director of Communications, who had been summoned out of the woods and back to campus on October 18. Jim is a Kalamazoo alum, a former English major, a poet, who returned to his alma mater when the Upjohn Pharmaceutical Company, where he played the formidable role of media spokesperson, began to disintegrate in the '90s. His notes from the meeting at 2:00 p.m. on Wednesday, October 20, read like a free-verse description of the tensions occupying the minds of upper administrators:

> Soccer game—black arm bands
> Vigil—holding for one student only
> politicizing the personal
> crimes against women political agenda
> —dehumanize our friend—

This initial list reflects how quickly Neenef's posthumous status had become a pressing issue: it appears near the top of the agenda, right after the black armbands to be worn at the upcoming soccer game. The Women's Resource Center's vigil for Maggie has already become problematic, both because there has been no corresponding honor for Neenef, and because the vigil has introduced the gender issue—thereby "politicizing the personal." If Maggie's death is placed in the context of "crimes against women," a political agenda must be at work. And Neenef's friends see this process as dehumanizing him in death.

The second stanza of Jim's notes struggles to rehumanize both murderer and victim:

Neenef—Odah

anger—murder   more than a victim

support that he was more than a murderer   more than this

                                                                  this single heinous act

irrationality that lurks in all of us

The last line offers a way out of the sticky problem of how to talk about
a human being who has killed two people: the irrationality that drove
Neenef abides in us all.

Jim's notes then move on to other corners of the crisis. The college
should have one point person communicating with the media and one
with the faculty (that equally troublesome crowd). Pat Ponto reminds
the group that the students have confronted death four times suddenly
this fall; for many it's their first confrontation with mortality.

On the public relations front, the annual "Preview K" weekend is
imminent; high-school juniors and their families will be making their
first visits. The shootings will be openly acknowledged. DeWaters and
Trowbridge are not on the Saturday tour.

This session of the Crisis Management Team was followed immediately by a meeting of the President's Advisory Committee, of which
Jim was also a member and for which he also acted as scribe. His notes
begin with an update: Counselors are working overtime to reach out
to students in need. Some parents are angry about the absence of metal
detectors in residence halls. DeWaters 201 will not be occupied this
term. Students have reached out to each other. But then:

 tension over political issue of violence against women
  >group wants to make statement on political issue
  >concerned over demonization of Neenef

The students' vulnerability and susceptibility to guilt are mentioned,
as are the "return to normalcy" letters to faculty and staff. Maggie's
funeral on Friday is announced. Jim will draft the President's remarks to
parents and prospective students for the weekend and get it to Jimmy's
office by 4:00 tomorrow. And finally: "200 emails [from] students overseas and on-campus to JJones."

Jim's notes from a meeting two days later, on Friday, October 22, note and comment on the upcoming symposium planned jointly by Women's Studies and the Women's Resource Center:

> Symposium
>> "violence against women"—reductive? simplistic?
>> who's in favor of it?

Five days after the deaths, the line has been sharply drawn. Whereas the cries for Neenef's humanization are recorded sympathetically, the symposium on violence against women is clearly a problem. It is critiqued in a way that denies its very foundation: "Who's in favor of violence against women? Nobody. And to characterize Maggie's murder this way is reductive and simplistic."

Eight years down the road, reading this record for the first time, I wonder, is it reductive or simplistic to call, say, the murder of Matthew Shepard an example of homophobic violence, or to label the 1963 church bombing in Birmingham as a racial crime? Conversely, isn't peddling the "irrationality that lurks in all of us" reductive in a way that serves to normalize the crime? By moving Neenef so swiftly to the context of "all of us," do we not manage to sidestep the chilling fact that he is one of the thousands of men who kill thousands of women in the United States each year?

4

The symposium on violence against women was set for Wednesday, October 27. Yet my sharpest memory of that week comes from a day earlier. I am sitting on the upholstered settee in the president's wood-paneled office, realizing—with all the hideous certainty that comes when you're about to release bodily fluids involuntarily—that I am about to cry.

The reluctance of the administration to call the murder-suicide an example of violence against women seemed inexplicable to many faculty and students. Indeed, that omission was part of what drove the organization of the symposium in the first place. We had among us considerable expertise on the issue that we believed could serve the campus, especially its shell-shocked students who were looking for some way to grasp what had happened. But we could also feel the resistance from the administration as we pushed, and I knew from over twenty years at the college that campus feminists were being cast as the adversaries.

So imagine my surprise when the phone rang on Monday morning, October 25, and it was Marilyn LaPlante asking if I could draft a statement for the president that framed the shootings and endorsed the Wednesday symposium. "Absolutely," I said. *About time*, I thought. What an opportunity: to inform the voice of the president, and thereby that of the college, telling the official story of what had occurred here. I cleared the decks, canceled appointments, closed my door, yanked out twenty years' worth of ragged files on domestic violence, and went to work. Later that afternoon I delivered into the hands of the president's assistant what I thought was a cogent, forceful statement. (See Appendix A.) It was grounded in statistics; it had been carefully sifted for polemical language; and it avoided sounding too much like me. It took on the Neenef-as-monster issue and the danger of campus factions, emphasizing unity. I thought Jimmy would find it comfortable to voice. At 4:00 p.m. I left for the monthly faculty meeting feeling confirmed and energized. I had asked Jimmy if he would announce the symposium in his opening remarks to the faculty, and he had agreed.

Over the fireplace in the Olmsted Room, where faculty meetings take place, hangs a dim oil portrait of the formidable Mary "Minnie" Senter Mandelle, who always looks down on us grimly, as if she doubts we're up to whatever task is at hand. The faculty sits in rows with two aisles. On this Monday afternoon the mood in the room was somber and tired, with little of the usual joking, sarcasm, or grumbling, overt or covert. Jimmy brought the faculty up to date on the college's official response to the shootings. And then he began to announce the symposium.

At that moment, I felt a palpable shift in the room, a tilt, a change in air pressure. Jimmy, who normally speaks with effortless confidence and assurance, began to falter. His eyes flickered. He hesitated. He couldn't remember the time of the event and glanced at me for information. He was something I had never seen before: nervous. The silence in the room deepened, as I've noticed it does when something is not being said. I left the meeting confused and ill at ease.

The next day, Marilyn called again. The statement I'd drafted was excellent, she said, but the president had decided not to use it. It had been decided that emphasizing the violence done to Maggie at Neenef's hands was too divisive. Marilyn, whose voice clearly registered that she knew I would be perturbed, was all gratitude and kindness. Not wishing to kill this particular messenger, I thanked her, saying that while I understood, I disagreed. I hung up, shaking, furious that my work had been rejected, that my time had been wasted, and that the college couldn't summon the fortitude to call this enormity by its name. Then I went on with my Tuesday.

That afternoon I got a call from the president's assistant, Margie Flynn, asking if I could drop by before I left campus. I dreaded the meeting, but you don't refuse to meet with the president unless you're declaring war. So, when I was done with teaching and office hours, I trudged up Academy Street to Mandelle Hall.

Jimmy came around his huge desk to meet me in his flawless white shirtsleeves. He looked genuinely stricken. He apologized profusely. He had no choice, he said; Pat Ponto had warned him that Neenef's friends were very fragile. The campus was on the brink of falling into Neenef's camp versus Maggie's camp. "That would be utterly disastrous," he said, his eyes begging me to understand.

I listened, nodded, listened, as I had planned to do. When he was silent, I said, "I understand. I really do."

"Do you?" he pleaded.

"I do, Jimmy. If I were president, I would take the advice of my director of counseling, too." I took a breath. "But I wonder if anybody is thinking about the women on this campus who are afraid, the women *I* have been counseling this past week, who *do* need to understand this as violence against women. They are fragile, too."

"Are they?" Jimmy asked, as if this were the first time he'd been aware of this population. And at that point, to my horror, I burst into tears.

At subsequent moments in his presidency when I was angry at him, I would think back to the moment Jimmy strode forward and put his arms around me. I'm sure I got mascara on his impeccable white shirt. We sat on his sofa and talked for a while, but I fled as quickly as I could. I prayed to make it to my car without running into anybody, but just outside the door to his outer office I met Carolyn Newton, associate provost and long-time biology professor. With sudden, deep concern she asked what had happened. "I just lost it in the president's office," I called over my shoulder as I rushed downstairs and out the door.

That night Greg Mahler called to check on me, but I was too mortified and exhausted to pick up. Looking back, I see that my expectations
of myself in this situation—that I should navigate this crisis, its politics
and its constantly shifting terrain, with transcendent self-possession
and, above all, never let the Boys see me sweat (or weep)—only helped
bend me to the breaking point. Still mortified the next morning, my first
accomplishment was to send the following e-mail:

Dear Jimmy,

I am absolutely horrified by the degree to which I lost it in your office.
The upholstery on your sofa will probably not recover. I know you'll say
it was fine, but my embarrassment is painful. In retrospect it's clear that
I should have postponed our meeting for a day or two. Thank you for
understanding and for taking time to meet with me.

Gail

Jimmy's response came at 11:28 a.m.—gracious, compassionate, and
also revelatory. Clearly, the wind had shifted again.

My Dear Friend,

Do not be horrified in the least. Members of our community shed
tears in my office often, the most being shed not by you at all but by many,
many others. You did not "lose it." And furthermore, you had every right
to be angry with me.

I am sending an e-mail to the entire community about tonight's Symposium. We are going to try for 11:30.

Remember above all else: your cause is right and just. I think it was
old Harry Truman who said, "When in doubt, try to do the right thing.
It will gratify a very few and amaze the hell out of everyone else." You
are doing the right thing. I am going to try to help, especially so that I can
again deserve the right to be your friend.

Semper,

JFJ

The message to the community is time stamped exactly two minutes
later.

To the members of the Kalamazoo College Community:

At the October 25th meeting of the faculty, an announcement was made of critical importance to every member of our community in the aftermath of last week's violent murder of Maggie Wardle and suicide of Neenef Odah: a symposium this evening that will explore the issue of violence against women. The symposium is sponsored by the Women's Studies Program, the Women's Resource Center, and the Women's Equity Coalition, and has been ably organized by Professor Gail Griffin. Tonight's meeting will feature Barbara Mills, a noted authority on the endemic problem of violence in our society and of violence against women in particular.

The Symposium is an ideal setting to start those conversations on our campus to which I alluded in the last paragraph of my letter yesterday. I should have linked my strong desire to see those conversations take place on our campus and tonight's event. Many different aspects of this societal pathogen will be discussed this evening, including in particular what those of us who are male can do to reverse the growing manifestations of violence against women in our world.

I urge each member of this community to attend tonight's symposium, which will start at 8:00 p.m. in Dalton Theater.

James F. Jones, Jr.
President

5

The context is unknown for the notes taken by Jim Van Sweden on October 27, the day of the symposium, but the subject matter seems clear.

There are fine, respected individuals who have an agenda and would like to use the power of the office of the president to advance that agenda.

Be slow to think about things. The notion that one situation is the same as another and therefore requires an identical response (or we are remiss) is a premise worth exploring.

Let people struggle toward knowledge—*it's Socratic*
            rather than mandate the information we think they should
            know and consider
what about complexity
de individualization
we think more in duality than we like to admit—there are far more than "two groups"

probably reacting more against any de-individualization of the two people who have been lost

Those "fine, respected individuals" with an agenda certainly included me. That the feminists on campus were being framed in those terms goes a long way to explain the sense of dissonance and unease I felt in the days before the symposium. Perhaps my strangest moment that night came before the event started. I was on the Dalton Theater stage when Jimmy walked in with Maggie's family. I had not been informed that they would be in attendance, but there was no way to see their presence as other than an endorsement. As they crossed in front of the stage, the president leaned up, I leaned toward him over the lip of the stage, and he said, *sotto voce*: "I owe you one." This was the moment I knew for sure that the Omilians were not at all hesitant to name what had happened to their daughter. I could only hope that what was about to occur would be somehow helpful to them.

The theater was sparsely filled—there were perhaps a hundred people there, mostly students. The utter absence of faculty beyond Women's Studies surprised and disappointed me. Several Student Services staff members, including counselors, were there, as arranged. In my introduction, I tried to make the connection that I sensed was so difficult for people to make, the connection between Maggie's and Neenef's deaths and the larger societal and cultural context. I began with the question of why such a link might be hard to see:

> If I stand in front of a class and say that four million women were physically abused by male partners or former partners last year, or that 75 percent of assaults on women by partners are inflicted during or after a separation, or that over two thirds of murdered women are killed by someone they know, half of those by partners or former partners, the class will look serious and no one will argue that this isn't a problem to be named. But when your friend complains about her boyfriend wrestling with her and refusing to let her up, or when you see bruises on your arm from when your boyfriend grabbed and pulled you last night, it's much harder to say, "Wait a minute: this is it. This is what they're talking about." . . . It is also very hard to stand outside an event like last week's and name it while it is washing over you emotionally. And finally, I think it is hard to

identify violence against women because to many ears, men who do that to women are monsters, terrible people whose entire identities are defined by that violence. Anyone who has studied violence against women knows this to be false. While there are patterns and behaviors associated with men who batter women, perpetrators are usually ordinary guys, liked, admired, and loved by many people, including often their victims. And that is the real horror of the violence that stalks women in this world.

Carol Anderson, assistant professor of religion, then took over and chaired the panel. Barbara Mills spoke first. Just the day before, she had been honored by the governor for twenty years of relentless work on behalf of abused women. Taking the mic and walking to the edge of the stage, she identified her task: to connect what happened here to what happens in society at large. She spoke of what we know about lethal relationships, for instance that the period during and after which a woman leaves is the most dangerous of all, and that coercion and issues of power and control are major symptoms. Mills then dispelled a couple of myths. The first is that perpetrators and victims are poor or less bright than the rest of us, a notion that is partly responsible for how difficult it is to acknowledge personal involvement in an unsafe relationship. The second myth is that women are safest from violence in the places where they live, including residence halls, when home is statistically the least safe place for women. "For women," Mills said in summary, "there is no 'safe place.'" I felt a little jolt of energy across the theater and in my own body.

Matt Filner, a young professor of political science, spoke about the politics of male power, and he too identified myths: that we can't understand it and that we can do nothing about it. He urged men on campus to consider how they benefit from male power and how they put barriers in front of women to secure it. He concluded by enjoining men to speak out against other men engaged in male violence. We know who they are, he argued; we need to say their names.

A student, Yoshi Bird, criticized what she saw as the lack of a "real" feminist presence on campus that would be more equipped to frame and address violence against women. Psychologist Karyn Boatwright read a lyrical piece recounting the multiple voices she remembered from her years as a therapist: the women's voices full of guilt and terror, including those of women being harassed in the workplace who wondered if they had the "right" to complain; the men's voices marked by the struggle with masculine conditioning that inscribes dominance and violence.

Finally, Stephanie Schrift, representing the Women's Resource Center, recalled how often during the first hours and days after the shootings she heard fellow students talking about other dangerous relationships. There are others at risk on campus, she concluded, urging her listeners to become more aware of the warning signs for potentially abusive relationships. Kiran Cunningham, assistant professor of anthropology, wound up the panel, as we had planned, by urging those who thought they were in dangerous relationships—including those who felt they themselves might become violent—to consult someone in Student Services or a member of tonight's panel.

The Q & A was short. One audience member wanted to know what questions men should ask themselves, and the response from Barbara was memorable: "Do you have feelings of severe jealousy? Have you ever thought, 'She doesn't have the right...'? Do you find yourself needing hypercontrol in the relationship?"

Jim Van Sweden's notes from the symposium conclude as follows:

> Maggie—warning signs—*looking back we can see the* signs now
> we must be vigilant
> i.e., because of an educational intervention we now see warning signs in this particular relationship.
> should we provide this intervention to all incoming students?

Below that last question, he has written and circled the word "Yes."

In planning the symposium, we had painstakingly called in all colleagues with counseling background to be available afterward, but nobody seemed to need them. The energy in the theater was subdued. Clots of women stuck around to talk. The WRC students had helped to distribute handouts that had constituted a large chunk of my work for the past week: statistics on violence against women, diagrams of the cycle of "domestic" violence, and a list of warning signs of abusive relationships. (See Appendix B.) Many women, I noted, were reading the list in groups, pointing and whispering. I heard about that list in a variety of settings for the rest of the year—and I heard about it again during my interviews for this book. Its impact exceeded any statistics or theory we could have presented, perhaps because it identified concrete, all-too-common behavior.

I went home still feeling uneasy. I had felt the same tension in the theater that I'd felt in the faculty meeting two days earlier—nervousness, stiffness, something being held in. I would feel it intermittently across the campus for the rest of the year.

In retrospect I think I understand the tension. But even in retrospect, knowing what I know now, when I try to imagine what might have relieved it, I get lost. Thinking about Simone's and Caitlin's experiences within the context of campus feminism, I wonder: Were we who were so invested in mounting the symposium only precipitating fruitless conflicts within and among our students, forcing information and analysis they couldn't yet use? Were we precipitous in asking the campus to see the Big Picture into which Maggie's murder so clearly fit? Or were we even, as some charged, co-opting a tragedy for purposes of forwarding our own politics or affirming our own claim to righteousness?

The last question I can answer with an unequivocal no. Among the planners of the symposium, students and faculty alike, I saw a sense of urgent obligation and service. Answering the first two questions is more difficult. Certainly many people, perhaps especially the students, were not ready for the Big Picture, the analytical approach. For adults, and perhaps especially for college professors, that approach is helpful, as it gives a horrendous event context and thus a measure of meaning. But in the weeks following the murder-suicide, the K students who had known Maggie and Neenef were very much on the level of the specific, the particular, the personal. A gun in a dorm. Blood. A murdered friend. A suicidal friend. A friend a murderer. Grief. Horror. Guilt.

We might have waited to mount the symposium, perhaps until winter or spring term. And we might have chosen to do so, had the college's various official responses not failed to speak to the gender issue or to address the danger women frequently face from the men closest to them. Based on what Stephanie Schrift had said, students were concerned about their own relationships and those of friends. Could we responsibly allow that silence to continue for months? At the time, at least, it didn't seem that we could.

For me the issue was fundamentally educational. I felt we owed students what we provided daily in our classes: frameworks in which to make sense of the world. How could teachers help students navigate painful conflicts except by teaching? Listening ears and hugs and latitude in deadlines were insufficient, in my mind. If we believed that knowledge is power, didn't we owe them knowledge—in the form of information, contexts, language, paradigms of analysis? Teaching is so often about clearing ways so that students might bring the unimaginable into the realm of the known. This process can be liberating, or it may be horrifying. More often than not, it is some combination of both. I wouldn't teach if I didn't believe that every significant moment, even the worst, is a teachable one.

The problem was that in our version of Maggie and Neenef's story the lesson was about gender, and it's possible that that story would never have been timely on the campus of Kalamazoo College. The silence I heard in the theater and across the campus was the same silence I have heard in classrooms when someone has raised the issue of men and women. It's something like the great white silence that occurs when race raises its annoying head. Talking about race is terrifying to most white people and can be very dangerous for people of color. Similarly, talking about gender seems to terrify male and female alike. It makes men angry and paranoid; it makes women fearful and anxious. The difference is that while most white Americans don't live in real proximity to, let alone intimacy with, people of color, most women do indeed live or have lived intimately with men. It brings danger "home" to suggest that intimacy between men and women is fraught with danger for women; it questions the foundation of heterosexual love and sex, and imperils the relationships in which the majority of women still tend to ground their sense of self, of value, of normalcy, and of safety. Is it any wonder that young people, especially, don't welcome Barbara Mills's message that for women there is no ultimately safe place?

6

The attempt to talk about violence against women met with particular resistance among Neenef's friends. If the collisions between abstract and concrete, political and personal were disorienting for most students, they were especially painful for people who loved and at least thought they knew Neenef. One such student was Navin Anthony.

I guess it was hard for me to understand that at that time because I knew Neenef, and he didn't seem like that kind of person; he didn't seem like a domestic abuser, the typical person who [commits] domestic violence. And I think when people started saying that, I was, like, "What are they talking about? I don't understand that. Because that's not a person that I knew, that's not a person I talked to every day." It seemed like people outside the situation saying this and making up a definition of what was going on. And it didn't make sense to me.

Navin's reaction probably represents what many other students believed—that there is a "typical" domestic abuser, a sort of person who does that sort of thing, and Neenef wasn't it. A pre-existing image of the guy who beats up women stands in the way of our seeing that it may in fact be our friend, our brother—in Navin's case, literally the guy next door.

Nancy El-Shamaa found it more difficult to dismiss the messages about violence against women—most women did—but at the time she, like many students, heard them as part of a larger effort to demonize her friend.

I was a nineteen-year-old woman who was just coming into her own about feminism and women's rights. I was just starting to see women's place in the world in general. So on the one hand I [felt the gender issue] HAS to be brought to attention. . . . And I can be pretty pragmatic and logical when I need to be, so while a lot of people would only think of him as a friend, a part of me, a pretty small part of me but still a part of me was thinking, "This kind of stuff happens to women all the time. Sometimes the men don't kill themselves as well, but they'll kill the women, and we should be angry about this." But most of me thought it was completely tactless and insensitive that a lot of his friends were kind of almost blamed, I felt.

But it was not only Neenef's friends who resisted the label. Sara Church first came up against the issue in Jerry Mayer's American Government class two days after the shootings. "That's when . . . I remember first hearing the 'd' word: domestic violence. I struggled with it at first and refused to buy it. That was a problem for older women, another group, not college girls, was my subconscious thought."

For some of Maggie's crew, like Erin Rome, the issue was, again, co-optation. "We were resistant to calling it violence against women," she says. "We didn't like the idea of them taking this horrible incident and turning it into a big cause." For those struggling to come to grips with losing Maggie, that loss was intensely personal; they didn't like people who didn't know her seizing her death and, in Katherine Chamberlain's words, "taking ownership of it." They thought of Maggie's murder—needed to think of it, in its enormity—as "an isolated incident." To make it symptomatic—to "politicize it," in Katherine's words—was to render it common and thus to rob it of its particular anguish and outrageousness, and on some level to take it away from the ones feeling that anguish and outrage.

It also shifted the focus. "We didn't want to talk about Neenef," Erin says. "We wanted to talk about Maggie." They wanted their own relationships with her to be honored. Katherine was "offended and annoyed that we were not being made central to the conversations that were happening," as if people who didn't know Maggie suddenly knew more about her than her closest friends. "I was not . . . ready for it to be labeled anything, except a really horrible tragedy," she says.

Yet seven months after Maggie's death, in a paper for my class, Erin would write, "After attending the violence against women panel, I was amazed by how exactly Neenef fit the profile of a typical stalker or abusive boyfriend. I wish so much that I had had that list a year ago, because it would have been a lot easier for me to recognize the fact that Maggie was in a potentially abusive and dangerous relationship. It would have made it easier for me to convince her to get out of her relationship before it got out of hand."

7

In some way, it always came down to Neenef: who he was and how we were going to speak of him. Maggie's lovely spirit we could consign to the angels and mourn. Neenef was going to be a more difficult ghost.

"What has happened is not characteristic of his personality," said Father Michael Birnie, the Odah family's priest at St. Thomas Church of the East in Ballard, Washington. "I was shocked, very shocked. He didn't seem to be that type of boy." His sentiments were echoed by virtually all of Neenef's friends. But many of them struggled against an undercurrent: what if he *was* "that type of boy," and they'd somehow missed it? Jennie Toner, an English major who had many good friends in Neenef's circle, says, "It messed them up more than it did her friends, in a way. I think they felt that they were somehow responsible for her death . . . that because they were bad judges of character they couldn't save her."

One of Neenef's friends, his "little sister" Heather Barnes, was a member of Writer in Residence Diane Seuss's first-year seminar that fall. The seminars tend to be places where new students can process the transition to collegiate life. For this entering class, the transition had just become exponentially more difficult. As a result, the hour when seminars met took on a deeper coloring after the first four weeks. Many faculty canceled assignments, lowered the reading load, and cleared space in class for the fallout from October 18. As Heather memorialized Neenef, another woman in Di's seminar insisted that his murder of Maggie had to be taken into any account of him. Heather—one of the handful who had seen the bathroom between DeWaters 201 and 203—was completely unable to focus on academic work, as were several others in the group. So Di scheduled an evening in the wood-paneled lounge in Humphrey House, the soulful old humanities building. They would meet and simply take time for their feelings. They could bring friends.

Word got out, and lots of people appeared, curling themselves into chairs and sofas and carpeted corners in "clumps," as Di puts it, leaning on each other, weeping. Among them were four of Maggie's closest friends, Erin, Kelly, Nandini, and Dan Poskey. That night, the conflict came into the open. "It was just weird," says Kelly. "And it was kind of like it was us against them." Di, with a master's degree in social work and an early career as a therapist, decided quickly to step out of the way and simply let people talk, only intervening to make sure everyone who wanted to speak got heard.

Erin remembers Neenef's younger female friends, like Heather, fighting for his memory. As she recalls it, their message was "Two people are dead here; it doesn't matter why." Maggie's friends' response was, "Yeah, it does! Your friend *killed* our friend!" Nandini's version of her feelings is even more blunt: "Grieve all you want, but shut up about it, because it's all his fault."

"Now looking back," says Kelly, "I realize they were grieving and they hurt just as much, but we couldn't see that at the time. I don't think he was a horrible person; I think he did a horrible thing."

Dan remembers Di saying, "You guys are only nineteen or twenty years old. It's so much to handle." In that moment, he saw himself and the others as if from the outside, "how young and innocent we really were, despite being away from our homes and feeling grown up. It was a very brutal awakening."

The "us against them" was precisely what Pat Ponto and her staff had been trying to prevent, but it was probably inevitable in such a case, on such a small campus, with everyone no more than two degrees of separation from everyone else. The tension between the two groups set in for good, cemented by some in Neenef's group who insisted that Maggie's "betrayal" of Neenef played some role in her fate—the ubiquitous and intractable need to blame the female victim. For Leza Frederickson and Erin Rome, going home to DeWaters at the end of the day became a particular trial. Leza recalls,

> I didn't want to go back to my room, ever. It was hard, because he had lot of friends who lived next to him on that floor, and several of them had the nerve to say it was her fault, and I remember hearing that and thinking, "How can anyone even say that?" . . . It was awful to hear, it really was. There was a guy who lived there and he had this poem on his door about—it was something about Neenef, and "may God be with him" and all this stuff. I had never felt so angry in my entire life. I know they had to grieve their friend, but it was hard to see that, it really was.

Meanwhile, others among Neenef's friends struggled to clarify their motives. For Navin, the talk about violence against women made communication harder:

> Some of [Maggie's friends] thought that we were defending him or that we were defending the whole situation. We lost our friend, and there were two people's lives that were lost. It wasn't just one person. It wasn't boy versus girl, it wasn't anything like that. I guess when people started to talk like this, I just didn't understand why people were taking sides on

this issue. Two really good people lost their lives, and why couldn't we just say it that way?

Occasionally, overtures between the groups were made. But only occasionally. Navin remembers,

It was so hard for me to talk to them. I knew her friends, and I knew I was getting looks from her friends, weird looks from her friends. I remember Erin Rome approached me and said, "Look, my friends are really upset about all this." And she was definitely—she was very, very kind and concerned about what I thought. And I know she was good friends with Maggie, and it was difficult for her to approach me and say something to me. I think she was really the only one.

How to mourn a friend without erasing his hideous violence? How to live in the reality of two lives lost without seeming to excuse the murderer? How to speak of the larger context of violence against women— "boy versus girl"—and still acknowledge Neenef's full humanity? What language could we find for Neenef? More often than not, we found none at all.

In the spring, psychology faculty Karyn Boatwright and assistant chaplain Jeanne Hess tried to move us toward a common language by inviting Marianne Williamson to campus. Williamson, author of *Illuminata* and *The Healing of America*, was a minister in the Detroit area who spoke and conducted workshops geared toward social justice, peace, and healing socially and culturally induced wounds. On an April evening she conducted a ritual in Stetson Chapel through which she attempted to address the rift across our campus with a controversial request: She asked men and women to apologize to each other, individually and collectively. At the end, she asked people to join hands and repeat a prayer that she would lead. The air in the chapel was very tense. "Marianne could feel it," Karyn recalls. "You could see that it was very difficult. It would be interesting to see, if it were on videotape—how people were reacting. They were coming together, but you could feel that in that moment people didn't want to touch. It's like couples, when they've had a tragedy—lost a child—they can't connect."

8

Within hours of the deaths, the question of memorial services had arisen. Greg Mahler recalls, "We did have a number of conversations about what's the appropriate thing for the college to do for him." There was no question about a memorial for Maggie, he says. "She was a victim of a violent crime. But what about him? And so that was something I really struggled with." As it turned out, he was the only member of the administration, so far as he recalls, willing to speak for a memorial for Neenef. Danny Sledge remembers Pat Ponto consistently keeping the fact of two deaths before the senior administration, but not her advocating an official commemoration of Neenef. The question was, according to Danny, "Should we publicly do anything for a person who was a murderer?" Glenn Nevelle, the ex-cop, was unambivalent: "Well, wait a minute, this is a murder-suicide, you know. As far as I'm concerned, there was only one victim, even though [Neenef] had his friends on campus. When you take somebody's life, you forfeit a lot of rights. . . . When life has ended, life has totally ended." According to Danny, President Jones was equally adamant—though his and Marilyn's interactions with Maggie's family may have had something to do with their position on this question.

Jim Van Sweden's undated notes from a Crisis Management Team meeting capture the tenor of the deliberations among the senior administration. A joint mass for both students at St. Tom's, next door to the campus, is mentioned. "Something other than a 'memorial' service for Neenef to help his friends" is suggested, "but how administratively should we get involved?" In a bout of soul-searching, the group discusses whether in backing off from a memorial for Neenef they are driven by "moral outrage" or "liability"—that is, the fear of a lawsuit from the Omilians. Fear of a demonstration is also voiced. Ultimately it is decided that an official memorial service for Maggie will take place in the chapel on January 14, 2000, and that a plaque bearing her name will be installed along with the other brass plaques commemorating students, staff, and faculty who have died while attending or serving the college. Jim concludes, "No plaque for Neenef. Any service will occur naturally from will of friends—small private ceremony." To my knowledge, no such small ceremony took place. It would probably not have occurred naturally; someone in authority would have had to organize it. And despite the focus on Neenef's friends, no one seems to have been willing to step up to lead this tricky project.

The issue of memorials was remarkably gnarled. It pitted the needs of some students against those of others, at a college that strives to serve them all. It set the needs and righteous claims of a victim's family against the needs of her murderer's friends. It brought moral issues and liability issues to the same table. The college's official institutional stance had to weigh against its internal responsiveness to community needs. In some way judgment or "moral outrage" wrestled with a kind of universal compassion that seemed, to some, to erase distinctions, to level perpetrator and victim. Was it Neenef's actions that ultimately mattered, or his humanity? Was he, finally, a murderer, or was he a student, just like Maggie? What were we going to do with him? Did Maggie's innocence and the terrible violation of *her* humanity finally trump any and all concerns about Neenef and his friends?

Kirsten Fritsch, who had danced with Neenef the night before he died, probably speaks for many who loved Neenef when she says,

> I felt, and still do feel, that we were discouraged from mourning the loss of Neenef . . . and of speaking of Neenef in terms of loss or grief. I remember that he was always made the "other," when he was referred to publicly at all. The chalk messages that covered campus after the vigil were all in support of Maggie and her friends, which is right, but there was no public support for Neenef's friends, which is immeasurably sad.

In retrospect, Danny Sledge agrees: "As an institution, we could have done something for Neenef and his friends."

Brooke Nobis, Maggie's old middle-school friend, remembers anger among Neenef's friends when a vigil was held for Maggie at the WRC but there was no similar vigil arranged for him. Brooke also recalls another facet of what Neenef's friends saw as his demonization: speculation about his ethnicity, his nationality, his religion, along with the predictable assumptions about Middle Eastern men in general. At a college that foregrounds international and intercultural education, Brooke was taken aback by the willingness, in some quarters, to set Neenef up as Alien and interpret him in racist terms. While this phenomenon was not widespread, it demonstrates how precariously close to the margins he dwelled on our very white, very Christian campus.

Interestingly, in the Public Safety Report, his race is indicated by the letter "U"—for "unknown." He was that ambiguous figure, the Middle Easterner (even though he was an American citizen), whose place in the American racial hierarchy is undetermined. Those without a firm racial identity are dangerous, as they subvert the whole system of racial classification. "Arab" or "Middle Easterner" carried its own load of assumptions, even before 9/11.

Yet Neenef was, in some sense, Unknown. All too unknown, his friends would say, by those vilifying him. Certainly the depths of his despair, his anger, and his violence were unknown to even his closest friends. For the college, perhaps understandably, the greatest unknown was how to speak of him publicly—that is, how to acknowledge his death. The official response to Neenef was silence.

"They should have said his name," says Caitlin Gilmet.

But before a month had passed, he would say it himself, in full. Neenef got to tell his own version of the story. Ultimately, it was Maggie who was utterly silenced.

KALAMAZOO COLLEGE
1200 Academy Street
Kalamazoo, MI 49008
FAX #(616) 337-7239

To: Detective Alofs   FAX # 337-8887
From: Tom Ponto
Date: November 12, 1999
Number of pages (including this cover sheet) 5

Attached please find the letter that I spoke to you about this morning. We have not been able to verify that it is authentic.
Please call me at 337-7225 if I can be of assistance in any way.

Thank you.
tmp

9

ANOTHER SAD CHAPTER

1

At 1:34 a.m. on Friday, November 12, twelve Kalamazoo students received this e-mail:

> This quarter has really been a tough one for me and many others. I would like to thank all of you so much for all of your help. You all have been the motivation for me to keep going during these grim times. I received this letter today (below). I know this is going to hurt to read, but I think that Neenef has some really important things to say. I guess Neenef wrote this before he took his and Maggie's life. All you can do is read it with care and learn from it. He would have wanted it that way.
>
> Please also visit the web site that Neenef's brother set up for him. This address is below. [The Web site no longer exists.]
>
> Thank you Neenef for being such an important part of our lives. Thank you for always being there for us. You shall never [sic] be missed.
> Yours Sincerely,
> Navin Anthony
> "May you rest in peace"

The letter that Navin appended is an e-mail forwarded to him on Thursday, November 11. Who sent it and how long it had been circulating in cyberspace is unknown. It reads as follows:

10/17/99

Here's the whole story. You can interpret it whichever way you like, but here's the truth that led to all the mistreatment, pain, and sorrow. We met in January of this year and at first I thought this was just going to be yet another one of those girls I'd get with and then leave and not think twice about it. The one thing that changed all this was two weeks after we went out she told me she was falling in love with me. No one I've been with had said anything like this to me so it came as a shock and I couldn't respond. But the closer we came to be the more I realized what it was about. I felt what I thought was love for her. We went through 8 months of this, the beginning being better than the end. She promised me that we'd work things out and that this month I was going to be home was going to be a good break for us to see how much we really loved each other. A week before I came back to school I hear that she had screwed another guy and this completely made me furious. It made me feel like I can't live with myself. And since I've been here this is how I've been feeling. She's had so much control over me that anything she said either built my self-esteem or broke it. And slowly and surely I wasn't getting any better. The more I tried to forget about her, and worse it would get. The more I said to myself I couldn't love her, the stronger that love grew. So it was a big conflict I had to deal with.

On the other hand, since the day she broke up with me based on a mistake she made, she was out dating, drinking, and having fun on my expense. I tried very hard to sit and try to understand the sudden change, but there was no explanation to I could come up with. It doesn't make any sense to me how a person can go from being the most caring, loving human being, to the most heartless and cruel person imaginable. It seemed that she didn't care for me after 8 months of trying to prove to me she did. This is what drove me over the edge a little more. To add to this, I've had nothing in the past 20 years besides grief and sorrow in my life. Having met Maggie I actually believed that life may not be so bad. And I believed this for 8 long months. Here's how it ends. Another sad chapter in the story of my life.

My purpose in writing this is for all—family and friends—to see that life is too short to be spent hurting one another. You can't love anyone unconditionally [sic—he certainly means "conditionally"]. Loving someone means never giving up on that someone. Never hurting that someone. And never saying I don't love you anymore. Once you truly fall in love with someone, as Maggie had done for me for the last 8 months, there's no way you can fall out of love with that someone. She did so much for me that I realized over the month I was home how much I have to change my stubborn self. And that's what I worked on all month. I had so many things planned to make her feel like the special person she was, but this is how it had to end. This is how much hurt she caused me. Not once had a thought such as this crossed my mind. NEVER. But seeing her do certain things, and hearing about those things just triggered this even more. I can't say I'm sorry for my actions because I hope to God all the people that get a hold of this letter realize how short life is to spend hurting one another.

To my family . . . I know it may seem as if I may have let you down by taking this path. Mom and Dad, instead of grieving over me, try to bring the family together more. Build the family as one unit. If one person hurts, the whole family hurts. That's what family is about. You can't have a family without the support of all. Remember the saying, one stick is easier to break when it's by itself. But when you add a few more, it becomes stronger. That's what a true, loving family is.

I know it may seem too much to ask for, but I would like for this to be read by all who were affected by this in any way. To see the truth behind it all.

Neenef Wilson Paulous Odah

2

When psychology professor Karyn Boatwright, whose field is counseling psychology, read Neenef's letter, her first response startled me. "Well," she said, "he's not crazy." What she meant was that there is no sign of clinical pathology beyond his statement that he has no remorse, a stance associated with sociopathic personalities. He talks about being over the edge, she observed, but he's clearly not, as he's writing this letter. Her colleague Bob Grossman, the senior member of our psychology department, a clinical psychologist with years of experience with seriously disturbed clients, agreed. "There is little evidence of and [are] few symptoms of emotional problems in the letter," he said, "other than of course the overwhelming feelings of pain and anger. No signs of psychosis for example." Bob cited Neenef's careful planning and premeditation as evidence of an ability to set overwhelming feelings aside and carry a plan out rationally.

Bob noted that Neenef's "mental pictures" after the breakup—of Maggie with other men; of her out enjoying herself "on [his] expense"—are extremely common among his students, male and female, when they describe the psychological experience of losing a romantic partner. So then, Bob asked, what differentiated Neenef? What made him so unable to live with those mental pictures that he went, in his own terms, over the edge? Bob identified three possibilities: First, did the suicide and/or the murder constitute, for Neenef, a kind of honor killing? "The last paragraph on family seems to be a bit unusual for our culture," Bob said, "so I would want to find out more about his background. Is there something in his culture that makes unfaithfulness extra painful/humiliating, so painful that deaths are the main or only way out?" Second, was the pain of Neenef's childhood and family situation enough to make the difference? And third, were Neenef's assertions of the unchangeable nature of love, which seem so extreme, simply "an exaggeration of our cultural belief that once you find true love it will last forever," or do they "reflect a more intense requirement of fidelity that is involved in some other cultures?" If Neenef's culture of origin did incorporate a more intense fidelity code, it may have been reinforced in Neenef's mind by the ultra-romantic rhetoric and imagery of Western popular culture and tradition.

Both Bob and Karyn spotted Neenef's intense need for control in his letter. He doesn't explain why Maggie's death is necessary, Bob noted. "Perhaps," he said, "the control issue is paramount for him," as implied by Neenef's statement about Maggie's control over *him*. Karyn also pointed out that Neenef has arranged it—and written the story—so that *he* is doing the leaving, controlling the end of the relationship, not allowing Maggie to make that choice. As Bob suggested the very masculinist concept of the "honor killing," Karyn noted the cold masculinism of Neenef's description of his initial attitude toward Maggie as "yet another one of those girls I'd get with and then leave and not think twice about it," as well as the mechanical hardness of his metaphors: "screwed," "triggered."

Where Bob repeatedly mentioned Neenef's cultural orientation as a possible factor, Karyn wondered about a gendered moral orientation. She reminded me of the groundbreaking work of Carol Gilligan in the 1980s. Talking to young people about moral decision-making, Gilligan distinguished the "justice" orientation that seemed to prevail in young men—a concern for what's right or fair according to established abstract principles—from a "care" orientation she heard in young women's accounts, which evinced a probing concern for the collective welfare and a search for alternate options. Neenef's letter, Karyn pointed out, epitomizes the former: behavior is judged in fairly rigid terms of guilt or innocence, wrong or right. For a guilty verdict, punishment ensues, inevitably and swiftly. This is the orientation Neenef brought to his encounter with Stephanie Miller and why it puzzled him so much that she seemed to have escaped punishment for her deviation from the sexual code for women. This orientation would have been deeply ingrained from childhood in Neenef—who signs his letter with his full name, which includes the full name of his father.

Since the "judge" himself is about to perpetrate a hideous wrong, the irony is almost unbearable. But from Neenef's perspective, as judge, what he is about to do constitutes not killing, not murder, but execution.

3

Almost certainly, this letter is what Neenef was typing so concertedly on his computer on the afternoon and evening of Sunday, October 17. This was most likely the project that made him too busy to talk to Heather Barnes and Stacy Lantz. The rifle had been in his room for eight days. He certainly planned to kill himself. But at what point did he decide to take Maggie's life as well?

In the letter, Neenef refers consistently to the act he is about to commit with the ambiguous pronoun "this." It may refer to two deaths. It may also refer to one alone, his own. "This is how much hurt she caused me" could imply that her death is the consequence of the hurt she caused, but it could also imply that *his* death is the result of hurt he couldn't bear, with which he wanted to punish *her* by letting her see its effect.

Almost instantly, it became part of the accepted version of events that Neenef had asked Maggie to come to his room on Sunday night to edit one of his papers, as she often had done. She had kindly agreed. This account seems to have come from J'nai Leafers' statement to police, in which she says that he had asked her to "read something." But the "something" is not identified further. It may well be that Maggie went to Trowbridge assuming that she would be helping Neenef with his homework. But given his obsession with making her comprehend his suffering, it is entirely possible that what he wanted her to read, and may have shown her, was this letter.

4

One of the recipients of Navin's e-mail was Maggie's friend Jeff Hopcian, who forwarded the message to Marilyn LaPlante at 7:34 a.m. that Friday, November 12. Marilyn sent it on to Tom Ponto at 8:13. Tom faxed it to Detective Alofs of the Kalamazoo Public Safety Department shortly after noon. It was discussed later that morning in the President's Advisory Committee meeting. Jim Van Sweden's notes read, "Widespread forwarding—all on campus will know by noon."

Indeed, by 12:12 p.m. Neenef's letter had reached a student named Riham Hossain, who forwarded it to the Women's Resource Center mailing list. At 12:49, Stephanie Schrift sent it to me.

Some members of the campus community, including Erin Rome, were furious that the letter got circulated at all. It was like giving Neenef a microphone and loudspeaker to broadcast his craziness far and wide. With his grandiose claim to "the whole story" and "the truth behind it all," it somehow gave him the last word. It put the blame on Maggie with appalling directness. It seemed to grant his last wish for the letter "to be read by all who were affected by this in any way." Indeed, a colleague to whom I showed the letter said he hoped I would not collaborate with Neenef by publishing it further.

But Neenef's letter contains precious truth. Not "the truth behind it all," to which he claims to have access, of course, but the truth (or as close as we can come to it) of how he saw his situation and Maggie's role in it, of how disturbed he really was—in fact, the truth of how a predator thinks, in particular about the woman he will kill. That is not just valuable but critical information if we are to understand what happened.

Among other imperatives, Neenef's narrative begs us to revisit entrenched notions of romance that emerged so clearly from his messages to Maggie the previous summer. What transforms his relationship with Maggie from the usual heartless hookup is not his feelings but hers: she says the L-word, the Open Sesame to his heart. Suddenly she moves from one category of female—*yet another one of those girls I'd get with and then leave and not think twice about it*—to another. His initial reaction is blankness, numbness, fear: *I couldn't respond.* At the other end of the eight months, Maggie jumps categories again—*from being the most caring, loving human being, to the most heartless and cruel person imaginable.* Madonna turns into whore. "Angel" becomes "feminist."

Neenef's despair and loneliness saturate his letter. But so do his rigidity, his judgmentalism, his dualistic thinking, his self-pity and self-delusion, and above all his horrifying facility in denying responsibility. *She's had so much control over me that anything she said either built my self-esteem or broke it.* His sense of self is entirely in her hands. This might be the crux of the matter: the man who is obsessed with control paradoxically convinces himself, and attempts to convince everyone else, that the woman he is bent on controlling is responsible for the violence he is about to commit upon her.

Thus he can speak of that violence, obliquely, as inevitable: *This is how it had to end. This is how much hurt she caused me.* "Had to" might mean this outcome was foreordained; more likely it means this end is *required.* It is the only possible end, the only conceivable judgment. Suddenly the abrupt invocation of Family Values at the end of the letter makes sense. It seems at once a reproof to his father (*If one person hurts, the whole family hurts*) and a statement of solidarity with the values and institutions his father represents, including the rigid judgments under which Neenef was raised.

Neenef's is one version of the story we struggled to tell in the fall of 1999. Even though he said we could "interpret it whichever way [we liked]," he clearly assumed that his readers would credit his version. It's worth noting that Navin, in the painful welter of that November, thought that it had "some really important things to say" and that recipients could "learn from it." The naivety of this response can't be held against kids like Navin who were vulnerable, shattered, confused, and utterly unprepared to grapple with such events or to read such a document. But the fact that Neenef's version of the story got any traction at all is the most powerful argument both for dissecting it and for making sure that other versions overpower it. We can, indeed, interpret it whichever way we want.

I have read Neenef's letter many times since the moment it appeared on my computer screen. It took several readings before his final metaphor snagged my attention—the one about the sticks. His sole alternative to the single, brittle stick is more sticks, so that the vulnerable individual is protected by the rigidity of the group. What would it have taken, I wonder, for Neenef to see a third option—the option of the green branch, which bends and proves difficult to break?

December 1999

Dear Alumni, Parents, and Friends of Kalamazoo College,

   Given that I am writing this letter within a few days of the new millennium, a statement about our vision of Kalamazoo College in the next quarter-century seems fitting. So does an observation of the critical role our endowment will play in the realization of our vision. These two subjects will garner the most attention in my letter to you. But before I comment on them, I wish to share a few words regarding the recent losses that our community has endured, including this fall the death of physics professor Benjamin Davies, the murder of sophomore Margaret Wardle, and the suicide of junior Neenef Odah.

   These three losses have been difficult for me. The circumstances of the deaths, the youth of the three individuals and the lost promise of their lives, and the emotional shock from the sudden realization that this idyllic campus is indeed part of what William Blake called the "valley of misery and happiness mixed" have left me greatly saddened. Yet even so, the responses of students, faculty, alumni, and staff to these tragedies have strengthened my conviction that Kalamazoo College is an extraordinary place to learn. While thinking of those responses recently and trying to find the words to describe them, particularly the educational promise implicit in them, I came across the following story.

   Some five years prior to his death, Albert Einstein received a letter from a nineteen-year-old girl grieving over the loss of her younger sister. The young woman wished to know what the famous scientist might say to comfort her. On March 4, 1950, Einstein wrote to this young person:

> A human being is part of the whole, called by us "Universe," a part limited in time and space. He experiences himself, his thoughts and feelings, as something separated from the rest, a kind of optical delusion of his consciousness. This delusion is a kind of prison for us. . . . Our task must be to free ourselves from this prison by widening our circle of compassion. . . . Nobody is capable of achieving this completely, but the striving for such achievement is in itself a part of the liberation and a foundation for inner security.

   A community like Kalamazoo College has distinct characteristics that break down the delusion of separateness and help widen circles of knowledge as well as compassion. These characteristics include a campus size and residential nature that transform a community into a family and a curriculum that combines the traditional classroom with career, study abroad, and individual research experiences. As a result of these characteristics, widening one's circle is so very possible here. Thus what I saw and felt in our several responses not only helped me cope personally with these tragedies but also gave me great hope about the future of the Kalamazoo College way of learning. . . .

Sincerely,
James F. Jones, President

10

ALL SURVIVORS ARE VICTIMS

1

At some point in the months following October, someone in the upper administration remarked, "I think we've lost a year."

"We were kind of like zombies," Kelly Schulte says of the group of women closest to Maggie. "We were expected to go to class, and she was in two of my classes, and it was just like there was a hole. I was supposed to go on, as normal. The college offered all these resources to talk to anyone, but then again you're eighteen; you think you can handle it on your own. We had each other, we had our parents, but . . . it was like the world kept going, but we were stuck in that day."

To a lesser extent, we all were. October 18, 1999, shadowed every succeeding day, and everything we did was somehow projected against its backdrop. The Counseling Center, radically understaffed on a good day, was swamped all year, but many of the people closest to the deaths, like Kelly, failed to seek help. At eighteen you not only think you can handle it, you often don't even have the experience to recognize the signs that there is something to handle. It's said that ours is a culture of victimization and pathologization, especially where kids are concerned, but by and large the ones I teach try to tough things out instead of seeking help. Their dominant ethos—especially the males'—is one of "strength": will, self-reliance, and avoiding adult authority. It's part of the same orientation that prevented Maggie, Neenef, or any of their friends from seeking adult help before October 18.

As the first unreal, stunned days stretched into weeks and months, most Kalamazoo students relied heavily on their peers, a "developmentally appropriate" response, as Pat Ponto's memo told us. Nancy El-Shamaa was one: "I went to talk to Pat a couple times a week. But I think the biggest support, the reason we all made it, was each other. Pat was very helpful . . . but it was the other students' support that really helped." Brooke Nobis had a built-in surrogate family in her little bungalow just off campus. "I just had a rock-solid group of girls I lived with," she says, "and I knew I could just sit on that porch until—sit with them and not even say anything. And that's what I did: I just sat, and they talked to me." Because she appeared on the list of Maggie's friends, someone from the Counseling Center contacted her, but she never returned the call. "I felt really comforted by the girls I was with," she says. Like many who lived through Maggie's murder, her memories become blurred after the week of October 18: "It then just became a really rough year."

The golf team, already close, drew even closer together after Maggie's death. The team included some fairly advanced partiers—with the exception of Sara Church, the well-behaved, serious one, the type who never turns a paper in late. "One night we decided that we were going to have a memorial party for Maggie," Heidi Fahrenbacher remembers. "So we got Popov vodka, and we drank [it] and smoked Marlboro Ultra Lights. Watching Sara try to smoke a cigarette—she was so—I kept having to take her for a walk around the block because she kept saying, 'I think I want to drink more,' and I was like, 'Sara, I think you are going to throw up.'" To raise money for some kind of memorial to Maggie, the team designed and sold arm patches in Kalamazoo's colors, orange and black, reading: "Stop Violence Against Women" across the top and, at the bottom, "Maggie Wardle, 1980–1999." The patches appeared on backpacks and jackets across the campus. I remember noting at the time that the golf team, at least, had decided what to call Maggie's death.

Despite his intimate confrontation with the carnage in his bathroom, Navin Anthony emerged solid, because of friends and also because he compartmentalized easily. "I remember I was able to sleep OK," he says. "I think the mind definitely has a way of saying, 'Put this out of your mind. This part of this incident was quite gruesome or quite traumatizing, but we will just close that off and not think about that too much right now.' I think I found comfort in some of my real close friends, and those were the people I really wanted to be around." He was also sustained by the closeness of the K community, students and staff alike. He says, "I remember sitting down with [associate dean of students] Barb Vogelsang and talking about things, and she said, 'Whatever you need, we'll get it for you.' It was such an open community."

But Navin, like other survivors, also discovered a paradox: that sometimes going through an extreme experience drives people apart instead of drawing them closer. His relationship with his roommate, Brian Newman, "was a little bit tainted. I think we associated each other with everything that happened. And we had our times when we could talk to each other, but there were times when I was like, 'I need to go talk to someone else.' And maybe I pushed him away a little bit, or he pushed me away."

For Kirsten Fritsch, the other DeWaters residents constituted a core group. "My friends were the most important in helping me to process these events," she recalls, "because we were all in it together, literally. That group of people that I was with when the events unfolded all experienced the same thing, and it was an experience that cannot really be shared with anyone who did not live there in the building." The staff at St. Thomas More, where she had gone to cry alone on the eighteenth, also sustained her. But her parents did not: "My parents, although they tried to be helpful, just didn't quite get the magnitude of the event. In the days that followed, I spent a lot of time at home, and it was clear to me that it wasn't quite real to them."

For others, parents were a critical source of security and stability. But those engaged parents constituted another ring of the extended Kalamazoo College community and were experiencing the deaths of Maggie and Neenef for themselves. Navin's father responded with an understated, laconic calm, but his mother couldn't dispel the terror of how close Navin had been to the shootings and how easily Neenef might have killed him, too. Brooke remembers a charged conversation with her parents within days of Maggie's death. Probably like many parents of K students that year, their imaginations were gripped by the intentionality of Neenef's behavior. *We know you and we trust you,* they said, *but we can't know the minds of the people you might be with.* This simple, devastating truth undercut a cherished parental credo: if you've raised your children well, they will make the good choices that will keep them safe. As Barbara Mills had said, there was no safe place. Jimmy Jones's "serene quadrangle"—the one we crossed every day, as well as the one in our minds—had been permanently breached.

2

The traumatized body goes into shock to protect itself against the outrage that has been perpetrated upon it. The traumatized mind often does the same. The difference is that the body knows when to relinquish its numbness; sometimes the mind and spirit do not. Many students, especially the younger half of the campus, the first-years and sophomores, relied on drugs, including alcohol, to keep them numb.

But perhaps the trickiest anodyne for our collective and individual traumas was the "return to normalcy." Some of us welcomed the policy, while others found it obscene. Danny Sledge remembers the quandary of how to make room for grief without allowing students to get "stuck." For Kelly Schulte, the campus's forward momentum was precipitous: "I'm not a psychologist. . . . And I'm sure that it's best for you to return back to normal, but when you're going through it, you need time to grieve. And I think they skipped over the whole grief portion of what happened." For others, the resumption of routine did indeed provide helpful, even soothing structure that kept chaos at bay and got the recovery process moving. As Alan Hill said repeatedly that year, sometimes we have to "perform" normalcy for a while, to "fake it till we make it," as he advised students. But business as usual sometimes became an anesthetic that kept feelings locked down and numbed; it mimicked forward movement while covering a hole that only got deeper. Karyn Boatwright observed that students "either withdrew or became more connected to people, it seemed. . . . I remember mostly that hole that people dug, to feel protected."

Sara Church's survival mechanism was her formidable sense of academic responsibility, which kicked in immediately on Monday, October

18. "I just remember not really comprehending what was going on," she says, "and trying to focus on my classwork, feeling like no matter what happened, I needed to be sure to not fall behind in the class work because that would just make things worse." Later, she and her roommate would marvel at the absurdity, "but it was our coping mechanism for the day." Kirsten Fritsch eloquently captures the way academic work functioned for those trying to live past October 18: "I think that, because the academic expectations at K are so high, losing yourself in work is one of the few viable options for coping with emotional strain on a daily basis. You want to push away the emotions for a few hours? Concentrate on a physics project. More interested in catharsis? Write an English or psychology paper. Want to just run away entirely? Work on your Study Abroad application."

Those academic expectations, after loosening for a couple days or a week, generally tightened right up again. However, for many of us on the faculty, after October 18, all bets were off, and the rules were suspended. We continued to factor the shootings into syllabi, deadlines, and grading in any number of ways, usually tailoring our decisions to the student in question. We improvised. Greg Slough, in chemistry, won lasting esteem and gratitude for enabling students to leave campus early and take the final exam long-distance, arranging for local high school teachers to administer it. Far from being deluged with imploding students, requests for leniency, or manipulations of the system in the name of October 18, I dealt with the opposite: students dedicated to getting work done on time and keeping up with the schedule—too dedicated, in fact, as if staying on track were the only alternative to tumbling into a dreadful void. I found myself prodding whole classes or individual students to take some time, to wander off-course a little for the sake of starting to grapple with the effects of serious trauma.

But some faculty stood by the schedule and the rules as if these structures alone were keeping them upright, which perhaps they were. Heidi Fahrenbacher's mother is still angry about what she saw as a broad institutional failure to cut the kids an academic break, as falling GPAs exerted even greater stress on a student body known for being driven and goal-oriented. Erin Rome, struggling to catch up in a computer science course, kept missing evening Spanish labs. In the tunnel vision of the survivor, she overlooked the step that might have helped: making contact with the prof. After she got a D in Spanish, her mother called the professor, urging her to take Erin's fall experience into account—to no avail.

3

In my hearing no one ever raised the issue of faculty or staff emotional well-being or described what we—not as teachers but as human beings—might experience in the aftermath of October 18. I remember suggesting to someone in the spring that bringing in a massage therapist for a couple hours a week, specifically for faculty and staff, wouldn't have been a bad expenditure of college funds. Karyn Boatwright notes, "I think that even some of the professors continue to dig holes, not talk about it."

Alyce Brady saw no choice but to keep the issue out in the open. She spent the weeks immediately after the eighteenth looking after the computer science brood for whom she sees herself as "den mother." "I had this whole group of students about me," she says, "and I was concerned, trying to reach out to them, almost entirely guys all the time." She consulted with Pat Ponto and Alan Hill regularly about the particular burden these students bore, trying to find a way to mourn Neenef without rationalizing or excusing what he'd done. Alyce agrees that they suffered from a form of guilt by association: *If my friend is a murderer, and I never saw anything wrong with him, what does that make me?* From them she learned that Neenef was not the brooding loner she saw in her classes and her office, or at least not only that, but also a gregarious, popular guy. The extent of what we don't and cannot know about our students gaped before her, as did the terrible questions: *What should I have known? What could I have done?*

In those days faculty and some staff often ate lunch around tables in the Quadstop, the snack bar on the ground floor of the student center. Alyce and her colleague Ray McDowell were regular attendees, along with Alan Hill. "It's possible that I was having free counseling and didn't even know it," she says. "In some ways, we *were* therapy for each other. Alan had known this kid and Ray had known this kid." Together they sifted, again and again, their recollections of Neenef, searching for clues. Alan and Pat repeatedly assured Alyce that there had been nothing to see, even had they been in her chair. A morose, struggling student under parental pressure, certainly; a potential suicide or murderer? Hardly. "They said that as professionals they find themselves feeling that [guilt] too," Alyce recalls, "even though they know it's irrational. And, they kept telling me, not just in this case but in any case: 'No. There isn't something you should've seen that you missed.'"

She and Ray McDowell forged an unusual collegial intimacy that fall. They were teaching sections of the same introductory course: "Really it's so tied together that we're team-teaching it, and Ray and I are doing it together for the first time." Neenef had been in her other class; Eric Page was in Ray's. "At the end of the day, one of us would just sort of wander into the other's office after everyone else had gone." They would compare notes on the students and check up on each other. "It was almost like having two marriages by the end of [the term]."

> Toward the end of December, Ray and I were talking, and I kept asking over and over again, "Do we need to be trained in how to recognize depression?" I mean, no one came out and said [Neenef] was clinically depressed, or whatever, but I just feared always that he had been, and there had been signs, if only I'd known what to look for. And I still wouldn't know. . . . But Ray finally went home—his wife is an MD—and asked her what are the signs of depression? So the next time I bring it up, he said, "Not sleeping at night, not eating," and he's looking at me the whole time, because what have I been eating at lunch? Almost nothing. I had no appetite, and I had been waking up at two in the morning and staying awake till four thirty in the morning. And he said "I'm not sure if any of these describe him, but they describe you."

Among the students Alyce most worried about was someone who had worked on a project with Neenef in her class and grown close to him. She'd left a message for him on the eighteenth and he'd shown up at her office and sat for a couple hours, talking about the friendship. "He worked really hard to live day to day," she says. As Halloween approached, Alyce and her husband decided to take Lauren, their three-year-old daughter, to a kids' event called the "Zoo Boo" at Binder Park Zoo in Battle Creek, half an hour east of Kalamazoo. On the spur of the moment, Alyce called the student. The outing, she explained to him, was "really for a three-year-old."

> "I'm not insinuating that you are three but, you know, if you just want to

get off campus for a day and just go somewhere else, you'd be welcome; we'd be happy to take you to Battle Creek and take you with us to the Zoo Boo." And he said, "Yeah, I think I'd like that." So he went to the Zoo Boo. He didn't follow that up; it wasn't like he frequently came to our house or whatever, but at that one moment, going with a family to the Zoo Boo—anything to get off campus. It was very uncomplicated.

Alyce's description doesn't really capture what happened there. The student got a precious afternoon's return to childhood; he got temporary parents and a little sister. Within that protective family circle, Halloween, in the form of the Zoo Boo, could do its thing, domesticating the horrible and mediating the unknown. At the end of the fall term, Alyce got a note of thanks from his parents.

Alyce had her husband and daughter; she had an empathetic colleague. And she had one more thing: "Marilyn was just a pillar of strength to me. I'd be walking by her and she'd be standing on the steps of Mandelle, and there was always something, like how am I doing." When she talked to Marilyn, everything seemed to get clearer. At some point during the fall, Marilyn contacted Alyce and asked her to send Neenef's advising folder up to her. In this folder would be the information released to an academic advisor when a student matriculated—SAT or ACT scores, address, Advanced Placement credits, high-school counselor recommendations, etc.—plus records kept by the advisor of courses taken, requirements met, and advising meetings. The simple request turned ferociously difficult for Alyce.

I couldn't do it right away. I think I actually looked through it and found the comment from freshman or sophomore year that said, you know, "He seems so passive or non-engaged," but not like "I'm really worried about him," or "He's going to murder his ex-girlfriend." Even just that little, [the fact that] I was worried about him at all: I was wondering "Did I call counseling?" I couldn't remember if I had called counseling.

I couldn't send [the folder] up there. And I couldn't put it back in my drawer. I just kept it on my desk. It was like a zombie or something. It refused to be alive or dead. . . . Ray and I probably talked a number of times when it was there, and I didn't mention it to him, but eventually I told Ray about it and I was able to send it out.

Speaking the name of the potent artifact to another person broke its spell. But before she let it go into campus mail, she photocopied the sheet with her early comment on Neenef, "as if somehow I couldn't let go of the responsibility."

4

Throughout the fall term, Pat Ponto continued to keep the administration apprised of student morale and to look for new ways to help students cope with what had happened. She wrote to a professional listserve, asking other college counselors for advice on commemorating October 18. Joe Abhold, Director of the Counseling Center at the University of Wisconsin–Oshkosh, responded, "I think it is important to remember that all survivors are victims." And some students were truly the walking wounded, slogging their way through post-traumatic stress as if somehow, on their own or with a little help from their friends and maybe a couple of visits to the Counseling Center, they could push their way back to a world they could recognize. On November 10, Pat Ponto gave the President's Advisory Committee a summary report: the center was seeing large numbers of students and frequent "crash-and-burn"—students spiraling downward academically and personally— as the term moved into its final three weeks. Counselors were seeing anxiety disorders, some suicidal ideation, one full-blown panic attack. Emotional cycling up and down was common. Faculty were reporting concerns about students, and the number of violations of the academic honesty policy seemed to be up. Everybody was looking forward to the long December break.

One DeWaters resident who had gone into the bathroom with Navin Anthony that night requested permission to move off-campus—a privilege normally unavailable to first-years and sophomores. Writer in Residence Di Seuss, her advisor and first-year seminar instructor, thought her situation warranted an exception to the rules and supported her request with written testimony. But the rules had their day, and the student's petition was denied. She left school.

Neenef's roommate, Eric Page, was in Karyn Boatwright's General Psychology glass. "Eric was a nice guy," she says, but he communicated best through art and computer science, not words. After October 18, he was "just terrified." "He wrote a little bit about it in Gen Psych, but it was clear he was traumatized. It was clear that he was having flashbacks; he was having dreams." She thinks he may have been seeing someone in the Counseling Center—certainly the staff would have sought him out as one likely to be in trouble. "I believe he was talking to someone but not having a good experience," says Karyn. And so, while she strongly encouraged him to continue getting professional counseling, she did something completely unique in her teaching career: she invited Eric to come in to her office at a regular weekly time. "I said, 'Come in and just talk. . . . Just come in and talk to me about whatever you want to talk about.'" Eschewing the therapist's role of questioning and probing, she simply listened.

During one of his visits, Eric pointed to a notebook he was carrying and said, "Those are Neenef's brains on my book." It was the one Gail Simpson had retrieved for him. Eric thought he had thoroughly cleaned it.

"And I nearly came out of my seat," says Karyn. "I just about threw up."

Eric continued to show up at Karyn's office for the rest of the term. Each week there was a place and a time set aside for him to voice his nightmares and a person willing to hear them.

Jeff Hopcian, who had gone into the bathroom between DeWaters 201 and 203, tried the business-as-usual approach, ignoring evidence of implosion. For a long time he didn't sleep well. "I felt drained," he recalls, "weighed-down. I should have found somebody, a friend, to talk to sooner. I started to fall behind in my classes, missing [choral] rehearsals and failing most of my commitments." One day during a private voice lesson, Jim Turner, K's vocal music director, finally confronted him.

He questioned me, asked whether I thought I was too good to attend rehearsals. He thought I was cavalier, snotty. The truth was I was missing rehearsals because I was overwhelmed. Couldn't sleep. Couldn't focus. Couldn't study. I was way behind in my classwork, on my way to failing. I was premed and my GPA meant more to me than I cared to admit. But falling behind doesn't bode well in the science world. My professors were giving me absolutely no slack. Not that I gave them a proper reason to. I was missing rehearsals to scramble together reports, lab data, and papers [at the] last minute. I was trying not to flunk out. Cavalier? Arrogant?

As if my absence from choir was a personal slight against him! I literally wanted to smack him. Instead I played it cool, as if nothing he said made the slightest difference to me. That made things worse. He pushed harder. When I opened my mouth to respond, I started sobbing. I couldn't stop. I think he was shocked. He asked my accompanist to leave. I told him parts of [what I had seen that night]. I told him I didn't know what to do. I was just trying to pull things together, my life that is, but I felt like I couldn't seem to catch up . . . couldn't seem to get things under control.

After that, I think he contacted somebody in the K-College administration and gave them my name. If not him then surely somebody else. All my professors sent me an e-mail and politely gave me extra time or make-up opportunities. I told Jim I would talk with my old psych professor—an ex-clinician—to whom I felt close. Some school counselors contacted me, along with a few other students who were particularly affected by that night. We all met together and had a group discussion. That was nice, but I didn't really participate. I think what really helped me move on was just giving myself a chance to talk about what happened and then being allowed a chance to get schoolwork back together.

Clearly, the mere act of breaking his silence was a crucial turning point for Jeff. But his friend Jennie Toner describes him as having "a wild look in his eye all the way to graduation."

Nick Duiker made it for two weeks. "I tried to go to class, but I wasn't sleeping." On his birthday, November 6, friends helped him pack up, and he went home, withdrawing for the rest of the term. He got a job, which helped, and like many others, he medicated himself. "I started drinking a lot more," he says. "It was kind of how I dealt with things. More avoidance, and I felt better. I felt better for not having to think about it."

In January, he returned to K. He didn't seek counseling, regarding it as "weak." Because he was repeating courses from the fall, he didn't feel the necessity of going to class regularly, leaving himself with too much down time. "So I started drinking a lot. It was almost all I did, morning, noon, and night. I was so pissed off at everything around me, God—at that moment my grieving process was pure anger. I was mad at the universe, mad at God, mad the world, mad at Neenef, mad at his family, mad at everybody."

One of his housemates, Veronica Minnard, "was my guardian angel at that time." She placed herself between Nick and self-destruction, insisting that he get help. Finally he began regular counseling with Pat Ponto, and the darkness began to lift—at least, he says, he wasn't crying constantly. The hardest part was the thought that Maggie's family might blame him. Virtually all the press coverage of October 18 said that Neenef might have been upset because he had seen Maggie at the Homecoming Dance with "another man." It was probably impossible for Nick not to fall into the survivor's fallacy, a version of *post hoc, ergo propter hoc*: X happened, and then Neenef killed Maggie; therefore, X caused Maggie's death. Nick danced with Maggie, and then Maggie died. In fact, the same cruel logic reappeared when Neenef's actions were explained around the campus.

Nick was incapable of attending Maggie's wake or funeral, but he visited her grave. One day while he was there, Martha Omilian appeared. "I introduced myself, and she gave me a hug and said it wasn't my fault. That day, the world lifted off my shoulders. I almost didn't get better until I saw her. I don't know if it meant anything to her, but that day—it was very brief, but I guess it was my turning point."

Nick's parents urged him to transfer to another school. "I said, 'I can't. I've got to graduate.' My grades weren't the greatest, but I graduated. That's all I cared about."

5

"We felt normal, or we thought we felt normal," says Erin Rome. "We kept doing what we had been doing." But in retrospect the veneer of normalcy that lay over Maggie's cadre of girlfriends is transparent, and Erin admits, "We all handled it really badly." They didn't like the grief therapist the Counseling Center hired and urged them repeatedly to see, though eventually two of them made appointments.

From the moment she knew Maggie was dead, says Kelly Schulte, "and probably through the end of winter quarter, I was on cruise control. Sophomore year was an awful year, all around." They all struggled for focus. Some of them took Incompletes in their courses and finished the work the following term. For a while their intimacy sustained them. Says Nandini Sonnad, "We had each other—there were a lot of us who were going through it at the same time."

The wider campus conversations went on without them. In fact, says

Katherine Chamberlain, "We didn't want it to be a public conversation," feeling that "it was more our issue than anyone's." Their grieving was collective, insular, and absolute, and like many mourners, they saw joy not only as impossible but as banished, prohibited. Kelly says, "I think for probably the first year we didn't think we were licensed to have fun if Maggie wasn't with us. Something so horrible happened, and how could we just go on and have any happiness in our life when this had happened?"

There is some agreement that of Maggie's crew of close women friends, her roommate, J'nai, was the one who went under. Karyn Boatwright believes that J'nai, a psychology major, suffered extended shock for which Karyn uses a metaphor of paralysis:

> J'nai as a student was just haunted. She stopped in her tracks. It took her at least a year and a half to begin fluidly moving again, to begin feeling any sense of normalcy. I honestly don't believe that she ever recovered. I mean, I believe that she is fine now, but I believe that she socially withdrew. I think she started drinking more; I think she developed less meaningful friends—that's just my observation. I watched her in class—I had her in a few classes, and she didn't seem to try to recreate those deep, meaningful relationships she had early on. She was shy, somewhat diffident to begin with, but [Maggie's murder] seemed to put her into a hole that she didn't seem to want to come out of.
>
> She eventually moved out of the room that she lived in. I don't know if she moved out by herself or if she moved with someone else, but that room became a place to avoid. She wasn't phobic about it, but it certainly wasn't a comfortable place for her. . . . I was a little bit disappointed in terms of the response [of the college] because they needed to be right there with her to help her adjust to the surroundings, to help her find her place. But from what I can recall, they weren't great about getting her a nice safe spot. It seemed she didn't have a good living situation after that.

Like so many others, J'nai pressed on with business as usual. But when she approached her senior year and the looming hurdle of the legendary Senior Individualized Project, she went to Karyn and made a remarkably wise, clear request. "She said, 'Karyn, I don't care what I work on [for] my SIP, I just want to go to a beach in California.' I knew that she just needed to [lie] on a beach; . . . she just needed to rest; she just needed to think." Karyn contacted a colleague at the University of California Santa Barbara with available space on her research team. So J'nai went to California, "worked at a coffee shop, and stayed on the beach for most of the summer. And after graduation, she went to the beach for a [another] year, in Mexico."

The one who didn't tough it out was Leza Frederickson. "Honestly, I didn't cope very well at all," she says. "I couldn't even focus on anything. I just had an absolute lack of focus. I couldn't do what I needed to do, because I was just stuck in this really dark place. I had never, and I don't think any of [us] had ever, experienced anything like that, and we all dealt with it in different ways, and unfortunately I just couldn't move on." In April she went home for a visit. Her parents wisely decided to keep her there. "I was not grieving properly; I was not coping well. I was angrier than I'd ever been. I'm not proud of the fact, but I drank a lot, and slept a lot—that was my coping skill. I was using to try to cope. And it was unhealthy, and I was in a bad place." Her parents got her into therapy. "If it wasn't for my parents' recognizing how badly I was doing, I probably wouldn't have [gotten help], because I was really . . . I couldn't see myself. I just wanted to drink and do whatever because that made me feel better. I thought I was OK, but I wasn't OK." Over the summer she began to emerge from that dark place, and she was able to return to K for her junior year.

The rest of Katherine Chamberlain's sophomore year was a "blank." Maggie died, she knew, because of Neenef—but she found herself unable to be angry at Neenef until she could stop fearing him, for he was still with her. She came to believe that violent death ushers in "a period of unrest" for the spirits of the dead. "When this happens, their souls are so jolted they don't know where to go." In her dreams, Neenef came into her room. She would wake terrified, feeling his angry presence. "I just felt like he was *there*."

According to long tradition, spirits sometimes find their way back into the living world through the vitality of nature. At some point in that year, at home in Mount Pleasant, Nandini took a photo of Maggie to a psychic named Joyce. Without any help from Nandini, Joyce proceeded to narrate the story of Maggie's relationship with Neenef, including its end and how Neenef's room was set up. She offered an explanation: Maggie was "a perfect soul and didn't have much to do here" on Earth, so she was taken elsewhere. According to Joyce, Maggie held no animosity for what was done to her. Look for her, Joyce advised, in nature.

Joyce also predicted that Nandini would have some kind of interaction with a brown-uniformed police officer. Nandini dismissed this; Mount Pleasant's cops didn't wear brown. On her way home, an accident on the road ahead stopped traffic for a while. Then a state trooper—wearing his brown uniform—appeared to wave her on.

A little later in the spring, a group of Maggie's friends were together on the campus and spotted a ladybug. Laughing, they reminded each other that this was a favorite species of Maggie the "bug dork." One day soon afterward, ladybugs appeared on Kelly's windowsill, and on Nandini's. Katherine and Kelly would make twice-weekly trips up to the Cooper Cemetery to visit Maggie's grave—and the ladybugs would be there, waiting. "We'd see them all the time," says Katherine, "but especially when we were all together. It was really comforting, like she was *around*. I definitely thought of her as a guardian angel," she says. For the next few years, she would call on Maggie's "wise soul" to be with her.

The others, too, were solaced by a sense of Maggie's persistence in their lives. Erin formed an important new bond with Emily Ford, who had just transferred to K in the fall. "We used to joke that Emily was like my guardian angel, that Maggie had something to do with it." Kelly says that the recovery process was like childbirth, involving some level of forgetting, of releasing excruciating details. The visits to Maggie's grave helped. "I used to bring her flowers and talk to her and write entries into the book that was there, and see what other people had written about her, and for me, that was healing."

6

Heidi Fahrenbacher quickly moved through the numbness and confusion engulfing her friends. As she remembers it, she was in shock for a day. She wept on the quad with her golf teammates. "And then in the days following, I got really angry." Coach Maurer had told the team to try to draw something positive from this disaster. "In [the] light of day," Heidi said in January 2000 at Maggie's memorial service, "there was nothing positive that came from this whole experience. I was filled with deep anger. The kind of anger that makes you want to run and run until your head clears."

She stayed angry for the rest of the year. Winter break was grim for her, with no academic pressure to occupy her mind. Oddly, she doesn't recall being angry at Neenef, though she says she probably was. A portion of her anger turned inward: "I really thought there was something I could've done. I really thought I could've done more. It was like 'She's dead, and it's all my fault.' I really thought that." If she'd told Maggie just a few more times not to have any contact with Neenef at all. If she'd intervened more obnoxiously. If she hadn't gotten so drunk on Saturday night and gotten kicked out of the Homecoming Dance. If she'd taken Maggie to the Zoo that Sunday night, so Maggie couldn't have gone to Neenef's room. If only one domino in the winding train of cause and effect had been removed.

She was angry at the college, too. "I was really mad that they only gave us one day off. I was so mad about that. I remember I was in Billie Fischer's art history class, and I told her, 'We need to talk about this.' She was like, 'OK'—and nobody wanted to say anything." Like many other students, Heidi couldn't find a space or a time for her pain and outrage, and the emphasis on gender violence didn't help her. "They wouldn't let me grieve. They wouldn't let me be sad. Instantly it had to become political. And we had to keep doing our homework. It was like 'Can't we just cry for a couple weeks?'" President Jones, of course, as the human embodiment of The College, focused Heidi's wrath, starting with his noon-hour address on the quad on Monday, October 18: "He said, 'They died.' And they didn't 'die'! I remember him saying that, and that pissed me off." She and a housemate made an appointment with Jimmy, at which Heidi enumerated the college's mistakes, and afterward she felt somewhat better.

Adding to the stress were the memorials for Maggie that seemed always to pull Heidi into a public leadership role she would rather have avoided. She designed the golf team's arm patches. She spoke at Maggie's funeral and at the college memorial service on January 24. "I had to be this spokesperson that I never wanted to be," she says. "I hate it. I hate talking in front of people."

Flailing around to find some response adequate to the enormity of Maggie's murder, Heidi found herself thrust into the center of activity, when inwardly her rage left her feeling alone. Unlike a great many of her peers, Heidi, in her rage, had the self-awareness to know she was in trouble. "I was so angry. I told my mom, 'I think I should go see a psychologist. If I don't I'll just be dealing with this years from now, and I would rather just get it over with.'" When she told her therapist how angry she was at Jimmy Jones for allowing the college to return to business as usual, he asked, 'Well, what would you have done?'" Eight years down the road, Heidi is more forgiving. "I was nineteen. I thought I knew everything, but looking back and as I got older, I was like, 'What *do* you do?'"

As the fall sank toward December, it began to seem to Heidi like her career at K was spiraling downward. Her grades plummeted, including her grade in German, which jeopardized Study Abroad. After weeks had passed and she assumed her expulsion from the Homecoming Dance would be overlooked, she was called on the carpet and told she would be on social probation. As this interview was coming to its close, Heidi says, she was finally asked how she was doing emotionally. She was OK, she said, and then she blurted out that she'd found out something about the police report that had disturbed her: Her sister had a friend who was responsible for typing the reports, and she'd let slip that when the police found the bodies, Maggie's legs were crossed at the ankle. In all probability, Maggie had fallen on her way to the bathroom door, one foot ahead of the other, and the back foot had fallen over the front. But in that environment of rumor and anxiety, some people made the assumption that Neenef had crossed Maggie's legs for some obscure symbolic reason.

"I opened my big mouth, and a red flag goes up, so they call the cops," Heidi remembers. Within twenty-four hours the police contacted her, wanting to know who had breached the confidentiality of the Department of Public Safety. Heidi stonewalled. "'I'm not telling you a thing. Uh-uh. I'm not getting anyone fired from their job.' But they wouldn't leave me alone." She finally told her father, who called a lawyer, who apparently called the college and then, getting no satisfaction, contacted the police and got them off Heidi's back.

As this crisis was developing, a problem with her scholarship was discovered. Her relationship with the college now complicated and almost entirely adversarial, she decided to transfer.

Then, in early December, something shifted. She captured it in a letter to President Jones—as angry, heartbroken, and somewhat inchoate as she herself was at the time. It started with a paragraph reminding him of the police harassment and the revocation of her scholarship. That she assumes—correctly—his awareness of both developments says something about the world of a small campus.

> As I drove home [to Plainwell] alone I thought about my decision and came to the conclusion that transferring might not be in my best interest. Sometimes one is required to fight the battles that need to be fought. So I ask you, Dr. Jones, do you sit and wonder especially at night if a murder like this could happen again on campus? I do. I do not feel safe walking alone at night. Not just on campus but everywhere. How many other students feel this way? How many students now wonder if their room-mate has a gun and is hiding it? How many students are afraid to start new relationships for fear of what will happen if things do not work out? I know that I am not alone. I know that you know this also.
>
> I propose a solution: Prevention. We as a community need to address the issue. We need to have seminars and workshops on anger manage-ment, gun control, violence, depression, self-esteem, and recognizing warning signs of unhealthy relationships. One panel is not sufficient. . . .
>
> Dr. Jones before we are academia we are first of all human beings. I understand that there is a concern among some faculty members that they feel that they are [not] adequately equipped to deal with Maggie's murder. I do not care if you do not have a degree in psychology or if a majority of the staff do not. We all have emotions and ears to listen, for no man is an island.
>
> I strongly believe that together administration, faculty, and students can use this incident to promote the healing process and to prevent this tragedy from reoccurring. If we reach only 1,300 students that is a start-ing point. Dr. Jones I am choosing to stay at Kalamazoo College because I do not quit; I fight for what I believe, and I also know that doing the right thing is also not always the easiest thing to do.

In his response, Jimmy wrote:

> It is perhaps not coincidence that I should receive your letter on the very afternoon that I was contemplating how best to get at the societal patho-gen of violence against women and be of some help not only to the com-

munity at large but also to those of you who are young women here. I constantly think about how I feel as the parent of a daughter three years older than you. I want you to know that I have no intention of doing nothing about the entire matter of violence and women. We are pondering a myriad of possibilities.

He says he is glad Heidi has decided not to transfer because the campus would have missed her smile—a comment that probably annoyed her even further.

That year, Heidi worked at the Lake Doster Store down the road from her home in Plainwell. On Fridays when she left work, she headed for the cemetery in Cooper. She would sit by Maggie's grave and talk or cry or just be silent. In the early winter, she was notified that she was going to Germany after all. Two years later, when she walked across the platform to get her diploma, Jimmy Jones shook her hand and embraced her. Heidi thought, "I don't wanna hug you. I'm still angry."

7

On January 21, 2000, Chimere McCrae, a first-year student at Montclair State University in New Jersey, was shot to death by her boyfriend, Price Hollace. He claimed the shooting was "accidental," but Chimere's family told police there had been tension in the relationship over the time she spent with her friends.

Just over two weeks later, on February 5, Thomas Nelford, a Columbia University dropout, came to the dorm room of his girlfriend, sophomore Kathleen Roskot, slit her throat, departed, and threw himself under a subway train.

Two days later, at Westchester Community College in New York, Joy Thomas was shot in the head by Olonzo Davis, against whom she had requested a personal protection order. Davis immediately killed himself. Thomas was critically wounded but lived.

8

The young women at the Women's Resource Center had a long year, doing unprecedented outreach, programming, and peer counseling, and keeping what was also their residence open to drop ins at all hours.

They had taken serious flak for commemorating Maggie and not Nee-nef, and their living room became a kind of haven even for people who wouldn't ordinarily have affiliated with the group, including Maggie's close friends. "I think they came in because it was the only place for them," says Stephanie Schrift. She remembers J'nai Leafers sitting among them, weeping. "And I don't think she necessarily wanted to be there; it was the only place she *could* be."

For the Omilians, the center became an important doorway to the campus, where they could be as close to Maggie as they could get, among young people who knew her and who were, in some way, like her. In a paper for a class of mine later that year, Erin Rome wrote, "One thing that did really help me to get through that terrible time . . . was the WRC. I thought [they] did an unbelievable job of trying to help people deal with what had happened, while doing [their] best to prevent it from happening again." She cited the October 27 symposium, the vigils, and the several times the WRC opened its doors to allow Maggie's family a place to come together with her friends, helping to create a bond that proved extremely strong and sustaining. For Erin, these rituals inter-rupted the struggle to carry on, clearing the way for the demands of grief.

> It was great to have an organized time and place to sit and talk. If it hadn't been for those times, I don't think my friends and I would have felt as comfortable calling Maggie's parents and going over to their house to talk. Every time I ran into a member of [the WRC], whether I knew them or not, they all seemed to know me. They continually asked me how I was doing, and encouraged me to come over and talk anytime, and to ask them for anything me or my friends might need. I have not forgotten that, and appreciated it way more than I could have vocalized at the time.

But the WRC women were operating in the face of fairly regular criticism from other quarters. Erin wrote:

> I read many of the letters written in the *Index* about the WRC, and heard many of the complaints. They upset me greatly, and at first I was furious that this organization that had done so much for my friends, Maggie's family, and our campus was being so terribly criticized. I finally came to a conclusion though, and that was the fact that this situation scared people.

It was a lot easier for them to think of this as an isolated incident than to admit it was part of a much larger problem, and something that could happen to their own sisters, or mothers, or cousins.

Sustaining this level of outreach, formal and informal, and doing so under fire took its toll on the group. Organizational work, like academic work, postponed grieving while seeming to substitute for it. As it did with most of the faculty and staff, collective responsibility seemed to trump self-care. "There was never a time for the women of the WRC to grieve," Stephanie says.

> That was something that we didn't realize, as a living-learning housing unit, [that we needed], because we weren't old enough. Our main concern was this huge tragedy, and we have to do something for [Maggie's] family. Essentially, we saw that as one of the main reasons we were there. . . . We had the women's power circles, we had the vigils, we tried to be a part of different events that the school was doing. But no one ever said to us, "Take a step back" or "Take time for [yourselves]" or "What are *you* going through?" I don't think that really happened until I graduated.

That voice should have been mine, and in this respect I failed them as their faculty advisor. I suspect I was too engaged in assisting their projects and not engaged enough in counseling them as young women.

The WRC women played a role that year whose political significance probably escaped them: they were Maggie's family's unofficial liaison with the college, functioning as an important source of information for the Omilians as they pushed to make sure Maggie's death generated institutional change. In return, the Omilians' support gave the organization clout it had never known before and has never known since.

Rick, Martha, and Rick's sister, Susan, were relentless in their concern that the circumstances of Maggie's murder be defined clearly and directly in official college communications. A meeting note recorded by Jim Van Sweden describes how Maggie's family has protested Jimmy's letter to parents of October 26, 1999, in which he outlines the steps taken by the college in the week since the murder-suicide. They are "very upset" that Maggie's death is not referred to as a premeditated murder. Jimmy's December letter to alumni, parents, and friends of the college incurs an even stronger rebuke. In it, Jimmy summarizes the autumn disasters as follows: "the death of physics professor Benjamin Davies, the murder of sophomore Margaret Wardle, and the suicide of junior Neenef Odah." It is as if, in Rick Omilians' words,

they were unrelated, separate issues, deserving the same consideration for the "lost promise of their lives." You made a similar statement on your Web postings during the week following Maggie's death about Neenef's actions against her, himself, our family, and his own family. At the time, both Bob [Wardle] and my sister, Elaine, objected to your wording and its failure to properly address this one incident as a murder-suicide instead of a murder and a suicide which were somehow not related or perhaps due to a lovers' spat. We respectfully request that you not do this again. Martha and I and all our family are fully aware that Neenef had friends and family connections on campus who are also trying to come to terms with what he did and we do have compassion for them. But it is necessary for all of us to call this incident what it was as we struggle to understand what was unleashed in Neenef that caused him to do what he did.

Martha was an especially frequent presence on campus. Danny Sledge recalled sadly, "Her entire body shook, every time I saw her." She and Rick got earfuls about the fear and anxiety across the campus. From the WRC in particular they got a good student perspective of what could be done to enhance women's safety. In November, they donated seven hundred dollars, contributed by family and friends of Maggie, to enhance the WRC budget. The funds, they wrote in their letter to Tom Ponto, were "to promote respect for women on your campus and to educate others in order to prevent violence committed against women in our society."

The pressure was clearly on. Marilyn LaPlante spent most of her year acting as the college's liaison with the family. I remember seeing her standing like a ship's figurehead in her red wool coat at the top of the stairs in the Hicks Center, waiting for their arrival and looking like she was steeling herself for it. Greg Mahler maintains that in the days following Maggie's death, Jimmy Jones made it crystal clear that he did not intend to operate in constant fear of a lawsuit. Other members of the administration weren't so persuaded. One senior official says that it was Susan Omilian who caused the most anxiety: as an academic herself, a researcher and also a lawyer, "Susan knew how to operate within the system." Neither she nor her brother or sister-in-law was about to be placated with words.

Among the "myriad of responses" that Jimmy Jones told Heidi Fahrenbacher he was considering was the Task Force on Violence Against Women that he formed in December, chaired by Marilyn and composed of associate provost Carolyn Newton, dean Danny Sledge, coach Lyn Maurer, two students, and me. Immediately, Rick asked that members of Maggie's family be able to meet with this group in January, when they would be in town for Maggie's official college memorial service on the fourteenth. On January 12 a letter from the president went out to the college community announcing the task force, including its two student members, Katie James and Stephanie Schrift. "The committee will seek in the broadest possible terms ways in which violence against women can be addressed on our campus," the letter read. "I expect the committee to recommend new or revised policies and to develop and encourage educational programs that help us understand, confront, and eliminate the behaviors that shape this particular form of violence."

It felt like a genuine mandate and also a kind of evidence that we had succeeded—faculty, staff, students, Maggie's family—in framing Maggie's death as femicide and bringing the threat of violence against women to the foreground on the campus as a legitimate educational issue. We met through the winter and spring, and on June 8 we sent to the president a report that included a record of our work, a list of resources already in place, a list of actions taken during the past academic year to improve the environment for women, and a long list of recommendations for various areas of the college. (See Appendix C.)

———————

During that grim winter term, David Barclay's twenty-fifth year at the college was celebrated with the usual ritual—a gathering in the Olmsted Room, a citation read by a close colleague, and then a reminiscence from the honoree. The campus atmosphere, Barclay recalls, "was so *heavy*." So in his remarks, he decided to go for humor, regaling the crowd with tales of his lifelong baseball addiction. At one point he glanced at the president. "And Jimmy was just *howling*. One had the sense that Jimmy was seeing this as the first opportunity in weeks to let go a little bit himself."

For the rest of the year, stories of violence against female students came out of the woodwork. One of Maggie's close friends confessed to Heidi Fahrenbacher that her boyfriend hit her. I remember a long, closed-door discussion in my office with a senior whose housemate's boyfriend kicked in the front door of their house to get to her. She was worried that he had a gun. Other women faculty could tell similar stories of advising frightened female students. We spent a lot of time carefully advising them to keep themselves safe and then following up with college authorities.

One story involved students I'll call Meredith and Evan. The "warning signs" handout sharpened the unease Meredith's friends already felt about this relationship. Evan absolutely controlled Meredith's time, they reported. He ridiculed her in public and private. He dictated to her. He steered her away from her friends, whom he badmouthed. He thrived on porn and made her imitate what he saw on the screen. They thought he wasn't hitting her, not yet. The friends were frantic, furious, helpless.

Meredith was a lovely, petite blonde woman. In creative writing classes she wrote adoring bad poetry about Evan, casting him as a hero out of myth. She seemed mired in romance to the point where she could no longer think or speak with any confidence. She writhed guiltily under her friends' opprobrium.

I and two other faculty members caught different parts of this story. All three of us knew Meredith from teaching her in class. Evan was a senior major in my department, enrolled in a senior seminar I was teaching at the time. A smarmy, slick guy who always seemed to me to be hiding something, he had made me uneasy since the first-year seminar three years before during which he had turned in a journal entry so full of anger and contempt that I had made a copy of it, just in case. The three of us decided we were uneasy enough that we should seek Marilyn LaPlante's counsel.

But before we could even make the phone call, Providence handed me a sword: Evan plagiarized a short paper in my seminar, so obviously that I found most of it on the Internet in about five minutes. When confronted, he seemed amazed that I intended to file charges instead of merely failing the paper. He couldn't fathom why it was such a big deal.

The judicial system ground into action, and Evan was found "responsible," the word they use instead of "guilty." But as it happened, there were other plagiarism complaints in his file. This was strike three. Within days, Evan was gone. Meredith stayed and graduated.

The effects of the murder-suicide seeped into many relationships. Kirsten Fritsch, reminiscing about the young man she dated for four years, says, "I can see that Neenef and Maggie's relationship shaped our relationship in very subtle ways. I was staunchly feminist and independent in ways that [my boyfriend] was never really comfortable with." She remembers believing that if they could argue without being actually angry, that would be a sign that they were OK. But she was "terrified of making him angry. . . . Deep inside, I had a fear that he might just snap and hurt me physically. Because I never did believe that Neenef was a hateful or violent person, and he committed the most hateful and violent of acts, so I had a fear that [my boyfriend] might do the same."

He never did, but one night, after the two of them had visited an exhibit of ancient weaponry, he mentioned that he might like to collect antique weapons someday. Kirsten suddenly began to sob. "That was in April of 2000, and the first time that I cried as a result of their deaths. I could only think that if my boyfriend had a weapon, even a rusty antique in a glass case, then that was a weapon that could kill me."

For Brooke Nobis, October 18 opened into a looming question that refused to be answered. She knew Maggie, from Plainwell through Kalamazoo College, first and foremost as one of the "smart ones." It's Maggie's intelligence that she recalls most clearly. If Maggie couldn't keep a deeply disturbed man from killing her, how on earth could any woman know whom to date, to trust, to allow into her life? If Maggie's smarts couldn't protect her, what protection was there for anyone?

She watched her housemates lead sometimes dangerous social lives, going home with strangers, drinking too much, taking the risks that pretty much constitute the norm rather than the exception in college life. That behavior was obviously scary. But what about the man you think you know? The friend, the "adopted brother," the guy you've dated for a while? Brooke notes, "I think that's the thing that probably lingered while I was here as a student, that I never got the answer to—maybe I never sought it out—but that probably troubled me the most: 'How does this happen?'" And if we can't fathom how it could happen, then it might just happen to us, and we'd never see it coming.

We all watched the young and not-so-young men on our campus wrestle with Neenef's ghost. Several of them formed an organization, Men Against Gender Violence. Others protested, in various ways, the "demonizing" of Neenef. Most remained silent. Marigene Arnold says that what scares men in the wake of violence against women is that the idea of the readily identifiable Bad Guy is shattered. It's "the notion that we don't know who it is. That it could be me or that everybody's going to think it's me." It's really the same dilemma that terrifies their women friends, trying to figure out whom to trust. Caitlin Gilmet remembers it well:

> When male friends had broken down themselves and then held our shoulders close to their wool coats while we walked past Maggie's casket, they were our allies in grief and recovery. Several of the young men who grieved with us had harbored crushes on Maggie. They were tall and formal, like my dad, but completely unequipped to deal with their loss. So we all stood there, in our formal clothes, trying to be the bravest, wanting to be there for one another.
>
> And yet what were we to do, when even the good guys could fucking kill you? What were we to do, when we'd cared about both murderer, victim, and—yes—victim? How could we stop this from ever happening again?

Issues of the *Index* from that year offer a compelling reading experience. The early October issues generally have that start-of-the-year hopefulness about them. The fifth-week issue, published October 20, is of course consumed by the murder-suicide, and the careful editorial decisions about how the paper was going to talk about their deaths are transparent. The front-page headline reads, "Grieving Students Pay Tribute to Wardle and Odah," and the article describes them as "the victims of a murder-suicide early Monday morning."

The following week there is a flood of letters attacking the WRC for conducting the vigil for Maggie only, and a letter from a male student defends the organizers and protests the coverage of that event in the preceding issue. But thereafter the murder-suicide vanishes from the pages of the paper unless its specter is raised by some specific development, like the January announcements of the Task Force on Violence Against Women and Maggie's memorial service. While many felt that October was relegated to the past far too quickly, Heather Barnes writes a letter to the editor in January protesting the memorial service as an example of the college's refusal to allow students to put October behind them:

> Why not let things go, and move on? I couldn't understand why some-one would want to reopen old wounds. Wounds that hadn't even had a chance to scab. I thought that the month of break was going to be healing for everyone, give [the] campus a chance to go home[,] take a breath and realize that life must go on. . . . Instead, not even a week into the quarter, one of the worst things to ever happen to Kalamazoo College is thrown in everyone's face yet again.

However, if the compiled issues of the *Index* from that academic year can be read as a single text, the near-silence about October 18 is countered by a powerful alternate narrative. In the absence of direct discussion of the murder-suicide, there is persistent coverage of what looks like an underground gender war. In January, the WRC sponsors a women-only self-defense workshop, scheduled before Maggie's death. They reserve part of the basketball court for the purpose. The "exclu-sion" of men is, of course, controversial, though hardly unheard-of, and many people understand why women might be unwilling to participate otherwise. During the workshop, a group of male athletes and an as-sistant coach show up at the gym for an intramural game for which they have reserved the court. The self-defense workshop is running over. The men hang around the fringes of the court, watching—in a fairly intrusive way. Despite being repeatedly asked, and then told, to get lost, they persist, unimpeded by their coach. The *Index* tracks the story for several weeks as the workshop's organizers file charges of violation of the college's honor code, the men are found "responsible," and the plaintiffs, in a truly impressive move, ask that the defendants not be punished but rather be asked to participate in a discussion with the workshop organizers so that they might understand the implications of male surveillance of women and invasion of women's privacy.

Other skirmishes in the ongoing battle are captured: A candidate for Student Commission is attacked for his sexist campaign posters. During Domestic Assault Awareness Week in April, the Women's Equity Coali-tion conducts a local version of the Clothesline Project, in which a line strung from tree to tree on the quad is hung with T-shirts inscribed with testimony about violence against women. The T-shirts are removed by unknown hands. The letters page regularly prints acerbic general attacks on feminism and defiant responses from WRC or WEC members.

I had remembered it as a hard year, a long year. What I had forgotten was how tense and bitter it was. To read the *Index*, the student version of campus life that year, is to see clearly that the gender anxiety raised by Maggie's murder was sublimated, only to erupt elsewhere. It was, in many ways, the urgent subtext underlying the entire year.

The *Index* headlines also preserve the struggle to name what had happened among us. The attention to the feelings of various student populations tugged against the need for honesty, for clarity. Sometimes the default to euphemism seemed unavoidable. I remember a poster announcing an event sponsored by the Counseling Center at some point that year, responding to what it called "the events of October."

10

After October 18, says Commission president Simone Lutz, "I was done. You couldn't have gotten me out of there faster." Her response was probably shared by most of the senior class. At commencement, virtually all of them, and most of the faculty, wore white carnations in Maggie's memory, and many of us wore the golf team's patches. Most of the juniors had returned from overseas in spring, and their re-entry—always difficult, under the best circumstances—was especially torturous, as the year had already been radically reshaped by an event they had missed. For the sophomores, Study Abroad would become, for better or worse, the great demarcation line. Once they crossed it, the murder-suicide would definitely be "past." For the first-year students, the entire collegiate experience would be stamped indelibly in blood.

———

The women's golf team helped to raise money for a second project: a bench on campus, affixed with a plaque bearing Maggie's name. After some touring of possible sites around campus, in which I participated, it was secured to the side of a gentle slope from the chapel down to the busy sidewalk that carries students up and down the quad, and a dogwood was planted beside it. It was dedicated on June 7, 2000, at the ragged end of that year. The dogwood was still flourishing on that June day. At the dedication, David Barclay spoke of the young woman he had known for a scant four weeks:

> I've been in college teaching for a long time, and I think that any of us who have spent some time in it, especially at a place like this, as a matter of course become talent spotters; indeed, I quickly realized that Maggie had the potential to be one of the very best history students of the decade. Moreover, she was just beginning to become truly aware of how bright she was, and just how important her contribution to all of us could be. So our loss remains terrible indeed—and that loss—a loss for myself, for my field of study, for this college, for all her close friends, for all who knew her, for the future that she was looking forward to so eagerly, and above all for her family—will continue to be with us.

Some of Maggie's circle of friends believe she was the glue that held them together. In any case, not even her spiritual presence could sustain them. As the year went on and they "came down," in Nandini's words, from the initial intensity of her death and their clinging to each other in its aftermath, they went into isolation—falling into those holes Karyn Boatwright described. At the time, says Erin, it didn't seem that the dissolution had anything to do with Maggie's death. "But thinking back now, we're sure that's why." Some 75 percent of parents who lose a child eventually divorce. No one has mustered statistics on friends. They went their separate ways into summer and then overseas.

But when they came back in the spring of 2001—years older, through the workings of the mystical time warp of Study Abroad—the ladybugs were still around. They found each other again, and Maggie.

Gaggles of Kalamazoo students who don't want to spend the summer in their parents' houses stick around, working on campus, many for Paul Manstrom and his Facilities Management, or Fac Man, crew, painting, scraping, hammering, plastering, cleaning, toting, lifting. It's a decent gig if one doesn't mind minimum wage, free housing in the empty (but not air-conditioned) dorms, and cafeteria food once a day. That summer, one of this crew was Caitlin Gilmet, and another was her new boyfriend, Mike Collins. She carries a powerful memory of one summer night in her room in DeWaters.

I'm not sure what really happened, but it reminded me of how intense the feelings were for many of us after [Neenef] died. The sun started to set, but we didn't bother to turn on the light; we were deep in conversation. There was this weird moment when we both stopped talking and looked up, like we'd heard something, and I felt suddenly panicked. Mike said, "He's here," and I nodded. I can't explain it, and I'm not sure I believe it, but it did feel like there was an angry, confused, incredibly sad presence in the room for about ten minutes. Mike seemed to connect to whatever was happening more closely, and said later he felt that Neenef wanted us to say his name, that we and everyone else were cowards for not daring to speak his name. We said his name out loud—I said his full name, Neenef Wilson Paulous Odah—and the spell seemed to break.

11

THE WHY OF EVERYTHING

1

"Odah shot Wardle and then shot himself."

This is the simplest version, the Public Safety Report version. Maybe it's the best version, or at any rate the safest. If only we could live with simplicity.

Simone Lutz says that in retrospect, she took "a very large life lesson" from the events of October 1999: "that some things will just simply never have answers." Yet she keeps wondering: "How can there be no answer to the Why? Maybe some people spend the rest of their lives trying to answer the Why of everything." Digging for the Why, we try to exert power over an event that flattens us, deracinates us, blows us wide open. It's a quest based in the illusion that we have some kind of control over the universe. But just as frequently we refuse that quest, claiming, as Jimmy Jones initially did, that we'll never "make any sense of this endless night." We sometimes want to keep horrific events distanced as mystery or abomination.

If I understand the horror perpetrated by a fellow human being, am I sympathizing with the devil? Will I lose my moral bearings? And must

I acknowledge that I can see myself in his eyes? Could I be the young woman turning to run to the bathroom? Could I be the young man with his finger on the trigger? Trying to answer the Why, we negotiate the fear of our own potential.

Finally, if we resort to mystery to explain our "endless nights," we learn nothing from them and certainly make no headway toward preventing them. We need to understand. We burn to understand. The trouble is that as we seek out a plausible story to explain what happened, we find not one but many. The truth is, indeed, out there—but it lies in the warp and woof of stories woven together.

2

The readiest versions, which proliferated on the Kalamazoo campus: (1) Neenef was a nice guy who suddenly snapped. (2) Neenef was a nice guy driven to the breaking point by (a) losing the woman he loved or (b) being betrayed by the woman he loved.

The first version won't hold. Sudden snapping does not exist in the repertoire of the human organism; there is only what a tree does: bending and bending and bending and cracking and bending farther and then, maybe, when the storm moves in, snapping. One cannot know Neenef's history without seeing him bend and bend in the months and weeks before October 18.

The second version, both variations, was especially popular. One reason might be that it is so available, endorsed by innumerable songs, by folklore and film. The fact that this version puts the blame squarely on the victim remains one of the most intransigent obstacles to women's safety in this world of ours.

Version 2b is particularly volatile. In my research, I sensed anxiety bubbling like lava under the question of Maggie's social and sexual behavior in the fall of 1999. I learned again an old, old lesson: that when women are hurt or killed by present or past intimate partners, their own behavior will somehow be called into question. People who loved Maggie are still clearly afraid that somehow her terrible death will be attributed to her own actions. It is time to ask the question directly: If we imagine, for the sake of argument, that Maggie had been cheating on Neenef—all through their relationship, let's say, for the sake of argument—would that "explain" her death? Legitimate it? Mitigate the responsibility of the person who bought the gun and pulled the trigger? Is it "normal" or "understandable" for a man to kill a woman who has been unfaithful to him? So much of our collective cultural lore says it is. Are we prepared to endorse it? If so, what price are we putting on women's sexual autonomy? And what are we saying about men—that they are all killers waiting for the wrong woman to push them over the edge?

All the evidence indicates that Maggie withdrew herself from the relationship with Neenef and began to see other people. It's what college students do and what they should be doing, in the pursuit of that crucial social education that runs alongside the academic one. They terminate one relationship and launch another, and often the two overlap. That Neenef wrote himself another story—that he and Maggie were just taking a break, that they would reunite in the fall—doesn't implicate Maggie. He didn't kill her, or himself, because of something she had done. Neenef killed two people for reasons having to do with Neenef. This doesn't make him a "monster," though what he did can justly be called monstrous. It does make him a perpetrator, one who, far from being "driven" by Maggie, acted with premeditation and care to arrange her death and his own. It is the trail of the shotgun that allows us to know that.

3

What about the gun story, which came to the fore the very morning after Maggie and Neenef died? For his trip out to On Target, Neenef concocted an ultra-normal American narrative as a disguise, and one peculiar to his present locale: a hunting trip up north. The mask extended even to the weapon itself, in his insistence that it have a camouflage pattern. Camo was in many ways his modus operandi, even the cultural camouflage of his various personae: the normal American kid, the fuggedaboutit gangster, the ninja with lethal hands.

The focus on guns, which so perplexed and annoyed many of us in the week following the shootings, can never be a satisfying answer to the Why, but it is a necessary component. As a report from the Violence Policy Center puts it, "women do not face the greatest threat of murder from knife-wielding strangers intent on rape or robbery, but from someone they know, most often a spouse or intimate acquaintance, who is armed with a gun. For women in America, guns are not used to save lives, but to take them." In 1997, 81.3 percent of women homicide victims were killed by a husband or intimate acquaintance using a gun—more than four times as many as were murdered by male strangers using all weapons combined.

In Michigan, no permit is required to purchase or to carry a "long gun"—a rifle or shotgun—and neither the weapon nor the owner must be registered. Assault weapons fall under this category and are as easy to buy as hunting rifles. The state requires no background check; the National Instant Check System goes into operation only at gun stores that are federally licensed. There is no waiting period for any kind of weapon, though the permit required for a handgun establishes one, de facto. Maggie's family was outraged that the college would not have been notified about a gun purchased with a driver's license with a Kalamazoo College address. But the address was simply a box number in Hicks Center, the student center, not including the name of the college. The clerk could not be expected to recognize it automatically. Would it even be legal for a store to notify a college that one of its students had made a purchase?

Gun-control legislation doesn't generally target shotguns; it usually aims to control assault weapons or handguns, the weapons more often used against other people. If a permit had been required for long guns in Michigan, it's possible that it would have discouraged Neenef's plan—possible, but not certain. He might have proceeded through the process of procuring a license, purchasing the weapon, taking the safety quiz, and getting the permit. In any case, the tighter controls on handguns were surely at least part of what prompted Neenef to decide on a shotgun, a weapon used very rarely in homicides, including femicides. Seventy-five percent of men who kill women with firearms use handguns.

The question of the extreme accessibility of guns in the United States—extreme in the context of other Western industrialized countries—is rarely discussed in terms of how people use guns in this country. If we set hunting apart for a moment, looking only at the use of guns on human targets, the statistics may be surprising: According to the FBI, guns are used most often in suicide (17,566 in 1997), followed by homicide (13,522 in 1997), with unintentional fatal injury far back in third place (981 in 1997). In the distant rear is the number for justifiable homicides by private citizens defending themselves: 193 in 1997. The most lethal gun-wielder in this country, then, is the person bent on suicide.

4

In my interviews with former Kalamazoo College students, many mentioned as flashback points the recent shooting rampages at Virginia Tech and Northern Illinois University. This scenario has been common and dramatic enough to define a new category of violence, the "school shooting," that constitutes another way of telling the story of October 1999. Though the crimes are vastly different in nature, the psychological and emotional link is potent: gunshots on a quiet campus, violence exploding out of nowhere in a community of young learners.

This dissonance, rather than logic, probably explains the number of people, students and parents alike, who were shocked that a gun could be smuggled into DeWaters Hall. In reality, there is nothing magical about the doorway of a dormitory that would stop a package, even a large one or a long one, from being carried inside from a small parking lot at the rear of the building, up a flight of stairs, and into the first room on the left. While many colleges and universities, like K, now have "zero tolerance" weapons policies, it's estimated that 8 percent of college men and 1 percent of women have working firearms on American campuses. No policy in itself is going to eliminate them because nothing short of turning campuses into prisons with forced searches and metal detectors at every door and window will make it more than a minor challenge for a student to get a gun into a building. In some quarters nowadays, there is a movement to repeal university weapons policies so that students may "defend themselves" against campus shooters.

As shocking as explosions of gunfire are on a college campus, they are hardly common. In fact, from 1995 through 2005, only .2 percent of the total homicides in the United States occurred in schools or colleges—225 total, about 23 per year. Nor can they be said to define a unique species of crime. Professor Dewey Cornell of the University of Virginia's Curry School of Education underscores the misapprehension: "Children and youth are safer in school than almost anywhere else, but you hear about 'school violence' rather than 'restaurant violence' or 'mall violence.'" Probably we are more alarmed by shootings in a school setting because these locations are child-centered, populated largely by our children, whom we think of as vulnerable and can't bear to imagine as victims. We invest these locales with an idea of innocence.

If the data call the category into question, the way in which school shootings are defined raises other problems. Media coverage and academic analysis generally fail to pay any attention to one critical variable: gender. With one exception—the shooting of two female students at Louisiana Tech in 2007—the perpetrators of our major shooting incidents at schools have been male. One has to wonder why this signal fact is less significant in defining the events than the physical location of the shootings. As Jackson Katz and Sut Jhally wrote in the *Boston Globe* following the Columbine massacre, "What these school shootings reveal is not a crisis in youth culture but a crisis in masculinity."

In several of the shootings the killer deliberately singled out female victims. The slaughter of fourteen women (and the wounding of nine other women and four men) in Montreal in 1989 is the most stunning example. The shooter, Marc Lepine, not only selected his victims for gender but voiced his motives, calling the women "fucking feminists" and leaving a three-page note that blamed women for his problems, along with a hit list naming fifteen prominent Canadian women. In Jonesboro, Arkansas, in 1998, two young boys killed five people and injured ten at their school—all but one victim female, as the media unaccountably failed to report. Media invisibility also accounts for the possibility that we may need to be reminded that the Amish school shooting in Nickel Mines, Pennsylvania, in 2006 was also a deliberate femicide: the shooter, Charles Carl Roberts IV, a man in extreme psychic distress apparently generated by the death of an infant daughter and his own sexual abuse of two female relatives as a boy, sent the male students out of the school before opening fire on the girls, killing five. Gender played a truly insidious role at Virginia Tech. After Cho Seung-Hui shot his first two victims in a dormitory—a female resident and a male resident assistant—the police interpreted the crime as "domestic violence," meaning they assumed the killer had found his victims and completed his mission. So even though the shooter was still at large, officers made the decision not to alert the entire campus. This decision enabled Cho to return to his own room, reload, and head for the classroom where he killed thirty more people.

Defining these kinds of rampages as school shootings has allowed us to shy away from the fact that where they occur is secondary to who is doing the shooting. If we frame these killings instead as explosions of male violence in venues with relatively vulnerable, substantially female populations, we might be less likely to talk vaguely about youth culture and campus gun policies than about the current crisis in masculinity when seeking solutions. To speak of male violence in schools, we would have to include all the other violence by intimate partners against teenage and college women, the kind that doesn't make the news.

5

According to Department of Justice statistics for 2005, the subgroup of women that experiences the highest rate of nonfatal intimate partner violence is, in fact, women aged 16–24. What this suggests, among other things, is that violence is as much a characteristic of short-term relationships like dating as of long-term relationships like marriage, and that we should look to high schools and college campuses as a likely place for it to occur. 33 percent of teenage girls report being physically abused by a dating partner; 26 percent report repeated verbal abuse. As of 2005, almost one in five teenage girls reports a boyfriend who threatened violence to himself or others when confronted with a possible breakup. At the college level, one 1996 study shows 21 percent of college students of both sexes reporting violence from a current partner, 32 percent from an ex. In a study of young Iowa women reported in 2003, no less than 60 percent reported being involved in an abusive relationship over a six-month period. Finally, one 1998 source indicates that from 39 to 54 percent of dating violence victims remain in the relationship.

Many young women are also stalked. In fact, stalking is a young crime, occurring in inverse proportion to the ages of perpetrator and victim. The act is now classified by the government as a form of violence against women. According to 2009 Bureau of Justice statistics, female victims of stalking outnumber male victims by a rate-per-thousand of 20 to 7.4. Sixty-seven percent of female victims report a male perpetrator, while male victims report male and female perpetrators in roughly equal numbers. It is especially easy to stalk someone on a campus—a contained area where people's daily paths are repeated and known.

And technology has taken campus stalking to a whole new level. National Institute of Justice statistics from 2000 show 13 percent of college women report having been stalked, 42 percent of these by a boyfriend or ex.

It is extremely difficult to replace our cultural assumptions about violence against women. We hear the phrase "domestic violence," and we picture a woman, probably poor, probably not white, probably helpless, deficient in self-esteem, undereducated, married to an uneducated drunk who beats her. Most of us do not imagine a bright, well-educated schoolgirl or college woman. Revising our assumptions about violence against women means feeling uncomfortable, because so many of us have raised our daughters to be self-respecting, assertive, informed, confident young women—like Maggie Wardle. Reality threatens the very notion that we can fight intimate violence by educating our girls right. In her book on college women's sexual mores, Lynn Phillips recounts that "thirty women at a small progressive college reported being pushed, hit, and verbally abused by their boyfriends—yet they still say they are in 'good relationships' and not 'male-dominated.'" To explain the baffling contradiction, I can only return to my own sense of the millennium girls as an admixture of feminist beliefs and what I would call "subfeminist" anxieties about being successfully and continually "mated," an undeniable part of being certified as a successful woman.

Granted, our behavior is driven by many things other than our conscious beliefs, and it may be that this disconnect is simply more pronounced among the young. According to Sally Goldfarb, who researches family law and violence against women at Rutgers School of Law, "College students may be more likely to accept traditional sex roles, in which the man dominates the woman . . . and they tend to go to peers for help, rather than to more informed older people. They are susceptible to peer pressure to stay in a relationship, which they often see as preferable to being alone, and they may be so inexperienced in relationships that they accept a violent one as normal." Also, if the statistics hold, a large portion of young women come to college already having experienced abuse from men and boys they lived with or from boys they dated. Tragically, child abuse schools its victims with devastating effectiveness to become abusers or to keep on being victims. Women usually do the latter.

But Maggie was not one of these. According to popular typology, she was nobody's victim—which did not stop Neenef from victimizing her.

6

One of the reasons that people on the Kalamazoo College campus resisted using the story of violence against women to explain what happened on October 18 is that there was no known history of violence between Neenef and Maggie. In our default narrative of the woman murdered by her boyfriend, the murder comes after months, even years of escalating brutality. But this version of the story, unfortunately, allows all of us—including the women in dangerous relationships—to ignore danger signals in the absence of physical violence.

Christina Nicolaidis and her colleagues studied thirty women who had survived an attempted murder by an intimate partner: one third of the survivors experienced no preceding violence. Prior research cites figures from 20 percent to 30 percent. But the overwhelming majority of Nicolaidis's subjects experienced other forms of controlling behavior: stalking, extreme jealousy, social isolation, economic deprivation, physical limitations, threats. "The intensity of the control varied greatly. For some it resembled romance"—as in the case of a man who continually brought flowers and gifts to his wife at work in what turned out to be a strategy for surveilling her whereabouts and behavior. Fourteen of the thirty women "said they were completely surprised by the attack. As one woman stated, 'I didn't realize what big trouble I was in until I was to the point of where I thought I was going to die.'"

What this research suggests is that these other forms of control are linked to violence itself, not merely symbolically but behaviorally. Our thinking about violence against women has to include these other controlling mechanisms, which do violence in and of themselves, but also can be precursors of physical violence. As Jennifer Tucker and Leslie Wolfe argue, "Verbal harassment and emotional abuse lie at one end of a continuum of violence that ends with brutal physical and sexual violence, even murder." But the abuse doesn't necessarily proceed stage by stage through the spectrum; it can jump from one end to the other very quickly. The intimate connection between controlling behavior and physical violence was corroborated in the monumental 2000 Justice Department study of intimate partner violence: "Women whose partners verbally abused them, were jealous or possessive, or denied

233

them access to family, friends, and family incomes were significantly more likely to report being raped, physically assaulted, and/or stalked by their partners," regardless of race or educational level. "Indeed, *having a verbally abusive partner was the variable most likely to predict that a woman would be [physically] victimized by an intimate partner*" (italics mine). Maggie Wardle qualified on all those measures except the one having to do with income.

Maggie was also stalked by her killer, by telephone and computer. Recent Department of Justice data suggest a "strong relationship between stalking and other forms of violence in intimate relationships." In a 2000 study, Judith McFarlane and her colleagues were more emphatic: "We found a statistically significant association between intimate partner physical assault and stalking for femicide victims as well as attempted femicide victims. Stalking was thus . . . significantly associated with murder and attempted murder." In this study, 49 percent of femicide and attempted femicide victims were stalked but experienced no other form of prior violence, "suggesting how important it is to recognize the serious risk of deadly harm presented by stalking alone." But when Maggie received persistent abusive phone calls from Neenef after their breakup, nobody called it stalking.

The perennial (and pernicious) question of why a woman stays in an abusive relationship has many answers, but this research helps us comprehend why really intelligent women make what seem to be really dangerous choices: they may not understand that their partners' behavior is threatening and can be a precursor to physical violence, including murder. The half of Nicolaidis's subjects who were blindsided by the murder attempt saw their relationships as full of problems, but control and violence were not among them. And one reason women may fail to recognize warning factors may be that they are preoccupied with "helping" men they see as suffering and troubled. Many of the women in Nicolaidis's study were "trying to help him or force him to change, and did not necessarily see themselves as frightened victims." That is, they saw these men as wounded birds.

Maggie Wardle was one of 1,195 women in the United States killed by male partners in 1999. In recent years, intimate partner femicide has represented about one third of all murders of women, and the incidence is higher for younger women: from 1993 to 1999, 45 percent of murdered women aged 20 to 24 were killed by intimates.

"Femicide" is now the standard term in academic studies when we talk about the murder of women. Many Kalamazoo College students wanted to know the purpose of accentuating the gender of the victim in a murder. To score a political point? To exacerbate the gender wars? One forthright explanation of the usefulness of the term femicide comes from Jacquelyn Campbell of Johns Hopkins University, one of the genuine experts on the issue: "If you want to prevent homicides of women, you have to look at the reasons why women are killed, because the reasons are different than the reasons for homicide in general. Using the term femicide really identifies these deaths for what they are." Another comes from Jeremy Travis, director of the National Institute of Justice: "violence against women must be understood as different from other forms of violence—the intimate nature of much of that violence, the setting of acts of violence within a larger context of a relationship characterized by power and control, requires a different law enforcement and criminal justice response." In other words, the term "femicide" is, first and foremost, pragmatic and utilitarian: it frames the deaths of women at the hands of men in a singular way, so that they can be more visible, better understood, more effectively prevented, and more effectively punished.

Ultimately, the word femicide challenges our ingrained assumptions about how safe our culture actually is for women. When the media ignore gender in relation to violent crime, they distort and obfuscate issues rather than clarify and illuminate them. Traditional studies of homicide ignored intimate-partner violence; traditional studies of domestic violence ignored unmarried partners and youth; traditional studies of intimate partner violence, amazingly, often ignored gender. Thus the picture never came into focus.

"Violence against women is predominantly intimate partner violence," concluded the National Institute of Justice in 2000. And within the realm of violence between intimates, there is a sharp gender difference. In general, 70 percent of intimate partner homicides are committed by men against women, 30 percent by women against men. There is also, in general, a difference of motive: "A significant portion of partner homicides by women occur in response to an assault, a history of assault, or threats," whereas "men's motives appear to revolve more around jealousy or imminent or actual termination of the relationship." Whichever way the statistics cut it, the impact on women's lives is extraordinary: Femicide is the leading cause of death for heterosexual women under forty, the second leading cause of death for young women aged 15 to 24, and *the* leading cause of death for young African American women in that age group. The developed country with the highest femicide rate is the United States, where, on average, four women are killed by male partners every day.

Far from exploding out of nowhere, Neenef's murder of Maggie was preceded by just about every warning sign except (insofar as we know) literal physical violence. And it occurred precisely when femicides overwhelmingly occur: just before, during, or immediately after the crisis of separation. The Justice Department's survey of 2000 included interviews with men who had killed their wives, who indicated "that either threats of separation by their partner or actual separation are most often the precipitating events that lead to the murder." In fact, most such murders occur within two months of the separation.

Why do men kill women who want to leave them? Like the other questions arising from Maggie's death, it is a gendered question: women by and large do not kill their male partners who want to leave. Ann Oakley writes that "violence against women is particularly likely to happen when men feel their power is threatened." This is why male unemployment frequently plays a role in stories of domestic violence: Western man's sense of power is deeply rooted in his economic success and ability to provide as chief or sole breadwinner. (The student corollary for this sense of achievement is, of course, grades.) What power is threatened when a woman leaves? The power to control the relationship—and, in fact, to control the woman. Daniel Saunders and Angela Browne report on interviews with men who killed their wives: "Separation or threat of separation was especially threatening, being interpreted by the men to represent 'intolerable desertion, rejection, and abandonment.' In killing their wives, men believed they were responding to an offense against them: the woman leaving"—a succinct summary of the state of mind in which Neenef wrote his final testament.

7

But it wasn't only a femicide. Two people died, as Neenef's friends passionately strove to remind us after his death. Another truth too simple to suffice. "Two people died" is only the husk of a story.

Among partner homicides committed by men, homicide-suicides are not a strange anomaly but rather "comprise a substantial minority of cases," around 30 percent. Only 10 percent of women who kill a male partner then kill themselves. Of murder-suicides as a whole, 94 percent of the perpetrators are male; in the 74 percent of murder-suicides that involve past or present intimate partners, 96 percent of the perpetrators are men. "The pattern of suicide following homicide is specific to men in partner killings," concludes Jacquelyn Campbell.

Why, we might wonder, when both stories begin similarly, does one end with a woman murdered and the other end with a woman murdered and a man dead by suicide? The greatest risk factors for following a femicide with suicide seem to be previous violence, prior suicide threats, and gun access—and the latter is a much bigger risk factor for femicide-suicide than for femicide alone.

The role of suicide threats deserves special attention. According to Alan McEvoy,

> Whenever a person threatens suicide in the context of ending a relationship, the former partner may be at serious risk of being murdered. In talking with scores of adolescents about dating violence, the author frequently asked students whether they knew of a situation in which a person had threatened suicide in order to coerce someone into maintaining a dating relationship. Approximately half of them indicated that they were aware of such a circumstance. When asked if anyone considered such a threat of suicide to be a threat of murder, however, nearly all students failed to make this connection.

It is likely most of them thought of the person threatening suicide as a victim, someone who was suffering, rather than a potential perpetrator.

Myrna Dawson distinguishes between the suicide that occurs as a remorseful afterthought to homicide and the homicide that is as part of an "extended suicide"—a single continuous act, a concerted whole. The former, relatively rare, tends to be perpetrated by older men with strong societal ties; the latter more often involves an intimate partner. In femicide-suicides involving intimate partners, the perpetrator often leaves evidence, such as a note, suggesting that the murder-suicide was a "planned whole"—just as Neenef did, referring repeatedly to what he was about to do in singular terms, as "this." It's conceivable that he bought the shotgun with the intent of killing only himself and altered his plan in response to something that occurred in the intervening days, perhaps even the Homecoming Dance itself. It may also be that he planned the event as a whole from the first. But there is no question that he planned it. Just as suicide is usually a carefully planned event, so is femicide-suicide. In fact, premeditation seems to occur more frequently in the latter than in a simple femicide, making it hard to talk about femicide-suicide as a "crime of passion."

Yet, as Saunders and Browne remind us, "there is a long legal and cultural tradition of viewing men's violence as being in 'the heat of passion' [and] attitudes from the past may linger about violence as being primarily 'out of control' behavior," explained, if not excused, on grounds of intensity of feeling. The desperate man who kills his lover and then himself constitutes one of the perverse narratives of romantic love most deeply embedded in the collective unconscious. Operatic, quintessentially tragic. The German *liebestod*, the love-death, supposedly an ultimate expression of passion, love at its purest. The script doesn't have to be invented; it is already written, stored in the cultural warehouse, readily available. The thick gloss of romance covers its real horror, its genuine sickness, so that it can be inscribed in chalk on a campus sidewalk as a love story: "Neenef and Maggie, together forever."

Media often contribute to the obfuscation surrounding femicide-suicide, either by using patently romantic language (e.g., "Romance Turns to Tragedy") to describe the crime, or by blurring its outlines, as Minna Nikunen explains:

> If the motive is outlined [in the press] it is most often quarrelling; and the reason for the quarrels is not given. A great portion of the headlines say that "a couple was found dead"; the fact that these deaths have initiators does not seem to be important. The couple is conceived of as a collective with common intentions. The moral order of heterosexual relationships is based on the idea of a common will and destiny which often disregards the woman's aspirations.

When the deaths of Maggie and Neenef were repeatedly explained in the media in terms of a "quarrel" that was overheard by other DeWaters residents, Maggie's family protested. Maggie's death was not the result of a quarrel, but of the source of that quarrel: Neenef's refusal to allow her to lead her life independent of him.

To obscure the perpetrator of a murder-suicide, to imply that it is an expression of "passion" or love, becomes another means of involving a murdered woman in responsibility for her own death, as surely as ascribing her death to her breaking off the relationship or her infidelity, supposed or real. Yet even in professional circles, where victim-blaming has become very unfashionable, there is still an entrenched resistance to putting the spotlight on the perpetrator. In a 1993 study, therapists were given written case descriptions replete with warning signs of violence. "Even when told that the case had a lethal outcome," Saunders and Browne report, "only a small percentage [of the therapists] focused on the problems of the perpetrator; many focused primarily on the underlying dynamics of the couples."

What happens when a relationship in which a man commits violence against a woman is analyzed in terms of "couples dynamics"? The therapist (or police or agency official) may be likely to focus on changing the dynamic (with the implicit goal of preserving the relationship) rather than on helping the victim escape danger. And a woman in such a relationship naturally wants to believe she can have some influence over the dynamics of which she is a part, so she focuses on "our problems" instead of on getting out. In other words, the way the problem is framed affects the victim's ability to protect herself. The way the situation is defined affects her ability to change it. She may, in fact, feel "empowered" by seeing her situation as something over which she has control, and that sense of agency may, paradoxically, keep her engaged with the abuser. Yet, as Koziol-McLean puts it, "many of the significant risk factors for femicide-suicide involve characteristics of the abusive partner"—that is, the trouble lies not in what the woman is or is not doing, but in who the man is and what is happening in his head.

8

It is difficult to say that the story of October 18 is in part about ethnicity and culture without seeming to say that Neenef killed because he was Iraqi or Assyrian or "foreign," a ludicrous and pernicious conclusion (but a relatively popular one: numbers of people of all ages explained his actions in terms of "their"—Muslims'? Middle Eastern men's?—beliefs about women). But surely Neenef's cultural displacement was a prime factor in the deadly synergy that exploded on October 18. Where gender was concerned, he described the conflict pretty well to Stephanie Miller during their brief romantic experiment. He saw himself as coming from a culture in which gender roles were different from those in the United States, but he was trying to adjust. The adjustment was undoubtedly impeded by his home environment, dominated as it was by a powerful, strict, demanding father—an overwhelming patriarch, in fact. For boys, regardless of cultural background, becoming a man often means either becoming or overcoming the father; Neenef could do neither. He was almost certainly torn between the image of his father as the model of a man and alternate forms of masculinity that could include his own gentleness, humor, and generosity. In fact, it is these latter qualities that so confounded his friends afterward: he did *not* behave like a traditional man around them.

Neenef found himself on a campus where students with international backgrounds are a small group, and those from Middle Eastern countries a miniscule minority. Peers from many ethnic groups loved him. But, as LaVange Barth explained, few of his white American middle-class friends could really have understood the expectations under which he labored, the pressure of being an immigrant having to prove himself not just to himself, his parents, his extended family, and his Assyrian community, but to America, and on behalf of all of them. Few of his white friends would have carried his sense of collective responsibility (although his African American, Middle Eastern, and Asian or Asian American friends knew it intimately). They wouldn't understand what it meant to know that when students, faculty, and staff alike saw him or heard his name, they would instantly think "Muslim," with all the baggage appertaining to that word in the white American mind. They wouldn't understand that his romantic choices were not entirely his own but were bracketed by his parents' desires and expectations. The late-adolescent anxieties about fitting in, standing out, conforming or rebelling operated on a completely different plane in his case, on a campus where he could legitimately say he fit in beautifully in many ways and also knew without question that he would never really be one of "us."

This is the main component of the isolation I kept seeing as I came to know Neenef through my research: not lack of friends but rather the marginality that persists no matter who loves you, no matter how many organizations you join or how many honorary cousins or sisters stop by your room every day. For Neenef, the marginality—the sense of "otherness"—conflated culture and family, as it usually does for students from non-Western backgrounds. The terrible pressure from home, plus the different sense of family values and obligations, were a constant reminder that he could not really be just another Kalamazoo College student, just another boy who gets girl and loses girl. For him, normal college life had very sharp edges.

9

And this is where the story of suicidal depression takes over. A 2008 mtvU-Associated Press poll discovered that some 9 percent of college students think seriously about suicide each year, and 16 percent know someone who has thought about suicide. The levels of stress and depression on campuses are among the factors that make them potentially lethal places. In fact, in 2005, suicide was the second leading cause of death among college students. If the garden-variety stresses of college are compounded by other factors, a young person can implode.

And it will probably be a young man. Suicide, especially by means of firearms, is a distinctively male form of violence: men commit suicide more than women by a factor greater than 4:1, according to 2006 statistics from the National Institute of Mental Health. In 1999, when Neenef died, the ratio for males and females aged 20 to 24 was 6:1. For the general U.S. population, suicide is the seventh leading cause of death for males, the sixteenth for females, but the third for people aged 15 to 24, as of 2006. While women attempt suicide at greater rates than men, 3:1, men complete the act much more often, in part because they use more lethal means—guns as opposed to pills. Racial differences are pronounced: white men comprise some three fourths of suicide victims and 80 percent of victims who use firearms.

Not surprisingly, the most common cause of suicide, including college suicide, is untreated depression. This elusive, grim, debilitating disorder is now a visible, regular part of campus culture at K; according to Pat Ponto, in the 1990s it usurped romantic troubles as the number-one issue that drew students to our Counseling Center, a story that, I have no doubt, would be reiterated by college counselors nationwide. The striking number of students coming to college on antidepressants or having them prescribed at some point during their college careers indicates a truly alarming development.

Equally troubling are the numbers of young people who do not seek help for depression, whatever story they're telling themselves. The most popular one is that they should be able to take care of their problems on their own, that it's weak to seek help, and that because there are "real reasons" for the way they feel, the problem is external, not internal. This particular narrative corresponds neatly with the notion that being a man requires utter self-reliance. Women report depression much more often than men, but men's resistance to seeking help explains most, if not all, of the disparity. However, in these confusing "post-feminist" days, I am growing accustomed to hearing women students talk in traditionally masculine terms about will power and self-reliance and avoiding "weakness."

It may be counterintuitive to link depression to violence; we often assume the depressed person to be lethargic and introverted, not seething on his way to the gun store. But in fact, depression often indicates lowered levels of the neurotransmitter serotonin in the brain, and normally, serotonin works to suppress aggressive feelings. Depression frequently renders people antisocial, irritable, and quick-tempered. "The psychoanalytic concepts of suicide as aggression turned against the self is well-known and accepted by psychiatric clinicians," write Rosenbaum and Bennett. "However, the possibility that the intense aggression may result in murder-suicide appears not to be so well known."

Depression is the most prevalent psychological disorder among perpetrators of murder-suicide, often coexisting with homicidal fantasies. In intimate partner scenarios, its onset coincides most often with the woman's exit from the relationship. A "trigger" incident—the breakup fight, the woman's declaration that she is seeing someone else, some other charged moment—can generate aggression that shatters the depressive "ceiling" and becomes violent.

In the Smizgirl-Ninjoda correspondence, a clear pattern emerges: Neenef gets angry, whether at Maggie or at himself or at his father; the distinction is often unclear. He flares up at her but then retreats into himself, refusing to communicate, often fixating on the computer screen, the anesthetic of choice for millions of young men. The inchoate, inarticulate anger percolates inside him. He fantasizes about killing romantic rivals, interfering friends, strangers in Chicago alleyways, professors. And Maggie.

10

We know a great deal now about the men who are likely to victimize women. They are often poor communicators; they are incompetent in managing anger; they are very likely to have witnessed or experienced physical abuse in childhood. All three describe Neenef. But as a portrait of the man who commits a femicide-suicide begins to emerge from the last twenty years of research, it tells a distinct story of its own.

A 1997 study of homicide-suicide perpetrators in Chicago found that they often demonstrate "extreme ambivalence" in what is called "attributional style," meaning they can't decide whether to blame others or themselves for their problems. In his exchanges with Maggie and in his suicide note, Neenef veers between blaming others—Maggie, his father, other students—and blaming his "stubborn self." It is easy to see murder-suicide as the enactment of this ambivalence: punishing the Other and then punishing the Self.

A pivotal 1994 study presented a typology of male abusers of intimate partners that distinguished three types. One was the antisocial type, described by Saunders and Browne as "intimate and controlling," though his "'distancing' attachment style may help him to let go of intimate relationships more easily" than other men. So he is not likely to kill a partner who threatens to leave. This category includes the true sociopaths, who are usually suffering prolonged post-traumatic stress from childhood and often abuse drugs and alcohol. A second type includes men whose violence is triggered by external stresses. These are usually inhibited, repressed men who experience a "break" that leads to a violent outburst. And then there is a third type, known in psychological parlance as the "borderline/dysphoric" type. He is likely to have experienced "emotional rejection in childhood and developed an 'anxious' attachment style and the greatest fear of abandonment." This man is less physically violent than others: "While he might be quite psychologically abusive, his physical abuse in the relationship often is not severe." He may have a history of profound losses and physical or sexual abuse; he is given to rage, depression, and suicidal feelings. If the antisocial type responds to a breakup by saying, in effect, "I hate you; get lost," the "borderline/dysphoric" will respond with "I hate you; don't leave me!" He is precisely the guy who is likely to commit a murder-suicide as a simultaneous expression of his rage and a defense against abandonment.

Another version of this personality is what George Palermo identified as the "jealous-paranoid" type of aggressor, which he says comprises 50–75 percent of all perpetrators of murder-suicide. This man is often depressed and has difficulty expressing anger. He also usually has "a history of jealous suspicion, verbal abuse, and sublethal physical violence." Palermo interprets the anxious attachment style of this type as a "pathological attachment toward the mother-partner."

In their overlap, these two portraits bear a striking resemblance to Neenef Odah—who, indeed, might have projected his intense love for his mother onto Maggie, a woman who loved caring for children and could be powerfully maternal in her dealings with others.

The link between these two "types" is what is normally called jealousy. It is the single most important predictor of violence against women. Virtually all reliable sources concur that sexual jealousy is a prominent warning sign of abuse. In a 1990 study of twelve perpetrators of both femicide and murder-suicide, "the presence of morbid jealousy" distinguished all twelve. This is why the moment the woman leaves ushers in the most dangerous period in her relationship with an abuser, and why, having escaped, she is by no means free or safe. This is also part of why many women stay with abusive men: they know that if they leave, the stakes shoot up.

Jealousy plays a leading role in the narratives of romance. It is the uncontrollable passion that sweeps away all constraint to seize its object. And it is commonly regarded as evidence of love. In Daniel Saunders' interviews with high-school and college women about their relationships, fully one third of the women in violent relationships saw their boyfriends' jealousy as a sign of love. But women feel jealousy, too. Why then don't more of them move from jealousy to battery and murder as so many jealous men do? It seems that for certain men, jealousy is less a personal feeling and more a desire for power and control, a byproduct of the social world of male privilege.

"The question of why some men have the need to exert power and control over their intimate partners is rarely, if ever, addressed," according to Rosenbaum and Leisring. "One logical answer is that they need to exert power and control over others because they feel impotent and powerless in their own lives." The point is unarguable, and also extremely pertinent to Neenef, who felt nothing if not powerless, failed, subordinated, blamed, rejected, and inadequate as a student, as a boyfriend, as a "foreigner," as a son—and thus as a man. Men on the margins—by dint of race, class, sexual orientation, ethnicity, physical ability, and any number of other factors—are likely to feel particularly powerless in their private or public lives in comparison to men closer to the center of a society and to its masculine ideal. Clearly, Neenef felt his distance from the ideal very sharply and tried energetically to compensate for it.

In their exploration of femicide, Martin Daly and Margo Wilson replace the term "jealousy" with "sexual proprietariness." The latter, they suggest, "implies a more encompassing mind-set, referring not just to the emotional force of one's own feelings of entitlement but to a more pervasive attitude toward social relations." In other words, social systems historically have dictated that women are, in fact, property: "Anglo-American law is replete with examples of men's proprietary entitlements over the sexuality and reproductive capacity of wives and daughters. Since the time before William the Conqueror there has been a continual elaboration of legal devices enabling men to seek monetary redress for the theft and damage of their women's sexuality and reproductive capacity." The root of most laws against rape, for instance, is the entitlement of men to the sole control of their property—women's bodies. So in many cases male jealousy includes assumptions about their rights where women are concerned.

How do such ideas apply to a young man like Neenef? Is he overwhelmed with unmanageable sexual jealousy because he feels powerless or because he feels entitled? Can he feel both? Can he feel entitled by his sex and his father's example to power over women's social and sexual lives, while also feeling powerless that he can't seem to enact this entitlement or live up to it? Minnesota Multiphasic Personality Inventory (MMPI) profiles of abusive men characterize them as "overly concerned about their masculine image." The men who "identify strongly with the patriarchal narrative of manhood yet feel, or fear, that they do not measure up to that narrative" are likely candidates to commit violence against female partners. This might help explain the extreme cognitive dissonance experienced by Neenef's friends, who wondered how a guy they knew as gentle, sweet, kind, sad, funny—*not* macho at all—could suddenly turn into a savage assailant.

Julia Wood, who has worked with male felons' accounts of intimate partner violence, has lucidly defined

> two contradictory, although not entirely independent, views of manhood that are woven into Western culture and embraced by some individual men. The first narrative holds that men are superior to women, which entitles them to dominate and hurt women and to expect women's deference. The second narrative holds that men should protect and not hurt women. Interestingly, many men in my study expressed allegiance to both codes of manhood, creating a tension that often legitimizes violence in a particular moment, followed by remorse for having harmed the woman.

As Wood notes, the narratives only seem opposed to each other; they actually "share the assumption of male superiority." That assumption, of course, is the root of the problem. These stories of Western masculinity wound themselves around Neenef's neck, as he clearly reveals in his veering from tyrannical appropriation to gentlemanly, chivalrous vows and repeated assertions that he would never hurt Maggie. Neenef's vacillations most likely confounded her as well, since women, too, internalize the stories of what our fathers, brothers, and lovers are supposed to be to us. Until we write and firmly establish a third story of masculinity, we are locked in the jaws of contradiction, in a crisis of masculinity.

11

The problem with the stories that shape our lives is that the really powerful ones are hard to read because they are so deeply inscribed. It is precisely because we take them for granted that they can do their work uninterrupted, teaching us to accept certain patterns as normal, to reject others as deviant. In any culture, the gender narratives are among the most deeply imbedded. They produce the narratives of romance that we hold dear, even as we might laugh at or parody them. Julia Wood writes:

> Western culture's romance narratives are not just the stuff of bodice-ripper novels, heartbreak songs, and fairy tales. They are also stories in

which we place ourselves and our relationships. They offer us characters, plot lines, and ready-made meanings for experiences that otherwise
might be incoherent. . . . Intimate partner violence reflects, embodies,
and reproduces codes of masculinity and femininity and gendered narratives of heterosexual romance that are deeply woven into the fabric of
Western culture.

It's crucial to remember that these narratives come entwined, like
strands of DNA, the feminine curling around the masculine curling
around the feminine, feeding each other. If the narrative of femininity
says that what women do is take care of people, defer to the male voice,
and take primary responsibility for preserving relationships, women
in dangerous relationships, even very smart, very strong women, will
have difficulty naming the trouble they are in and seeking to escape it.
The much-documented relationality of women has a dark underside. A
woman has often learned "to identify the satisfying of others' needs and
complying with others as *a need of her own*" [italics in the original].
Such conditioning amounts to nothing short of a recipe for abuse and
entrapment.

In 1989, the United Nations reported that "based on all of the available research evidence it appears that violence against women in the
home is a universal problem, occurring across all cultures and in all
countries." As U.S. senator, Joseph Biden said that "the single greatest
danger to a woman's health is violence from men." In other words, the
pervasiveness of male violence in women's lives is not exactly a secret or
a crackpot theory propagated by die-hard second-wave feminists. And
yet we have enormous difficulty talking about it, on the Kalamazoo
College campus and in society at large—mostly because of what Ann
Oakley calls "a deep-seated reluctance to admit that 'normal' ideas
about gender and ordinary imbalances of power are both implicated
as causes." We cling to explanations that involve the psychology of
particular individuals or the dynamics of particular couples or the assumed traits of ethnic or religious groups so that we can avoid examining the narratives of gender that have written themselves across our
own lives, our institutions, our communities. To do so would mean
reading the whole story, beginning with toys in the store, harassment
on the street, and porn on the computer, and ending in prostitution, sex
trafficking, and femicide. To do so would also mean to acknowledge

that between any man and woman, whatever their relationship, falls a shadow. "Not all men are abusers," writes Lorraine Radford, "but it is hard for women to know who is and who isn't. It remains that the threat of violence, even when it does not occur, shapes women's behavior." Men's behavior, too, I would add, insofar as it is shaped by the threat of violence within, the threat posed by the legacies of masculinity. Finally, to examine these narratives would be to enable ourselves to rewrite them—not to erase them, for what is written is indelible, but to super-scribe a new story for women and men, one that doesn't end in death.

If we speak of the death of Neenef Odah and the murder of Maggie Wardle as individual tragedies only, we keep those events alien, deviant, far from us. If we look at them in their various contexts, as events in ongoing narratives of culture, family, ethnicity, mental illness, collegiate life, and gender in which we are all included, we have brought them close to us. We have implicated ourselves in the meaning of what happened in DeWaters 201 one October midnight.

We all felt implicated, in the weeks and months that followed. Some more than others, of course; there was guilt enough to go several times around. And there was the single question that hung over the campus and, for me, still hangs there: why was no one worried enough to take action, some action that would have drawn attention to the danger facing both Maggie and Neenef?

That question might have a spectrum of answers. At one end is the vast and terrifying answer: the cosmos and the lives we live in it are only marginally, occasionally, and momentarily under our control, despite our illusions to the contrary; violence and other horrors spring up randomly, without pretense of justice or even of causality, defying our attempts to understand or prevent them. At the other end is the most mundane answer: no one had all the information that I have presented here. It was dispersed across and beyond the campus. Some of it was known only to Maggie and Neenef themselves. Interested parties understood only as the proverbial blind men understood the elephant—partially, in fragments.

Along the spectrum lies another answer, one that has become, for me, a critical variable in any discussion of femicide or general violence against women. It has to do, once again, with narratives—with the stories embedded in our minds about who commits such violence and who suffers it. The cardboard cutout Abuser: physically big, macho, mi-

THE WHY OF EVERYTHING

sogynist, and habitually violent, as well as working-class, non-white, a heavy drinker. (Sleeveless undershirts are colloquially known as "wife-beaters.") No amount of empirical information seems to be able to dislodge him from his comfortable place in the folds of our brains. Neenef, to most people, was none of these things. He was, we know, capable of misogyny, but maybe only slightly more than the average college guy. He was violent, too, but sporadically, and mostly verbally; before October 18 his physical victims, so far as we really know, were wood and glass. His friends mostly remembered him as funny, gentle, especially warm and sympathetic to women. Their howls of protest when he was talked about as an abuser came, I believe, in large part from the dissonance they felt between the imaginary Abuser in their heads and the actual Neenef they knew.

The iconic Abuser has a female counterpart who is less often discussed: the woman who is, in her essence, a Victim, weak mentally and physically, hyperdependent on men, without will of her own—and again probably working-class and non-white. In this story, the woman stays with an abusive or dangerous man, refusing to stand up to him, refusing to leave, refusing even to see the abuse or the danger. In this way, she becomes a collaborator, the victim we love to blame, the one who deserves her fate. Thus it is that the first question asked about a situation in which a woman is abused by an intimate male partner is not *What's wrong with him?* or *How did he get that way?* but *Why did she put up with it?*

This figure of the Victim has played a large role in the struggle of Maggie's friends to comprehend what happened to her. Most of them resisted seeing her death as belonging on the spectrum of violence against women, especially at first. Many, perhaps most, have changed their minds in the interim between then and now. But in their conversations with me, I often noted that an explanation of past feelings suddenly slid into present tense. Nandini Sonnad believed that the talk of "violence against women and all its trappings" cast the woman as Victim, and her Maggie was the opposite: a self-reliant woman, nobody's victim. "Maybe I don't like to think that somebody like Maggie was capable of getting herself into that kind of situation because we thought of her as stronger than that. . . . I don't know if she always did" stand up for herself, says her friend, "but she accomplished it" by leaving Neenef. Nandini still can't bear to see Maggie as one of those women who "put up with it." She prefers to see her death as random, unrelated to her relations with her killer, "as if a stranger on the street had grabbed her and thrown her in a van." Kelly Schulte echoes Nandini's thinking: for her, the most important thing is that although Neenef was able to control Maggie's behavior to an extent, Maggie was not weak. "I just don't want it portrayed that she was a weak person."

This Victim "inaction figure" strikes me as even more dangerous than the Abuser figure in distracting us from seeing what male violence against women is really about. Where did these bright, worldly young women get this notion that a woman beaten or killed by a man is a certain type, one who "gets herself into" abusive situations? Does the answer perhaps lie in the confusion over the hot-button word "victim"? In the decades that have intervened since the time when we could talk about genuine victimization without seeming to imply something about the victim's character, the word has been anathematized. Our popular culture has confused an experience—being victimized by a crime, for instance—with a personality type or character trait: the victim as Victim, as a weak or self-pitying person, done in by her own character flaws. (Nandini believed Maggie couldn't be a victim because she was "stronger than that.") Above all, we want to believe that we can "refuse to be victims" by conducting ourselves in a certain way or by being a certain kind of person. When violence overtakes us, then, we have somehow failed: a recipe for guilt and for the very victim-blaming from which Maggie's friends so passionately wish to protect her.

Without these figures, the story gets much more frightening—if the abuser might be any "type" of man and if the victim might be a strong, smart, self-reliant woman. But this view also opens another way to approach violence against women. Instead of looking for types of people, we must look at behavior, keeping in mind established warning signs, acknowledged patterns that characterize abusive or dangerous relationships. If we had understood how to do these things, how to be on the watch for these recognizable signals, and if enough of us had seen them and been willing to speak up, could we have saved either or both of the two lives lost on October 18? That one nagging *Why*—Why did none of us see catastrophe coming clearly enough to intervene?—is the one that goes to the heart of what a community is and what it might be. It is the one that haunts us all.

CONCLUSION:

HAUNTINGS AND VISITATIONS

1

The college kept DeWaters 201 "offline"—unoccupied during regular academic sessions—until Neenef's class had graduated, but not Maggie's. In the summer of 2000, Dan Poskey went to visit some friends housed in DeWaters while they worked on campus. Suddenly he realized that he was in 201. "No one really discussed it (most of the people in the room hadn't been good friends of Maggie's), but we all knew." He walked toward the bathroom door, "trying to picture what the last few seconds of Maggie's life were like and what her last thoughts were. Then I felt sick and wanted to leave."

In the fall of 2001, which would have been Maggie's senior year, the room was occupied again. That September, the golf team was helping to move the new students into their lodgings. Maggie's teammates Sara Church, Kelly Schulte, and Nisse Olsen were assigned to help in DeWaters. "Unfortunately," Sara recalls, "when I walked past, the door was open, and the new occupants were playing Michael Jackson's 'Smooth Criminal,' and I still can't really enjoy the song anymore."

Some students were aghast that the room was not permanently closed—treated as a damned space, as it were. Others wanted it turned into a women's resource center. The college, of course, needed the space to house students. Today, when I look up at the second-floor corner window, I wonder if the present occupants have any idea. "The murder-suicide" is certainly part of vague campus lore, but the room number has not entered into collective memory.

A few of us continue to gather, on or near October 18, at Maggie's bench under the dogwood. A few Octobers ago, as I was approaching the site, I saw Martha Omilian coming slowly from another direction. I had heard that she developed multiple sclerosis, so I was not surprised to see her walking hesitantly, with a cane. But I was grieved. MS is stress-related; it seemed to me in that moment like the outward manifestation of the toll taken on her by Maggie's death. I approached her and must have asked the appropriate stupid question, "How are you doing?"

"Well," she said, "you know I have MS?" I nodded and mumbled something. She shrugged. "But after you've been through the worst, nothing else much matters."

We walked together up to the bench. After a few words and a little silence as people gathered, Rick Omilian said, "I'm wondering if students hear about Maggie now. Do they know about her? Does some kind of education take place, so that the story gets passed on?"

A silence fell over the group. As seconds passed, it became uncomfortable. Finally Vaughn Maatman spoke, saying something vague about how Maggie's story had become part of the story of the college.

It was all he could say; none of us could call up one consistent educational legacy specific to Maggie's death, or Neenef's. Later I went back to my files from the Task Force that met during the winter and spring of 2000 and found our report to the president. Looking over the second section, "Actions Taken During the 1999–2000 Academic Year," I saw how many were to have been made permanent. Among them was an annual Violence Against Women Awareness Day, which I had hoped would be marked on the anniversary of Maggie's death but which never got traction, probably because no one was assigned responsibility for making it happen. That's the story with most of the recommendations, I suspect: they got lost in time, distance, budget shuffling, and staff turnover. Administrations change; hardly anyone in authority in 1999 is still there. No one has been assigned real responsibility for women's safety, and individuals whose full-time jobs lie elsewhere in the college cannot take it on. A half-time position in women's programming was indeed created in Student Development, thanks to some creative money-moving by Danny Sledge, and was filled successively by two talented, committed young women with very little institutional weight. The position has since vanished.

As for the third section of the report, comprising our recommendations: the Task Force did not continue for three years, never did the recommended assessment, and never proposed continuation or replacement by another advisory body whose primary concern would be women's welfare. One significant improvement is that the policies and procedures around sexual harassment and assault have received an overhaul, but not in response to the murder-suicide. Instead, the change resulted from continuing complaints from women students that filing sexual harassment and assault charges precipitated them into an exhausting, confusing, and sometimes punitive labyrinth. Finally a group of students in one of Karyn Boatwright's classes undertook, as their final "action project," to research such policies on other campuses and to recommend "best practices" to the powers that be at K. They did an exhaustive job, and, lo and behold, officials were designated to follow up with the college's lawyers, and new policies and practices were implemented—in 2007.

Finally, there is no Women's Resource Center on the Kalamazoo College campus today. As a student living-learning unit, it depended upon student interest to keep it going from year to year. For a while there, from the mid-90s through the first few years of the new century, the interest amounted to a kind of passionate moral commitment. And then it waned. If a group of students proposes a "house" organized around so-called "women's issues," and if their proposal is successful, such a resource will exist on campus. But it will not have the stability or the influence of the old WRC.

Violence against women probably appears in the curriculum and in the classroom more often today than in 1999, partly because of a general raised awareness, partly because of greater student willingness to talk about it, partly because of intentional faculty and staff efforts. It's a fairly inescapable topic in women's studies classes. But a women's self-defense course, offered sporadically, never took root in our curriculum. Once in a while a vocal student will raise the question. The usual answer is that finding an instructor proves difficult.

I could go on.

So here is my answer to Rick's question today: Several of us, a rapidly diminishing number, remember October 18 and the days that followed. Others of us have heard the story of how Maggie and Neenef died. Those of us who were around were changed by it in all kinds of ways. But apart from the bench and the dogwood, I don't think the college itself has been changed by those deaths in any substantial way. Institutional memory can be very short.

There is one interesting pedagogical ritual that takes place in memory of Maggie. In Karyn Boatwright's General Psychology class, she sometimes selects a day where she can leave the room during one of the laboratory sessions and arranges in advance a staged fight between a male and a female student in the hallway outside. A real fight: "yelling and throwing chairs and throwing books and screaming," says Karyn. To date, only one student has gone into the hallway to check on what was going on. When the next class period comes, Karyn proceeds as if nothing has happened, but the lecture for the day turns to the psychological research on why people fail to intervene when others are in danger. Karyn presents case studies to the students—for instance, of Kitty Genovese being stabbed while bystanders watched. The students "are just incredulous," she says, and then they move to judgment, voicing righteous indignation. "Then," says Karyn, "I get them."

The psychological research indicates not lack of caring but diffusion of responsibility, she explains; if no one else is taking action, we decide that what's happening must be OK. In other words, our failure to act is not an individual failure of compassion but a communal failure of responsibility.

She tells them the story of October 18, including the fact that numerous DeWaters residents heard screaming and fighting and rationalized it as a normal couple's argument. The students overwhelmingly fail to make the connection to the uproar in the hallway during the preceding class or to suspect Karyn of staging it.

2

For the Omilians, life divides very clearly into Before and After. "After" quickly pulled to a focus on the twin vectors that converged in Maggie's death: endemic violence against women and the proliferation and ready accessibility of guns. They have worked steadily to keep Maggie's story alive on the campus and beyond, and to make her story work for others. In January of 2000, they sent a letter to alumni encouraging financial support for the new projects related to violence against women. In October of 2000, as the first anniversary neared, Rick sent a lengthy editorial to the *Index*. His sister Susan lectures and conducts workshops all over the country. She came to campus on October 16, 2000, for the first of several visits in which she told the story in the context of her knowledge of violence against women—an expertise colored dramatically by Maggie's murder.

Rick and Martha have been significantly involved in local and national movements to bring sanity to the American love affair with guns, including the Million Mom Marches that take place on Mother's Day in the national and state capitals. At their first such march, in Lansing on May 14, 2000, Rick looked back, in that gesture familiar to survivors of the unbearable, to that land of glory, the now-distant Before:

> A year ago on Mother's Day, we celebrated at a dinner with our daughter and son, and Maggie gave her mother a rose bush for the garden. It is planted and now preparing to bloom alongside the other plants that she bought for her mom on Mother's Day over the years. . . .
>
> A year ago, we were watching Maggie finish up her first year at Kalamazoo College, proud of her for making it through her freshman year. She was an excellent student all through her years of school but this was a particularly tough year for her. She loved science and history and had decided to be a lawyer.
>
> A year ago, as we looked out into our backyard, we watched Maggie with her camera, chasing butterflies in order to capture their beauty on film. . . .
>
> A year ago at this time we were impressed with the friends that Maggie had made at college. She was a good friend, with a fine sense of humor and compassion for others.
>
> But last fall in the early morning hours of the eighteenth of October, our beloved 19-year-old Maggie was murdered by her ex-boyfriend on

the Kalamazoo College campus. He sought to control and possess her, using her compassion and feelings for him to keep contact with her even after she had clearly and firmly broken up with him. In hindsight we can see that he hid the problems he had from all of us and had focused all of his anger for his life in her. *And he had access to a gun.*

On October 24 of that year, an editorial by Rick appeared in the local paper, ending with a call: "Remember what happened to two lives, two families, two sets of friends, an entire community because one angry person had a gun."

In 2001, Michigan Lieutenant Governor Dick Posthumous convened a Domestic Violence Homicide Prevention Task Force, which held hearings around the state to gather information for a report and recommendations to the governor. Martha and Rick attended the Kalamazoo hearing, placing a photo of Maggie on the table before the committee and their bank of microphones. The subsequent report resulted in new legislation passed in 2002 that made two dramatic changes. First, police were given the authority to make an arrest without a warrant in assault-and-battery cases and required to do so in domestic violence cases. Second, it redefined "domestic violence" to include dating and former dating relationships. Barbara Mills advised her staff at the YWCA Domestic Assault Program "that the addition of dating relationships to the legal definition of domestic violence in Michigan was due to testimony of Martha and Rick Omilian. . . . Members of the Task Force said that the testimony was so compelling that it was included in the final report and was introduced as part of this legislative package, despite opposition." The Kalamazoo County assistant prosecutor concurred: "The parents of that young lady spoke very openly and very poignantly about how [the definition of] domestic violence should be extended to dating relationships. And Posthumous got the ball rolling."

On June 15, 2001, Rick and Martha met with Jimmy Jones for a private ceremony in which Maggie was granted a posthumous BA, by vote of the faculty. Later in the afternoon, we processed down the quad, all of us wearing white carnations in Maggie's memory, many wearing the golf team's patches. Near the end of the long roll of graduating seniors, her name was read. We'd all been told that a moment of silence would follow. But, true to form, the seniors did what the seniors thought was right, and when the words "Margaret Lynn Wardle" were spoken, they erupted in applause that went steadily on for a long time.

3

Martha Omilian says that for the parent of a lost child, the worst fear is that the child will be forgotten. Telling Maggie's story has helped them survive her death.

For Wilson and Susan Odah, the road has understandably gone in the other direction, into silence. After Neenef's remains were shipped west, they were never heard from again by anyone at the college. After the murder-suicide Rob Wardle attempted to contact Neenef's brother, to no avail. In my own search for Neenef, I contacted his parents directly and then his family's Kalamazoo connections, to no avail. One cousin initially corresponded with me but indicated that she would need to consult with her family before agreeing to be interviewed. I never heard from her again.

I did not pursue the family beyond these initial contacts, and I don't find their silence surprising. If my child died by his own hand after taking the life of someone else's child, I very well might wish not to speak of it beyond my immediate circle, not ever. There is not only terrible grief but soul-destroying shame in such a death. On top of this, add the humiliation of the immigrant who has come to the new country to succeed, to make good, to establish the groundwork on which one's children will thrive.

The culture of the global West, in particular contemporary U.S. culture, values revelation and confession. We tell. We prescribe therapy for grief and trauma because we believe (rightly, in my view) that the way out is to tell the story until you own it and it no longer owns you. We publish memoirs—especially in the past twenty years—in which we reveal our worst nightmares to legions of strangers. Or we go on television to do it. Or both. Our media respect no boundaries of personal space or experience. We import our sexual nightmares and fantasies around the globe through our films. But there are still cultures in the world where telling the truth publicly, airing our secrets, being "uninhibited" is not an inherent good. There are cultures where, for better or worse, what happens in and to the family stays there, and profound personal wounds are addressed in deep privacy.

In fact, I respect silence. In some way it even seems to me a proper response to the enormity of Neenef Odah's final night. As a writer I respect silence the way a musician does, or the way a painter attends to the empty space on his canvas or the sculptor does her work in intense consciousness of the negative space around and in her construction. The less silence my world allows me, the more I crave it, savor it, honor its beauty and profundity.

And yet I chose to tell this story, and to do so I had to enter two families' worst nightmare and switch on the glaring overhead light. I may have been wrong to do it. But ultimately I had to accept that I am a child of the culture of Telling, and I am also a writer who believes that untold stories are more often damaging than not. I believe, with Mark Doty, that "we live the stories we tell; the stories we don't tell live us." And I believe that if this story doesn't live and work its changes, then Maggie's death, and Neenef's, too, is meaningless.

Some of Neenef's friends also claimed their silence when I contacted them. One said the events were still too painful to talk about. Another struggled for a long time and then said that without the Odahs' sanction, she couldn't participate in the project. A third, after an even longer struggle, ultimately couldn't be sure of my intentions. I think all of them feared seeing their friend "demonized" once again. I also suspect that their own confusion and ambivalence, unresolved after nearly a decade, is the source of much of the pain.

Among his friends who agreed to collaborate with me, the one who seemed to have achieved a kind of clarity is Frank Church, now a chef in New York. He has no trouble reconciling the Neenef he loved with the one who murdered Maggie: We all have the potential to get lost, he said, to wander into the dark, to have it get so bad that we "implode." His Neenef was an active, positive part of the campus community who then did a horrendous deed that we all have the potential to do. But for Frank, that deed did not put Neenef beyond the pale of the community. His violence, no less than his humor or his willingness to join in the dance to help out a buddy, made him one of us.

For Nancy El-Shamaa, now a physician in Michigan, that reconciliation of the dark and light in Neenef has been harder. "It really shook me, the whole murder-suicide really shook me, because there was this friend that I cared for so much that had it in him to do this, and over time I realized that if he could, then anyone could. Because he wasn't inherently an evil person. And I still believe that: he took someone else's life, but he was sick, more than anything." Having grown up "surrounded by really stable, loving people," Nancy's faith in human nature was radically undermined by Neenef's action.

> It wasn't just a friend dying and taking an innocent girl with him—which actually for me was harder, the murder more than the suicide; it was just a complete change in how I saw people, how I saw the world. I was *so* trusting. I'm not nearly as much as I used to be. Not that I think everyone's Neenef, not that everyone is going to react like Neenef. But humans are flawed, and really, really damaged. Humans can be very dangerous.

October 18 precipitated Nancy into the chiaroscuro of the world that she would probably have entered anyway in the natural course of development and education, though not so quickly and violently. "I don't believe in good and bad people anymore," she says. Neenef still remains in her heart, unresolved. "He was introverted and he did keep a lot to himself. But when he was with a few close friends, he was just a riot. That's the Neenef I'm trying to hold on to."

Caitlin Gilmet is working in college fundraising now, work that she says has everything to do with October 1999, and the sense of community she felt afterward, essential to her ideal of a liberal arts college. She looks back on October 18 as the watershed moment when innocence gave way to grim experience. Like Nancy, she struggles with memory.

> It's hard to remember him clearly, harder still to separate the friend I had from the person who ended Maggie's life and his own. I hate what he did, and I hate how it changed K and the innocent life we'd had there. I don't mean to defend him, especially not at Maggie's expense. She was so wonderful, and I kept thinking when I went back to K for our reunion that she would have continued to be such a light in the world. But I don't believe he was a monster. He needed help, and he deserved to be loved, and he was also a young person with a life full of hope and potential. I can't distance my friend from his actions, but I wish there was a way to remember him that felt honest and fair.

I still miss him sometimes.

"I still see it in my mind," says Chris Wilson, now a Washington, DC, lawyer. "The images just stick with me." The story needs to get out, he believes, because its implications are so far-reaching. For Chris, who is African American, the heart of the story is cultural conflict. The murder-suicide was, he says, a hard way to learn about the potentially terrible consequences of the friction occurring among "people in small communities . . . coming from different backgrounds." Emotionally it's still intimate for Chris, still close, and the guilty question that lurks in the background of others' reflections moves straight to the foreground in his:

> I'm still upset that there's a chance I could have acted and prevented all this mess. I'm still upset about some people's reactions to Neenef and how they were able to characterize him as this horrible villain, when that's not the person I knew. I'm still upset that he would take those means and not be able to control his emotions. I think I still have all the same emotions about it now that I had back then. And I actually don't dwell on it that much anymore, but there's still this nagging feeling that maybe, maybe, maybe—maybe I could have done something.

Neenef's death left Kirsten Fritsch Paulson with a new attentiveness to her emotional environment. She describes it as a kind of mythic Fall from innocence into consciousness.

> Before their deaths, I can honestly say that I would have never intervened had a friend or acquaintance become seriously depressed or started behaving strangely. Not because I didn't care, but because I wouldn't have noticed. Things like that just weren't on my radar at the time. Now I consciously make myself available when my friends and family are in emotional distress.

In fact, Kirsten was the person who called the police when she thought a friend might hurt himself. "I did face that person's anger for a long time," she says. "But at least he's still around to be angry with me."

I have also been the shoulder cried on when a marriage was ending, the person confided in by a teenage relative who is considering coming out as bisexual, and the person my mom calls when she's having a shitty day. Maybe it's a maturity thing, but I'm glad to be in that role now. Draining as it can sometimes be, I would now rather have emotional distress on my radar and be able to at least listen, if nothing else, than to be blissfully ignorant. Which I was back in October of 1999.

Like Kirsten, Navin Anthony left K with a new attentiveness to suffering, along with the haunting question of what he or others might have failed to notice in Neenef:

> All I can do is hope that if I ever come to a situation where someone needs my help—and I think Neenef did, and maybe I wasn't quite attentive, or maybe I wasn't thinking about things the right way. But I'll think about them and think about how precious life is, and how you need to be able to listen to people and not take them for granted. If I had known how many problems he had, what exactly was going on in his mind. . . . If you ever think that someone needs to talk about things, I think it's important to actually take that time and do it. Don't just take it for granted, what they need to say. Sometimes there's a little more underneath what they're saying. And maybe Neenef wanted to come out and say more, or maybe he was saying more and we didn't listen.

Navin, now practicing medicine in the Detroit area, manages and contains the images in his memory bank through a kind of professional compartmentalization. "There are certain parts of the whole situation that I try to block out, that I don't think of," he says.

> I still have that picture of the bathroom in my head. It's always there. I'm really happy I didn't see what was in the room, first of all. And I guess the doctor in me says, "Wow, that was someone's flesh, that was someone's body parts," and I depersonalize it. I don't know if that's good for me or not. I think, "They're not living anymore."

The fragility of the body, the transience of life—these are also fundamental medical lessons. The gore on the bathroom tile gives way to a positive lesson:

I learned how precious life is. And that's how I treat my patients every day. I see people, and I think, "Someone could put a gun to your head and try to kill you. That's how quickly your life could end." And if you can try to help someone, no matter what they have—diabetes, high blood pressure—if you're able to help them and listen to their story, you can change their life a little bit.

Navin, too, had to learn the lesson about human complexity. Initially, knowing Neenef as "a great guy," he sought an external source for his violence. "Maybe I was trying to defend him more." In the intervening years, the locus of Neenef's violence, in Navin's mind, has moved inward.

Now I wouldn't exactly defend him, I would just say that he definitely was disturbed. There was definitely something in him that motivated him to do this. There's other sides that I didn't quite grasp. You never know the power of what people can do. I'm amazed at all that happened, but at the same time, pure and simple, he killed himself and he killed the girl that he loved. And that's unexplainable to me.

At the core of the story of October 18, for Navin, is that ultimate mystery—the unknowability of others.

The true essence of Neenef was only known by himself. Everything—his troubles, his day-to-day things that made him pissed off or made him happy—he only knew. To think about what he did—the will power and his feeling and his emotion, everything—it was so powerful for him. It was so strong in his head that he and Maggie should be together. It was so powerful, the influence his family had on him, and maybe the love he didn't see from his family or from Maggie. . . . I think about the terrorists that bombed the World Trade Center: their religious beliefs were so deep[ly] embedded . . . that they thought this was the way they could get back at the U.S. . . . When you look at it that way, how do you know what Neenef was thinking?

It's hard for Navin to draw any lasting truth from October of 1999. He considers the possibility that "maybe their lives weren't in vain. Maybe it made us better, the people who were affected by this."

4

Maggie's death focused Stephanie Schrift Fletcher's vision very sharply. She had already chosen a women's studies concentration when she lived in the Resource Center, and she went on to get a master's degree in women's studies in religion. Then she joined AmeriCorps in California, working with high-school peer-counseling groups. This work afforded her the precious opportunity to revisit October 1999. She identified the students' struggles with her own college experience and noted how much death many of them had seen in their lives.

> I remember realizing, "This is a time when I can really go and feel what I felt four years ago." Everything I do with my students is about safety and empowerment and just making sure *they* know who they are and *they* know what they're comfortable with and *they* know their boundaries. Because what I see in high school students right now is that boundaries— *their* boundaries—are not drawn. They don't want to make people feel bad. That's what I hear the most: "I don't want to make so and so upset or angry with me." And so they would rather be tortured themselves . . . than be healthy.

"Every day," she answered when I asked her if Maggie's death continues to affect her life. "Every day."

Brooke Nobis Buys worked for several years in K's Career Development Center and then moved to a local foundation. She married in 2007 and had her first child the next year. The question that haunted her after Maggie's death—"How does this happen?"—got answered during her last year at K. "I fell into a really bad relationship here my senior year, and you know that you're in it, and you know it's not good, and you know it's not healthy, and you know that's not something you would normally place yourself in, and you still keep going through it. And I remember thinking that of Maggie: 'Maggie's smarter than that. How did she get . . . ?'"

For Brooke, a dedicated runner, a strong mind and body are fundamental. Like many young female runners, her conviction that the streets were hers to run on led her to some grim realizations about a woman's place in the world. She talks about a business trip to Minneapolis where she did a lot of walking and encountered debilitating street harassment.

Her own violent reaction startled her: "I want[ed] to beat the shit out of them." Then, realizing how much more trouble that particular response could get her into, she had a glimpse of the limitations on female mobility. She sees a clear connection with Maggie's death. "Somehow it's all in the same circle."

The summer after Maggie died, Sara Church interned at the U.S. District Court. Then she studied abroad in Clermont-Ferrand, France, during her junior year. While she was there she undertook what K terms an Intercultural Research Project by working with SOS Femmes, an organization in the Auvergne region that assists victims of domestic violence. In the course of the internship she listened to phone calls from victims, observed meetings of organization staff with victims, and accompanied one victim to court.

> I heard survivors asking why their loved ones would want to hurt them, and asking what they had done to deserve this abuse, while describing their partners pushing them down stairs while they were pregnant, or partners who controlled their every move, restricting or prohibiting contact with friends and family. Though I could not always understand all that the survivors said, I could hear their scared, frantic, emotional voices, and see the tears running down one woman's face as she asked us why her husband would treat her like an animal and call her *la poubelle*, or trash, every single day.

When Sara got back, she was on fire. She immediately began planning a Senior Individualized Project internship as a victim advocate with FirstStep, a similar organization in the Ann Arbor area. She wrote a superb account of her experience there. In the introduction, she said that "before the morning of October 18, 1999, during my sophomore year, the characteristics and implications of domestic violence did not concern me too much. I had not seriously thought about it." In the conclusion of the report she writes, "My own awareness of violence against women and the accompanying myths and attitudes in our culture in general has also heightened, from Shakespeare's *Othello* to blockbuster movies. The voices of these survivors, along with Maggie's memory, will remain with me, serving as a constant reminder that we, as a society, need to end violence against women." Sara sailed through the University of Michigan Law School and practices in Washington, DC.

Heidi Fahrenbacher, who survived after October 18 like an engine running on anger, finally got to the bottom of it. "I was really mad at myself. I really thought there was something I could've done. I really thought I could've done more. It was like, 'She's dead, and it's all my fault.' I really thought that. I did." Heidi still lives in Plainwell, where she has her own ceramics studio, Bella Joy Pottery. Several years back, she and her mother invited Martha Omilian to join them in a local knitting class, and since then, she and Martha have bonded. "She is like my second mom." They share a certain refreshing bluntness. "I remember when [Martha] said, 'I just don't give a shit anymore.' And I was like, 'Oh, I like you!'"

Today Kelly Schulte works for a Washington, DC, public relations firm. She believes that after the first year full of events, the college "swept [the murder-suicide] under the rug" in the service of public relations. Beneath her satisfaction with her rewarding job she feels another variety of the guilt I heard about so often from survivors, not for what she didn't do in 1999 but for what she is not doing today. "I think about this from time to time," she says. "So this happened, and I was a part of it, and what have I done? And I've done nothing." Kelly begins to weep. "I just feel like I should be an advocate or get involved somehow to prevent this or stop this from happening to other people. I know Susan [Omilian] has done so much work, and she has essentially dedicated her life to this, and I've done nothing, and I feel really guilty about that."

We talk about how sometimes an enormity like Maggie's murder can inform and inspire one's life in other, less direct ways. And in the final moments of our conversation, her memory turns directly to Maggie's continuing presence. "I can so see her smile; I can hear her laughing; I can so hear her voice."

> Today, when I was outside my building, a butterfly just flew by. So I just thought, maybe Maggie knows that I'm talking to you today. When I'm having a good day or a bad day, whatever the situation, if a ladybug flies by me, I just think it's her. She was such a bug dork. I feel like she's around. I feel like she's here. I think, "What would she be doing tonight? Would she be living in DC? Would she be married?" I think what the rest of her life would be like.

Leza Frederickson also relies on the ladybug visitations. "Whenever we thought about her they were there, in swarms—and it was just amaz-ing. Whenever I see a ladybug, I think about Maggie. I'll never be able to think about a ladybug the same way again." She has a butterfly tattoo in memory of Maggie. After that very rough first year, Leza found her way through the dark. "I still think about her a lot, and I can talk about her now. I still get upset when I think about her, but I know it's OK; I can talk about her now." Like most of Maggie's friends, she has turned 180 degrees in regarding Maggie's murder as domestic violence. "I think that's absolutely what it was. I didn't [at the time], but I had never had any experience with that. I don't think I even really knew what it was at the time. But I've read a lot about it and know a lot about it now, and I think that's absolutely 100 percent what it was."

Leza, too, cries in the course of our conversation. In the background as I talk to her are the urgent voices of two small children. "I want them to grow up and be beautiful people just like Maggie was," their mother says. "She was just the most amazing friend. She put her friends before herself. She had a gift."

A post-interview e-mail arrives from Nandini Sonnad, who is living the theatrical life in New York City:

> So I just had to share this with you. . . . I was amazed that I remained so composed during our conversation, but as soon as I hung up the phone I lost it. I was sad and angry and frustrated all over again. I left my apartment a few minutes later and hadn't walked ten yards from my door when something struck me square in the chest—it was a butterfly! I saw another one the next day. And there are never butterflies roaming Manhattan!

Katherine Chamberlain works in Washington, DC, now, like Kelly. She, who was plagued by Neenef's angry spirit, remembers staunchly resisting the efforts of his friends to portray him as another victim. "There's no way I'm going to feel any sympathy for someone like him," she thought. Now, if not sympathy, what she feels is "sadness and pity." She sees him as fundamentally self-absorbed, his murder of Maggie "the quintessential act of absolute self-obsession. He just wasn't able to see anything else." In the intervening years Katherine has come to a clear conclusion about the events of October, one that rejects any whiff of redemption: "This didn't happen for a reason, in my opinion," she says emphatically. "There is no reason she was taken from this earth."

Erin Rome Zabel lives and works in Virginia now. A new mother, she thinks about what Maggie will miss. Voicing a concern common to Maggie's friends, she says, "I feel so cheated for her, that this now defines her life." As the years pass she seems to feel more, instead of less, about Maggie's death. She is perplexed by why she and the rest of the crew didn't connect the dots to get the picture of how dangerous Maggie's relationship with Neenef was; like Leza and others, her view has changed radically.

When she thinks back on the fall of their sophomore year, what she remembers is endless phone conversations and wishes she and Maggie had gotten together more. When they did, Maggie expressed a particular affection. "She'd put her arm through mine, or put her head on my shoulder; she'd tell me loved me all the time."

On Erin's dresser sits a photo of her with Maggie, taken in Erin's room on the day she moved in, in September of 1999. Her mother was taking the photos that day. "We remember taking one of me and Leza," but neither of them remembers taking this picture of Erin and Maggie. "So my mom had this roll of forty pictures or something, and she probably had it developed six months after Maggie died." On the roll there was no picture of Erin with Leza, but the Maggie photo appeared. "It's just the weirdest thing," Erin says. "I always have it with me."

J'nai Leafers Wallace works at a college in west Michigan. Our talk left me with a single sensory image, one of brittleness, as if she had spoken from within a carapace of some kind. While she readily agreed to speak with me and kept contact after our conversation, her answers were short, matter-of-fact, unyielding. In an effort to track her emotional and spiritual road since 1999, I asked what enabled her to graduate, get married, get a good job. "I don't know," she said. "What other option was there?"

My enduring image of Nick Duiker is my first glimpse of him: a big former football player with a sad, kind face, hobbling on crutches. A damaged man. Nick lives with an autoimmune disorder that affects his joints and mobility. After 1999, he jumped the premed track. He got a social work degree and now works with boys at the St. John's Home in Grand Rapids, Michigan, a residential center for troubled kids and adolescents. Founded as a Catholic orphanage over a century ago, St. John's is now a nondenominational nonprofit that happily takes the kids no one can deal with, the ones who are acting out our collective nightmares as a society. The St. John's philosophy, according to their Web site, is unequivocal:

> Our strength lies in a philosophy that has been honed for more than 100 years and through the lives of more than 10,000 boys and girls. We believe that, above all, children and teenagers need to be loved—and you can't just say it, you really have to do it. We believe that behavior—even that of the most troublesome child—is far less important than the child's perception of himself, other people and the world at large. If St. John's changes a youngster's perceptions, he will change his behavior on his own—and forever.

Among other things, this could have been written with Neenef in mind. And it was with Neenef in mind that Nick changed the course of his life.

At the table where we sat, Nick's story of October 18 fell out of him as if it had lain waiting for someone to hear it. Afterward, telling me about his life since K, he said that the work he was doing was quite intentional. As the young man who had clearly spotted Neenef's violent potential where most others missed it, he felt he owed his life to the attempt to rescue boys heading in the same direction. His message to them, as he phrases it, is unambiguous: "It doesn't matter how big or strong you are or what you can do to people. It doesn't matter at all."

The turning of the year is tricky for Nick. He feels the approach of Maggie's August birthday each year, and the early autumn is always hard. Now a devoted stepfather, he got married in October specifically to "make some happiness" in that haunted month.

5

Jimmy Jones assumed the presidency of Trinity College in Hartford, Connecticut in 2004. Provost Greg Mahler became academic vice president at Earlham College in Indiana in 2007. Dean of students Danny Sledge left the college, as did associate dean Vaughn Maatman. Professor Marigene Arnold retired in 2006, after thirty-three years. Pat Ponto and Alan Hill endure in a still radically understaffed Counseling Center, valiantly working against the surging tide of student struggling.

Marilyn LaPlante postponed her retirement for a year in the wake of the murder-suicide. Finally, in 2001, she retired, with big plans to travel with her long-time partner. In 2003 she began to have digestive problems and was diagnosed with cancer. She died early in 2005.

In the early years of the new millennium, a student named Brandon Young took David Barclay's British History course. In an office conversation, Brandon disclosed his struggle with clinical depression. "And all I could think of," says Barclay, "and I don't think I told him this, because with people with depression it probably makes it worse—all I could think of was, 'Well this is British history, and Winston Churchill had the famous "black dog."' And I kept thinking, 'Oh God, if there was just some way we could reach this young man.'" One winter day, after Brandon hadn't been seen by his friends in a while and they couldn't rouse him by pounding on his door, Gail Simpson from Security was called to "key in." She saw his body hanging in the closet and quickly closed the door.

For all of us, the shadow fell again. For Barclay, "all the old thoughts came back, about students," about the terrible fragility beneath their energy and strength and their delusions of indestructibility. Of Maggie's murder, he says,

> It permanently changed me, that's for sure. And again this has to do with the contradictoriness of the human condition, as pompous as this sounds. On the one hand, I feel more distanced from this current crop of students than I have from any previous crop of students, part of it being because of Old Fart status, but part of it having to do with culture shifts. But at the same time I feel closer to them than I've ever felt because—and here I'm going to sound really mawkish—more than ever before, having seen Maggie, having seen Brandon, having seen these others, even when they are bullshitters, they're precious human vessels. . . . It makes what I do, whether as a research scholar or as a classroom teacher, more important; because of that fragility, somebody has to be the bearer of the story. And so my function as a professor, and it became clearer to me than ever before, is to be the bearer of the story. At least one bearer of one story or set of stories. And I think I became more conscious of that after Maggie than ever before.

October 1999 drove Barclay to the foundations of his professional mission, and even further back than that: "In a sense it brings me back to my Baptist roots, of bearing witness. And all of that became clearer to me, I think, after Maggie."

Alyce Brady went on directing the computer science program. When the vagaries of our computerized registration system left us all weeping and babbling incoherently, she served as Acting Registrar and has recently been named to the post for the foreseeable future. For Alyce, the events of October have not leant themselves to clarification as readily as computing systems. She remembers Pat Ponto asking her, in 1999, if she had ever had a student like Neenef. "I responded, 'Yeah, I've had a lot of students like this!' And, you know, do you refer all of them to counseling?"

She told me she'd recently come across her class list from the fall of 1999. There was his name, with a blank where the grade should be. Shortly after this, going through alumni folders, she came across one without a name. Inside were a note from the student she'd taken to Zoo Boo, another from his parents, thanking her for her care of him, and one other item: a photocopy of her advising notes on Neenef Odah.

Her eyes suddenly fill. "And I still can't let go of the feeling that I was responsible, seven years later."

6

For three nights straight I dream of October 1999, but indirectly. On the first night, I dream there is a conspiracy around Maggie's death, secrets and plots, grown men whom I don't know but who are somehow involved, informants trying to clue me in. On the second night, I dream there is a fire in one of the residence halls at K, and we are trying to clear the students out. When I wake, I think immediately, inexplicably, of how "fire" is a noun and also a verb. The third night's dream is the most extensive and lucid. I am driving to various locations in the dark, filling the trunk and backseat of a car with Halloween decorations. I know that this has something to do with Maggie's death. At one stop, her mother is waiting—not Martha Omilian but some dream doppelgänger. She has many items for me, which she helps me load with a sad smile. As I drive off, she is standing in the middle of the road, that smile on her face.

Remaining unconvinced that the story has become "part of the story of the college," I decide to tell it publicly in October of 2006, shortly after I have begun researching it and ten days before the seventh anniversary. My venue is Stetson Chapel, during our weekly Friday common hour. I give the mostly student audience a short version of the story as clearly as I can. In closing I dwell heavily on the question of a community's voice, or lack thereof, and of our collective responsibility to people we suspect are in danger.

Afterward, outside, I spot Kate, a student in my first-year seminar, weeping, being consoled by another woman from the same class. I barge right in and eventually get the gist: In the dorm where Kate is living, a male student is terrorizing several of the women—shoving into rooms, grabbing women's arms, threatening, and otherwise drawing an edge of violence and intimidation. A woman he has just begun dating, says Kate, has bruises on her thigh.

This story has a good ending: I get Kate into the dean of students' office; wheels start to turn; ultimately the male student leaves the college just ahead of expulsion. My point is that one story can release another that lurks in silence. The tale of October 18 was told, and it broke something in Kate open enough so she could tell her story, too, so that her situation could be changed. This truth has a shadow, however: Kate and the women in her dorm were willing to put up with dangerous harassment for a long time. No learned response sent them to any authority figure who might have helped—it took Kate's hearing Maggie's story. For me, the relentless question continues to be, What taught these women to accept such a vicious status quo for any period at all?

Asking other people how they were changed by the events of October 1999, I start to wonder how they changed me. There was a time when, if a student on the verge of disclosure asked me to keep it confidential,

I readily agreed. Now I refuse. If I hear even a whisper about suicide, guns, abuse, or threats, it goes straight to the Counseling Center and the dean of students. Also, I now have a very sharp understanding of the specific dynamics of potentially abusive relationships, so I can talk to students more directly about them. I have a much clearer sense of why violence against women is so hard to combat, now that I have been up against the convoluted resistance to naming it. Finally, I live with a weird sense that horror incubates under the calm surfaces of lovely small campuses. Thankfully, that awareness stays dormant most of the time, but now and again it will wake up and shake me.

———————

Somewhere in the course of excavating the story of October 18, I start to listen with new ears to the music I love, what's now called "classic" rock. I start violently when listening to the Jimi Hendrix cover of the traditional ballad "Hey Joe":

Hey, Joe, where you goin' with that gun in your hand?
Hey, Joe, where you goin' with that gun in your hand?
I'm going down to shoot my old lady,
Caught her messin' round with another man.

Similarly, I am happily immersed in early Beatles when I hear for the first time lines that I've known since I was thirteen:

Well, I'd rather see you dead, little girl,
Than to be with another man;
You'd better keep your head, little girl,
Or I won't know where I am.
You better run for your life if you can, little girl,
Hide your head in the sand, little girl,
Catch you with another man,
That's the end, little girl.

This was our soundtrack—what we danced to, cruised to, got high to, got laid to. How deeply woven into our cultural consciousness this is, I think, this "romantic" plot of the man "driven mad" by jealousy who murders his lover. How deeply was this story imprinted in me? How often does a kid need to hear different versions of a song before that kid has it by heart?

On the night after Halloween I honor the Day of the Dead in the Mexican way. I put a candle in the window, along with bread and fruit, to summon the hungry spirits wandering abroad. Maybe one of them will be Maggie's, I think to myself. And then it occurs to me that spirits don't come by special order. You don't know who you might get. It might be Neenef's tormented spirit that is out there tonight, unresting, looking for shelter, spotting the small light in my window.

Talking to these former students, whether I knew them or not, I find myself becoming protective. Nearing thirty, when they talk about October 1999, they become twenty again, lost in the reverberations of shotgun blasts in a residence hall. For me the aftermath of these conversations is sometimes crippling self-doubt.

There's Jeff Hopcian, who had been waiting for Maggie downstairs in DeWaters Hall, who walked into the bathroom and saw what he saw, who staggered through his life for the next weeks, trying to be OK, trying to get back to normal and pass his classes, until pressure from his choral director cracked the dike. Jeff, whose friend said that after October 18 his eyes had changed. Another friend remembered talking to him at a party later that year and realizing he was "marked." Jeff was somewhat embarrassed by his friends' memories of him. He felt less entitled to his damage than others. *What about her parents, and his?* he asked me. *What is my wound, compared to theirs?*

In a *New Yorker* interview with Sean Penn, I read the following: "Hunting isn't necessary in the world we're living in. A man can go and hunt elk if he wants. But the woman can get to the market sooner than that and bring home the food. So what's left? Violence. That's it. There's no identifiable venue for the system of alpha."

I read the passage again and again, trying to comprehend. In the absence of the hunter role there's nothing left to a man but violence? Really? No other "venue" for this immutable System of Alpha—and neither the will nor the imagination to seek or create another system?

It's everywhere, this masculine dead end. I have known this for thirty years, but now I know it all over again in some other, terrible new way. On *A Prairie Home Companion*, U.S. Poet Laureate Billy Collins is explaining mistakes that writers make. One of them is the sudden, unwarranted switch in the narrator's point of view. He offers an example: "I pointed the gun at her head and pulled the trigger. Suddenly shots rang out." The audience roars.

In an article called "The Music of Prose," fiction writer Richard Goodman is explaining how prose, as well as poetry, has rhythm:

> One of the best ways of looking at the idea of rhythm and music in prose is to write the same thing in three or four different ways. . . . So, for example, let's turn to murder. Here are four ways of telling the reader you shot a woman:
>
> I picked up the gun and shot her.
> I picked up the gun, and I shot her.
> I picked up the gun. I shot her.
> I picked up the gun. Then I shot her.
>
> Each of these sentences provides the reader with all the information about the killing he or she needs. But you can provide the reader with various melodies with each of these choices, and each one is slightly different.

These choices. Each one is slightly different. Not different enough. *You can provide.* Whom do you see when you say, "you"? *Rhythm and music. Various melodies.* Same old song. *All the information he or she needs.* Hey, Joe, what is it in the masculine imagination that, when called upon to improvise a generic plot, so swiftly has a gun pointed at a woman's head?

———————

I find myself carried off by fantasies in which Maggie escapes. Neenef raises the gun, she spins and runs for the bathroom door, yanks it open, tears across the tile floor, bangs into Navin's room, slams the door behind her. She locks it, Navin locks his hall door, calls Security, calls 911. There is one blast from 201, one only. Maggie is terrified, shocky, traumatized, maybe even hurt. But she is alive.

Sometimes these visions are so real that I have to pull myself back to the present and the sickening knowledge that it didn't happen, that she never made it to the bathroom. This story cannot be rewritten. But for a moment, it's like those dreams that seem so real you can't shake them on waking. The imagining feels almost strong enough to reach back through time and snatch her to freedom, to the rest of her life.

December 2006. An e-mail from an old friend at another college. Claire, the younger daughter of our mutual friend, Kate, has been murdered by her ex-boyfriend. He had held her overnight at his apartment; the next day she got away and, with her family's help, made plans to go into hiding. But he followed her, found her, and shot her in a parking lot. Then he shot himself.

I remember the day Claire was born. I remember a tough, spirited, vociferous little girl. On a brilliant white January morning in upstate New York, I sat with Kate and Claire and Kate's older daughter, Moray, and watched Nelson Mandela walk to freedom. I haven't seen Claire since.

I am shaken to my shoes. The world is unbearably frightening. That men and women are living intimately with each other all over the globe seems incredible and dangerous.

Three months later I journey to Virginia with two other friends to be with Kate. When I get home, I feel like I've been in another country, off the edge of the map, the land of unimaginable grief where time cannot pass.

7

On the road to Plainwell, I first pass the cemetery in Cooper and then, having some time to spare, turn around and go back. The first time I came here I had no idea where Maggie was buried, but I found the grave within minutes. It is marked with a rose-colored stone bench. Across the top it bears her name and dates, followed by a verse:

Grieve not nor speak of me with tears
But laugh and talk of me
As though I were beside you.
I loved you so. 'Twas heaven here with you.

When I pull into the driveway of the octagon house, the first thing I notice is the gardens, tall, lush, teeming with color—the kind no yard of mine will ever have—evidence of a genuinely inspired gardener. Inside, a cupola over the living room allows fierce August light to pour into the house. Martha is no longer working at the psychiatric hospital; she is on disability leave. Rick has told me that she has strong days and bad days; today seems like a strong one. Three cats roam the house—Callie, Soot, and Dexter, who is part Manx and has an engaging crook in his tail.

A small side table in the living room is a little shrine: a picture of Maggie surrounded by small stuffed animals, a statue of the Virgin, and other mementos. Martha says she probably shouldn't keep it up, and I wonder, aloud, whyever not.

Martha and Rick have experienced many of what they term Maggie's "interventions" in their lives and especially in Rob's. They live in the confidence that her spirit is present and engaged with them. "I *know* my spirit will be with Maggie's," Martha asserts emphatically, "so I just try to do a good job while I'm here."

She asks me if I would like to see Maggie's bedroom and walks me into it. The shape of the house means that the room is triangular and snug. There are photos everywhere of Maggie and her family and friends. Insects are carefully mounted within framed cases—a spider, a butterfly. Against one wall is a narrow single bed with an appliqué duvet cover; a big pale-pink comforter is folded at its foot. This is where Susan Omilian sleeps when she visits. I touch the comforter briefly.

After Maggie died, Martha had a recurring dream: that she would come into this room to speak to Maggie, who would be reading in bed, a big book covering her face. She would lower the book, and her head would be swathed in gauze, as it was in her casket.

Eventually that dream vanished. Now Maggie appears in her mother's dreams as she was in life. They sit and talk together. "Now," Martha says, "they're *visitations*."

At the end of a hot summer day, I sit on my porch. The western sky is a weird, gleaming apricot, with the earth darkening to black. It's a combination I've never seen before, probably produced by some atmospheric dance between a long, dry, hot spell and the cold front full of rain that has been predicted for tonight. As I sit in the gathering dark, whispers of rain come and the heat drops palpably, minute by minute. It feels like some big, heavy thing is slipping from me. Looking out at that luminous sky cut by inky branches and leaves, I think about the conversations that have occupied my days. I think about people—some of whom don't know me and have no reason to trust me—handing over their memories to me. I think about memory and the persistence of the past, how grief and guilt go on and on. I want to send out some benison upon them all, a soft rain, a gentle night.

It's midsummer. Everything feels suspended. Five blocks away, on campus, the quad is a surreal green, deeply quiet, spellbound. In a matter of weeks the first stirrings of fall energy will begin to wake it. The early rumble will swell steadily to the brilliant September afternoon when we will assemble in our regalia in double lines in front of the chapel for the hike down the hill, into the clicking of parental cameras and the eyes of the daughters and sons being given over to us. And we will move into whatever story starts here.

ACKNOWLEDGMENTS

First and foremost, I thank the people who gave me their stories. Several of them knew me very little or did not know me at all and had no reason to trust me with their memories. For many of them, it was very difficult to reenter the events of October 1999. My examination of how the murder-suicide affected our small campus community would have been fruitless without their collaboration and generosity. I am especially grateful to those who thanked me for telling this story or told me that it was important to do so; those affirmations kept me going.

Of that group, Maggie's mother, Martha Omilian, and her stepfather, Rick Omilian, come first. They are understandably very protective of Maggie's legacy, and they are experts on how the story of her death might be mistold. Their trust, manifested in their welcoming me into their home, sharing personal memories and memorabilia of Maggie, and encouraging me in my work, has been precious to me. I hope they consider this book an act of witness in their daughter's honor.

I would also like to thank Kalamazoo College for several generous gifts that made this book possible, most importantly the Ann V. and Donald R. Parfet Distinguished Professorship, which funded parts of my research, and the sabbatical leave that enabled me to write the manuscript. Additionally, the college's Andrew W. Mellon Foundation Exchange Grant allowed me to tap the expertise of colleagues at the University of Michigan. The Friday chapel program in recent years has also given me space and time each October to tell this story and to see its power for current students and staff.

The staff of the Upjohn Library—Robin Rank, Stacy Nowicki, Liz Smith, Heidi Butler, and Kathryn Lightcap—was unfailingly eager to help with my research, including securing archival materials. Sally Arendt, administrative assistant in the Dean of Students office, also aided my research by retrieving important internal communications from 1999. And I'm especially grateful to my colleagues on the Faculty Development Committee, who approved both my sabbatical proposal and my application for a student-faculty research grant.

Which leads me to Kathryn Prout, 2009 Kalamazoo College graduate, who leaped at my offer of a research assistantship and spent the summer of 2007 doggedly unearthing scholarly literature that fed my knowledge about the many contexts in which the two deaths at Kalamazoo College could be understood. It was encouraging to struggle with another literary type through the wilderness of social-science scholarship, but more importantly, it was a great gift to work with a passionately intelligent young woman compelled to understand the dynamics of violence against women.

Through the Mellon Exchange Grant, I interviewed three members of the University of Michigan faculty whose expertise provided important context for this story: Daniel Saunders, professor of social work, who gave me invaluable leads to research on perpetrators of femicide and femicide-suicide, as well as access to his department's library; Ann Lin, professor of political science, who shared her knowledge of the Assyrian and Chaldean communities in the Midwest; and Carol Jacobsen, professor of art, whose work on behalf of women who kill violent partners has carved a path toward a just future.

I'm very thankful for the assistance of Lee Kirk, Kalamazoo City Attorney in 2006 and my comrade in the 1968 Youth for Understanding Chorale, who facilitated my access to the Public Safety Report that formed the platform for my research. This report makes electrifying and horrifying reading on its own.

The initial readers of this manuscript were two old friends whom I solicited because of my deep respect for their critical eyes. The first was Catherine Frerichs, director of the Pew Faculty Teaching and Learning Center and professor of writing at Grand Valley State University. The second was Marigene Arnold, professor emeritus of anthropology and sociology at Kalamazoo College. Their honest, wise, perceptive responses were critical in bringing the manuscript to maturity.

Annie Martin, acquisitions editor at Wayne State University Press, was first effusive in telling me the effect of this story on her and the people in her office, and then fierce, precise, and demanding in getting the manuscript ready. That's what you want in an editor. Her suggestions for revision, in collaboration with Kathryn Wildfong, editor-in-chief, made the process infinitely easier for me. But when Heidi Bell took over to copyedit the manuscript, I got an advanced course in what every writer needs to know about the limits of her own vision and the powers of a really accomplished professional editor. Having taught writing for over thirty years, I became a quietly humbled student, and I am deeply grateful.

To Pam Polcy, shaman, guru, holy spirit, teacher, my deepest thanks for "sitting with me," as she would say, during the longest, darkest days of my life, through which this book was completed. I am here in no small part because she was there.

It might seem strange to thank Philip Seymour Hoffman. But it was on a winter afternoon in 2006, sitting alone in a multiplex watching *Capote*, that I finally heard an internal voice say, very clearly, that this was the book I needed to write. And that was because Hoffman's performance so sharply brought to light the terrible dilemmas of writing someone else's story, especially when the story is one of terror and trauma.

That winter, as usual, I was teaching my creative nonfiction workshop, and I had been taken aback by my students' interest in precisely this question. Their concern was a significant factor in my determination to write this book. Two years later, the winter 2008 workshop put up with endless stories about my struggles with this project, but I thank them most of all for the eruption of applause that followed my announcement at the start of one Tuesday class that Wayne State wanted the book. I also thank the many students who have told me how eager they are to read what I've written and who have kept asking me, along the way, "How's the book?"

And finally, I thank the handful of people who posed the question "Why would you want to write about something like *that*?" They made me figure out the answer.

Statement drafted by Gail Griffin for President James Jones Jr., October 25, 1999.

One week ago, the Kalamazoo College community suffered a profound shock from which it will be recovering for months and years to come. We have lost two members of our community to the violence which, tragically, has come to characterize U.S. society. Students, faculty, and staff of the College have rallied to see each other through this nightmare, with the deeply appreciated support of alumni, parents, and the larger Kalamazoo community.

In order to move ahead in our struggle to comprehend what has happened on our campus, we must look at it in a larger and even grimmer context. We must begin to acknowledge that an event that seems extraordinary is, in fact, devastatingly common. The rampant male violence against women in our country and our world has struck too close to us to be ignored or denied.

In order to confront this reality, we must first face the most difficult fact of all: that men who commit violence against women are not necessarily people we identify easily or readily as dangerous, as evil, or even as disturbed. They may be people we know, like, and love, as many on this campus loved Neenef Odah. It would be a great deal easier to prevent such disasters if those tending toward violence were obvious monsters, but they are not. They are complex, multifaceted individuals, as we all are, and their violent acts stem from sources and forces that must not be oversimplified. We only start to comprehend the violence that threatens women's lives when we see that it does not come solely from a small class of criminal, openly misogynist, or habitually violent men. It can come from our brothers, our sons, our friends. Our challenge is to sustain our love for them while struggling to understand their actions. To do so demands that we turn to the larger societal context.

The cold facts paint a horrible picture: 90 percent of murdered women are killed by men, two-thirds of them by a man known to them, and 30 percent by a male partner or former partner. Four women die each day at the hands of male partners. The suicide or attempted suicide of the perpetrator is a common feature of this deadly scenario. Over half the women in this country are battered at some point in their lives. Women are much more likely to suffer male violence while or after leaving the relationship. Finally, while studies indicate that 10 percent of high-school students experience violence in dating relationships, among college students the figure rises to 22 percent, the same figure for the adult population in general. In other words, the college years, the time we regard as one of opening doors and widening possibilities, are also the time when our society's patterns of violence against women become firmly established.

In the cruelest of ironies, we are now entering the final week of Domestic Violence Awareness Month. We must pledge ourselves as an educational community to do all we can to break those patterns—through institutional policies and procedures that guard women's safety; through interventions as friends, teachers, and mentors in situations where we perceive women to be at risk; through study and discussion of the phenomenon of male violence against women. To this end, this Wednesday's symposium, sponsored by the Women's Studies Program along with the Women's Equity Coalition and the Women's Resource Center, can help us initiate a new level of discussion. Let us use every possible means to reach beyond factions and personal loyalties toward a common goal: a campus where violence is identified in its roots, where women's welfare is taken seriously, and where women students, faculty, and staff can be safe.

Do You Know . . .

The Warning Signs of Potentially Abusive Relationships?

(A note on pronouns: abusers and victims can be of any gender, but the vast majority of cases involve men abusing women.)

He is controlling and possessive . . .

- He restricts her contact with friends or family and is often very critical of them.
- He monitors her communication with others by phone or e-mail.
- He is intensely jealous of her interactions with other men.
- He invades her privacy—her home or room, her diary, her e-mail, her phone, her possessions.
- He grills her about what she did at work or school.
- He controls finances and decision-making.
- He refuses to accept her termination of the relationship.

He seems to be two different people . . .

- He has a Jekyll-and-Hyde personality, often showing a charming, gentle, charismatic side to others.
- He seems deeply penitent and loving after an emotionally or physically violent episode.

He is desperate and extreme about her . . .

- He may push for commitments too early in the relationship.
- He threatens to kill her or himself if she leaves him.
- He says he cannot live without her or she cannot live without him.
- He seems obsessed with having her for himself.

He is verbally abusive . . .

- He puts her down, privately or publicly, insulting her intelligence, her body, her looks, her sexual behavior.

- He plays on her guilt or her love for him.

- He makes her question her perceptions or her sanity, or he accuses her of being crazy.

He disparages women in general . . .

- He denigrates her women friends.

- He talks or "jokes" about the inferiority or untrustworthiness of women, the need to keep women in line, the need for men to "be men."

He is violent . . .

- He loses his temper easily over small things; his anger seems out of proportion, unpredictable, or frightening.

- He grabs her, twists her arm, pushes her, pulls her, or otherwise uses physical force.

- He is cruel toward animals in general or toward her pets.

- He was physically violent toward a former partner.

- He throws things, kicks things, punches things, breaks things.

- He demands sex; he forces her or badgers her to perform sexual acts that she resists or refuses.

He disowns responsibility . . .

- He denies being verbally or physically abusive.

- He blames her or someone else for violent incidents; she "drove him to it" or "made him do it."

- He excuses the abuse on grounds of his great love for her.

She shows signs of physical, sexual, or psychological abuse . . .

- She excuses his actions to herself or others; thus, she can't name what's happening to her.

- She speaks of the inferiority of women or the need to keep relationships or homes intact at all costs.

- She accepts responsibility for his verbal or physical abuse.

- She wants to end the relationship but fears what it will do to him or how he'll retaliate.

- She has recurring, non-specific aches, pains, or ailments, which can signify stress or abuse.

- She speaks disparagingly of herself, especially in relation to him.

- She makes significant lifestyle or appearance changes to benefit or appease him.

- She has bruises or seems physically hurt.

Improving the Environment for Women at Kalamazoo College
Report of the Task Force on Violence Against Women
Kalamazoo College
June 8, 2000

It is imperative that Kalamazoo College addresses the environment for women within our community. In October 1999, sophomore Maggie Wardle was the murder victim of a former boyfriend in his residence hall room in DeWaters. Following such a terrible and tragic event, it is imperative that we review our policies, procedures and educational programs and take whatever steps we can to try to avert such acts in the future. Though we continue to address student reports of sexual harassment by peers and inappropriate and unwanted sexual activity and abusive treatment of women, we know that there are many more women students who do not report abusive behavior and do not seek the help of the judicial structure of the college or the court system. We also know that women students who protest this demeaning, abusive and violent treatment are often subjected to personal ridicule and threats and that we are likely to be officially aware of and respond to only a minority of those incidents.

Our culture has experienced a well-documented backlash against some of the progress toward equality in the past twenty years. Attitudes, images, and speech that objectify, demean, and threaten women have become distressingly more acceptable. We must realize that the Kalamazoo College community is not isolated from larger societal and cultural trends. Women students here report feeling unsafe and unequal, as they do in the world beyond the campus. Our mission is "to prepare (our) graduates to better understand, live successfully within, and provide enlightened leadership to a richly diverse and increasingly complex world." We must achieve this for our students regardless of gender. By addressing several areas, we can help women feel that they, too, are the full beneficiaries of the incredible education that Kalamazoo College offers.

The Task Force on Violence Against Women has worked this year to better understand the institutional practices and policies that interfere with a healthy environment for our women students and to encourage programs, activities and reviews that could be helpful. The position of the Task Force is that these educational activities must be embedded in the very fabric of our college for institutional change to occur. Thus while it may not look like the Task Force has done great things this year, we are proud of the activities that others developed this year to address the issues of violence, which were supported and encouraged by the Task Force to begin this "embedding" process.

The recommendations of the Task Force stem from discussions of the Task Force on Violence Against Women, concerns raised by the Women's Equity Coalition and the Women's Resource Center, concerns expressed by the Women's Studies Faculty, concerns raised by the family of Maggie Wardle, suggestions by a consultant from the National Center for Higher Education Risk Management, and concerns of the Student Development staff. We intend for this outline of proposed activities to provide the focus for continued work by the Task Force and for a proposal for a federal Grant to Combat Violent Crimes Against Women on Campuses under the Violence Against Women Act coordinated by the national Violence Against Women Office. The report, responding to the charge by President Jones, will also be sent to all appropriate administrators who have responsibility for areas that have been asked to provide some action by the recommendations. Those names are included in parentheses following a category of recommendations.

Task Force on Violence Against Women, 2000

GAIL GRIFFIN, Professor of English and Director of Women's Studies
MARILYN MAURER, Professor of Physical Education and Director of Women's Athletics
CAROLYN NEWTON, Professor of Biology and Associate Provost
PATRICIA PONTO, Director of Counseling
DANNY SLEDGE, Dean of Students
HEIDI FAHRENBACHER, Sophomore

CATHERINE JAMES, Senior

STEPHANIE SCHRIFT, Sophomore

MARILYN LaPLANTE, Vice President for Experiential Education and Chair

Things in Place to Address Concerns

1. A Task Force on Violence Against Women charged by the President to organize and make clear a college-wide focus on these issues.

2. A newly created half-time position for a Women's Resources Coordinator to help with programming across campus on the topics of concern to and about women.

3. A curriculum in Women's Studies to provide courses and special programs on these topics.

4. A Student Development staff knowledgeable about women's issues and dedicated to educating others so that appropriate changes can occur to make the environment more hospitable to women.

5. The student organizations, WEC and WRC, that sponsor special programs and collect materials for all students on topics of interest to women.

6. A student organization, Men Against Gender Bias, that devotes itself to educating men about the issues of gender bias and encouraging them to combat it in their daily lives.

7. A judicial system that has special procedures to address sexual misconduct and an automatic dismissal penalty for proven sexual assault.

8. Social policies for students that define, prohibit or control sexual harassment, discriminatory harassment, alcohol use, drug use, sexual conduct, assault and abusive behavior, weapons, and team initiations.

9. A First-Year Experience that provides support to new students and delivers materials and programs on topics of transition from home to college.

10. Protocols for responding to victims of sexual assault, suicide gestures, hate-crimes, and violence.

11. Significant library and media materials on the broad topics of gender issues, violence, women's studies, women's issues, etc., and a

staff willing to purchase new materials as requested.

12. Students, faculty and staff who are interested in the topic and willing to work to eliminate violence within our community.

13. A faculty development fund that enables faculty to participate in conferences and workshops on topics in order to bring back new ideas for courses and for the community.

Actions Taken During the 1999–2000 Academic Year to Improve the Environment for Women

1. At the beginning of Winter Quarter, President Jones named a Task Force on Violence Against Women charging the committee with seeking "in the broadest possible terms, ways in which violence against women can be addressed on our campus;" and expecting from them recommendations for new and revised policies and educational programs "that help us understand, confront, and eliminate the behaviors that shape this particular form of violence."

2. The WEC and WRC sponsored their annual weeklong focus on domestic violence.

3. Pamphlets on stalking and sexual assault were distributed on campus during the Domestic Violence Awareness Week.

4. A lecture by Susan Brownmiller on violence against women was also a fund-raiser to support the YWCA Domestic Assault program.

5. A group of male students and faculty organized a discussion on the topic of men addressing violence against women. That group then organized themselves into a student organization, Men Against Gender Bias.

6. The Men Against Gender Bias held a residential life program on the topic of violence against women that included a discussion of the female perspective on violence against women and the male perspective on violence against women.

7. A coalition of student organizations under the leadership of one student organized a concert with proceeds donated to a local agency to use to address domestic violence. An educational effort was offered in the lobby of Hicks as tickets were sold.

8. A second student organization sponsored a dance to collect money

to donate to the YWCA Domestic Assault Program.

9. The Campus Life Committee began planning for a Violence Against Women Awareness Day to be held in the Fall Quarter of 2000–2001. The CLC will implement this first program and then the Women's Studies Program will assume continued annual responsibility for it. We hope it can become as strong and effective as its model, the Martin Luther King, Jr. Celebration.

10. The Women's Studies Program sponsored a talk by Sue William Silverman, author of, "Because I Remember Terror, Father, I Remember You."

11. WS 600 (a spring course) committed to the topic of violence against women.

12. Gail Griffin updated an information sheet on Dating Violence Awareness and that was distributed on campus and will be used during the orientation program in the fall.

13. Special materials will be distributed in the summer mailings to entering students and to parents of both entering and continuing students.

14. The Director of the First-Year Experience has started planning for a program for first year students to be offered in the fall.

15. Two resident advisors were added to the residential system to add a greater student staff presence in the residence system.

16. A new half-time position has been created to add support to the residential life program with particular emphasis on RA training and program development that will address the issues of violence in relationships.

17. President Jones authorized a new half-time position to focus on addressing women's issues. That position will be housed in Student Development and will be staffed starting in Fall, 2000–2001. The new person will help to develop specific programs on campus on issues of importance to women and will support others who are offering the same types of programs.

18. The Residence Life staff went through a special training session on domestic violence. That session will be incorporated into the RA training program to help RAs address more effectively the understanding of and response to violent behavior in the residence system.

19. The golf team created a book bag patch in memory of Maggie Wardle, a member of the team, to remind students to end violence against women.

20. The Student Development staff and members of the Task Force on Violence Against Women worked with a consultant on reviewing our judicial procedures and our protocol for responding to incidents of sexual misconduct. Rewriting our policies and procedures will be done during the summer.

21. Two faculty members arranged for Marianne Williamson to speak on the topic of healing a community.

22. Funding has been made available to support the increase in counseling hours available to students.

23. We have agreed to develop a handbook for women. That will likely be started as independent materials and then developed into a complete handbook as a SIP project of one our students.

24. We will work with the GLCA [Great Lakes Colleges Association] Women's Studies committee to discuss the possibility of offering the next GLCA Women's Studies conference at KC with a special focus on addressing violence against women on college campuses.

Actions We could Take to Improve our Community

Advisory Structure (President Jones)

The Task Force on Violence Against Women provides a campus-wide focus on these very specific issues and can work to embed the recommended activities into the on-going structures of the college. Only when that is accomplished will we see the institutional change that signifies an environment that is safe for women, is concerned about their particular needs, and is peopled with enlightened men and women. We recommend that the Task Force be continued for at least three more years and expanded to include Dr. Carol Anderson (representative from Women's Studies), Andrea Plevak (sophomore), Dawne Bell (senior), and the Women's Resources Coordinator (yet to be appointed). To be most effective, the Task Force should also include a representative from the YWCA Domestic Assault Program who can keep the college representatives in tune with national and community issues and a representative from the Kalamazoo judicial system who can help the college coordinate with the judicial system to use full legal opportunities to help eliminate crimes against women. At the conclusion of the three-year time frame for the Task Force, the members should review the impact of their work on encouraging real institutional change and might at that time suggest the continuation of the Task Force or some other advisory body that could be beneficial to the on-going activities of the college.

Judicial System (Danny Sledge, Vaughn Maatman)

Our students report that the system is intimidating and that it is difficult to know to whom to speak when reporting an incident that might be a violation of one of our policies. We do not have a stalking policy, though that is one of the major crimes of violence against women and we have had a few incidents. Students do not see that there are resources to help free themselves from abusive relationships. Students do not feel that the sexual harassment and discriminatory harassment policies inhibit intimidating activities by others. The statement of the process is too legalistic to clearly define it within an educational context and set it apart from the court system.

ACTIONS:

1. Rewrite the process to improve the effectiveness.

- Rewrite the procedural sections to make them more "user friendly" and remove the legalistic language.

- Rewrite the student rights of the hearing process as separate lists for the complainant and for the person accused to clarify the differences.

- State more explicitly the educational context in which the judicial system operates.

- Use videotape as the transcript for a sexual conduct hearing to provide more information for the appeal process.

- State explicitly that students may invite an expert witness in cases of sexual conduct violations.

- Develop an option for an administrative panel to hear complainants of sexual assault to remove the barrier of concern about confidentiality.

- Include a recommendation in cases of sexual assault, domestic violence, or stalking that students file criminal charges as well as institutional charges and outline the process for such action.

2. Improve access to the judicial process.

- Develop a clearly defined and more effective access route for making a complaint, particularly for women who have been victimized.

    a. Clarify the types of complaints that go to the Dean of Students, those that go to the Provost, and those that go to specific administrative offices.

    b. Develop an "ombudsman type of role" to hold the initial discussion of a complaint with a student, provide an advisory relationship to the complainant, and route the complainant to the appropriate authority as defined above.

    c. Name a female staff or faculty person as the first access to students reporting complaints of sexual harassment, sexual assault, violent relationships, and safety concerns.

    d. Develop, train, and publicize the names of a specific group of faculty and staff to whom students can turn for guidance when they have been victimized.

- State clearly that there is no time limit for reporting crimes of violence to eliminate a barrier that often impedes the reporting of a sexual conduct violation.

- Do not extend the option of mediation to sexual assault hearings.

3. Develop important policies and procedures.

- Add a section to the social policies that defines the crimes of violence against women, and include the appropriate specific policies within that section.

- Expand the "Assault and Abusive Behavior" policy with examples and specific penalties for the most serious forms of abuse.

- Expand the "Posting of Signs" policy to ban the posting of pornographic images and messages in public areas of the campus.

- Develop a policy against stalking, including cyberstalking.

- Expand the jurisdiction of the judicial system to include students who have paid deposits for admission but are not yet enrolled and for six months beyond graduation to graduates of the college who committed a violation while enrolled.

4. Improve the training process for people involved in the judicial process.

- Train the members of the Judicial Council and the Harassment Advisory Board to better understand how gender issues impact the disciplinary system and how to help women have access to the system.

Addressing First-Year Students (Zaide Pixley, Danny Sledge)

Both males and females are arriving at college with less understanding of gender issues and needing more directed and effective education on this topic. It is essential to work with entering students very quickly on some of the topics, because unwanted sexual attention and rape can occur within the first few days of the opening of a new quarter and the arrival of new students.

ACTIONS:

1. Prepare informational material that can be sent to prospective new students in the summer mailing describing the potential for unwanted sexual attention, rape, and other crimes of violence against women. Perhaps this should be written expressly for men and for women.

2. Prepare informational material of the same sort as above but written for parents to encourage them to help their sons and daughters prepare more effectively to deal with this type of negative activity.

3. Develop a First-Year Forum on gender issues, safety, and the policies that define the expected behavior of our students.

4. Hold separate residence hall meetings for women and men to discuss the residential policies that address gender issues and safety for students in the halls.

5. Create and deliver handy reference lists of phone numbers to report sexual assault, hotline to talk about suicidal thoughts, Security office, KDPS.

Security (Danny Sledge, Glenn Nevelle)

Women report a lack of confidence in the security staff understanding the particular needs and concerns of women about their safety and welfare.

ACTIONS:

1. Add new security officer positions so that there are at least two officers on duty at all critical times of the night.

2. Develop a training session for new security officers on the impact of gender issues in safety and security.

3. Review the concept of a "Safe-Walk" program and incorporate some version of it under the umbrella of the Security program.

4. Put "call-box" phones in the residence hall lounges, hallway near the Counseling Office and the BSO room in Hicks, lobby of Light Fine Arts, inside entrance of the library, inside entrance of Olds-Upton, unless there are currently campus phones available in a public space within a building.

Public Information (Danny Sledge, Lisa Palchick)

Students need more visible reminders of contact people, how to handle emergency situations, serious societal problems that occur on campus, etc.

ACTIONS:

1. Place signs in computer labs defining the use of the computer to download pornographic material and giving instructions about how to respond.

2. Place information in computer labs about the definition and prohibition of computer stalking.

3. Laminate and affix posters in bathrooms naming contact people, the process for reporting sexual assault and protective steps to take following an assault.

4. Provide more public information about suicide prevention and telephone number of the 24-hour Suicide Prevention Help Line.

5. Place more signs around campus on topics of alcohol and sexual assault, violence in relationships, date-rape drugs, stalking, hate crimes, etc.

6. Do a poster campaign designed to break the code of silence that many students adhere to.

7. Develop a woman's resource handbook that will include information about gender issues, resources available to women, community

agencies that address women's issues and provide community resources, safety procedures, etc.

8. Counseling staff develop materials that identify symptoms of alcohol use, suicidal thoughts, eating disorders, abusive relationships, etc., that help a student to know when to seek help for a friend.

Programming (Danny Sledge, Vaughn Maatman, Richard Berman, Gary Dorrien, Pat Ponto)

Because some students learn more effectively by attending programs on specific topics of interest, we should regularly be providing programs to address the issues of violence and safety.

ACTIONS:

1. Arrange for 2–3 LAC [Liberal Arts Colloquium] events each year on topics of violence, gender issues, and safety.

2. Offer men-to-men dialogues on a regular basis.

3. Work with the coaching staff to involve athletes in the various program opportunities and men-to-men dialogues.

4. Counseling staff offer one "For Men Mainly" and "For Women Mainly" program on a regular basis.

5. Residential Life staff offer programs on related topics on a regular basis.

6. Student Life staff offer, on a regular basis, programs on how to talk with others about differences.

7. Career Development staff offer, on a regular basis, programs on sexual harassment in the workplace.

8. Implement the annual weeklong program to address Violence Against Women.

Curriculum (Greg Mahler, Gail Griffin, Amy Elman, Lyn Maurer)

ACTIONS:

1. Add a regular offering on the topic of violence against women in the Women's Studies curriculum.

2. Add a women's self-defense class for PE credit.

Other (Danny Sledge, Tom Ponto, Vaughn Maatman)

ACTIONS:

1. Redesign the Judicial Policies and Procedures area of the Web site to make it easier to locate the specific policies and procedures one needs.

2. Use the Web site as a source of interactive information about important student issues such as sexual intimacy and abuse, relationship abuse, suicide, alcohol abuse, etc.

3. Design specific protocols for responding to a student concern about sexual assault that can be distributed to faculty, to RAs, to work supervisors, to friends, to health center and counseling center staff, to student development staff, etc.

4. Add a section on "Managing the Grieving Process" to the Emergency Protocol for Responding to the Death of a Student or Faculty.

Funding (President Jones)

ACTIONS:

1. Continue funding for the half-time position of Women's Resources Coordinator.

2. Provide a budget for the Coordinator to use to help fund special request programs.

3. Increase program budgets in Counseling, Residential Life, Dean of Students office, Student Commission, Security specifically to add programs on the topics and materials suggested above.

4. Increase the program budget in Women's Studies to enable the expansion of the curriculum to out-of-class programming.

5. Increase the staff in Counseling to provide specific counseling on women's issues and violence against women.

6. Provide a budget for the annual Violence Against Women Week.

Chapter 1

1 *If you were a painter:* James F. Jones, "Surviving the Fall: Murder/suicide at K-College the latest in a string of tragedies." *Kalamazoo Gazette,* sec. A, November 14, 1999.

6 "Kalamazoo Alma Mater," music by R. F. Holden, lyrics by W. F. Dunbar, *Kalamazoo College Songbook,* 1933.

Chapter 2

10 *seemed to instinctively know:* Rick Omilian, "Family Remembrances of Maggie," read at the Kalamazoo College Memorial Service, January 14, 2000.

11 *enthralled by small organisms:* Rick Omilian, Memorial Service.

11 *bug geek:* Kelly Schulte interview.

15 *She was the only girl I knew:* Posting on Maggie's Web site: www.remembering maggie.com/guestbook.html. January 18, 2000.

17 *giggled a lot:* Brooke Nobis interview.

17 *feisty and sometimes catty:* Ibid.

19 *She was very humble:* Kelly Schulte interview.

20 *I looked forward to practice every day:* Leza Frederickson, Memorial Service.

20 *She had this way of making:* J'nai Leafers, Memorial Service.

20 *She told me the truth:* Leza Frederickson, Memorial Service.

21 *She blossomed from a shy, quiet academic:* Beth Hartman Green, "K-College Must Continue To Build Its Sense of Community," Opinion, *Kalamazoo Gazette,* sec. B, November 28, 1999.

21 *getting away from being a girl from Plainwell:* Caitlin Gilmet interview, July 23, 2006.

21 *I see her walking:* Memorial Service.

Chapter 3

31 *but not much less:* Memorial Service.

52 *She wrote that her political values:* Memorial Service.

Chapter 4

56 *in the form of instant messaging records:* Public Safety Report.

56 *The record begins with a long exchange:* In instant messages, each new line represents a new entry, and because the messages are "instant," sometimes responses overlap, so that one person responds to the other's second-to-last message. The typos and misspellings have been mostly left as they stand. The asterisks seem to represent kisses.

Chapter 5

89 *knew every bouncer:* Nandini Sonnad and J'nai Leafers, Memorial Service.

91 *He began to abuse her over the phone:* The abusive phone calls were described by J'nai Leafers in her statement in the Public Safety Report. The face-to-face abuse was recounted by Heidi Fahrenbacher in our interview.

91 *In October, he accused his roommate. . . . Another DeWaters acquaintance, Vaughn Preston:* Public Safety Report.

98 *said it was the worst day ever:* Qtd. in Lynn Turner, "Killer's Actions Baffle Friends," *Kalamazoo Gazette,* sec. A, October 20, 1999.

98 *were sucking face:* Nate Cooper, Public Safety Report.

101 *acting slutty:* Navin Anthony, Public Safety Report.

101 *upbeat and normal:* Brian Newman, Public Safety Report

102 *she said Neenef wanted her to come over:* J'nai Leafers, Public Safety Report.

Chapter 6

124 *began our meeting by quietly but firmly stating:* James F. Jones, "Musings on the Presidency: A Reflective Primer," in *On Assuming a College or University Presidency: Lessons and Advice from the Field,* 15–24 (Washington, DC: American Council on Education, 2005).

126 *Thomas would later say:* Sue Youngs, Kalamazoo Department of Public Safety, e-mail message to author, July 16, 2007.

Chapter 7

133 *the recording of Jimmy delivering it:* "Pres. Jones a.m. press conference," October 18, 1999, compact disc, Kalamazoo College Archives.

138 *As is his wont, he began with a quotation:* James F. Jones Jr., "Comments to the Campus Community, October 18, 1999," Kalamazoo College Archives.

137 *Something from the ninth level of Dante:* James F. Jones, personal communication with author, June 28, 2006.

139 *We have two dead students:* Lynn Turner and Mark Fisk, "Students Search for Answers," *Kalamazoo Gazette,* sec. A, October 19, 1999.

139 *Similarly, the foregrounding of gun control:* Michigan's senior senator, Carl Levin, would frame the story in these terms as well on Friday, October 22, 1999, reading a synopsis of what had happened at Kalamazoo College into the Congressional Record.

144 *I was in disgust:* Qtd. in Lynn Turner, "Killer's actions baffle friends," *Kalamazoo Gazette,* sec. A, October 19, 1999.

152 *said he seems to remember Odah:* Public Safety Report.

153 *She clarified that she first heard:* Public Safety Report.

Chapter 8

169 *Women's Equity Coalition:* This latter group was the feminist student organization, differentiated from the Women's Resource Center, which was a living-learning unit dedicated to service to and programming for women on campus. Sometimes the personnel for the two groups overlapped.

176 *After attending the violence against women panel:* Erin Rome, Response Paper, Literature of Women, May 15, 2000. Used with permission of the author.

176 *What has happened is not characteristic of his personality:* "A 'Devastating' Murder-Suicide: Police say Seattleite killed ex-girlfriend at Michigan college," *Seattle Post-Intelligencer,* October 19, 1999.

Chapter 9

185 *This quarter has really been a tough one:* Public Safety Report.

187 *"he's not crazy":* The observations of Karyn Boatwright and Bob Grossman should in no way be taken as professional, formal clinical assessments; they are merely the immediate insights of professionals in the field.

Chapter 10

203 *"I think it is important to remember":* The e-mail from Joe Abhold to Pat Ponto, October 5, 2000, is used with permission of Pat Ponto.

214 *I read many of the letters:* Essay, Literature of Women, May 15, 2000.

216 *they were unrelated, separate issues:* The e-mail from Rick Omilian to James F. Jones was given to me by the author.

216 *they wrote in their letter to Tom Ponto:* The letter from the Omilians to Tom Ponto, dated November 19, 1999, was given to me by the family.

221 *the WRC sponsors a women-only self-defense workshop:* A backstory not covered by the *Index:* President Jones hedged on cofunding the workshop until the Omilians chimed in with their support of the event.

Chapter 11

227 *women do not face the greatest threat:* Violence Policy Center, "When Men Murder Women: An Analysis of the 1997 Homicide Data," (Washington, DC: Violence Policy Center, 1999), www.vpc.org/studies/dv2cont.htm.

228 *In 1997, 81.3 percent of women homicide victims:* Ibid.

228 *According to the FBI, guns are used most often:* Ibid.

229 *8 percent of college men and 1 percent of women:* M. Miller, D. Hemenway, and H. Wechsler, "Guns and Gun Threats at College," *Journal of American College Health* 52, no. 2 (2002): 57–66.

229 *they are hardly common:* Sierra Bellows, "How Safe Are Our Schools?" *The University of Virginia Magazine* Spring 2008. www.uvamagazine.org/short_course/article//how_safe_are_our_schools.

229 *Children and youth are safer:* Qtd. in ibid.

230 *What these school shootings reveal:* Jackson Katz and Sut Jhally, "Crisis in Masculinity," *The Boston Globe,* sec. E, 2 May 1999.

230 *The slaughter of fourteen women:* Jane Caputi and Diana E. H. Russell, "Femicide: Sexist Terrorism Against Women," in *Femicide: The Politics of Woman Killing,* ed. Jill Radford and Diana E. H. Russell, 13 (New York: Twayne, 1992).

230 *In Jonesboro, Arkansas:* Sabrina Denney Bull, "Violence Against Women: Media (Mis)Representation of Femicide" (speech presented at "Women Working to Make a Difference," the Institute for Women's Policy Research's Seventh International Women's Policy Research Conference, Washington, DC, June 22–24, 2003) www.iwpr.org/pdf/Bull_SabrinaDenney.pdf.

230 *the shooter, Charles Carl Roberts:* "Police: School Killer Told Wife He Molested Family Members," *CNN.com,* October 3, 2006, www.cnn.com/2006/US/10/03/amish.shooting/index.html.

230 *After Cho Seung-Hui shot his first victims:* Lucinda Roy, *No Right To Remain Silent: The Tragedy at Virginia Tech* (New York: Harmony Books, 2009).

231 *highest rate of nonfatal intimate partner violence:* Bureau of Justice Statistics Office of Justice Programs, "Intimate Partner Violence and Age of Victim," United States Department of Justice, 2005, http://bjs.ojp.usdoj.gov/index.cfm?ty=pbdetail&iid=1003.

231 *33 percent of teenage girls:* "love is not abuse: statistics," Liz Claiborne Inc., 2010, www.loveisnotabuse.com/statsistics.htm.

231 *confronted with a possible breakup:* Ibid.

231 *At the college level, one 1996 study:* C. S. Sellers and M. L. Bromley,

"Violent Behavior in College Student Dating Relationships," *Journal of Contemporary Justice* 12, no. 1 (1996): 1–27.

231 *In a study of young Iowa women:* R. Barri Flowers, *Male Crime and Deviance: Exploring Its Causes, Dynamics and Nature* (Springfield, IL: Charles C. Thomas, 2003).

231 *remain in the relationship:* B. Caponera, *Guidelines for Counseling Adolescents in Sexually Coercive Relationships* (New Mexico Coalition of Sexual Assault Programs: 1998).

231 *2009 Bureau of Justice statistics:* Katrina Baum, Shannan Catalano, Michael Rand, Kristina Rose, *Stalking Victimization in the United States* (Washington, DC: United States Bureau of Justice Statistics, 2009).

232 *National Institute of Justice statistics from 2000 show 13 percent:* Bonnie S. Fisher, Francis T. Cullen, and Michael G. Turner, *The Sexual Victimization of College Women* (Washington, DC: United States Bureau of Justice Statistics, 2000).

232 *thirty women at a small progressive college:* Lynn Phillips, *Flirting with Danger* (New York: NYU Press, 2000).

232 *College students may be more likely:* Qtd. in Tina Kelley, "On Campuses, Warning About Violence in Relationships," *New York Times,* Metro sec., Sunday, February 13, 2000.

233 *Christina Nicolaidis and her colleagues studied:* Christina Nicolaidis, et al, "Could We Have Known? A Qualitative Analysis of Data from Women Who Survived an Attempted Homicide by an Intimate Partner," *Journal of General Internal Medicine* 18, no. 10 (2003): 788–94.

233 *prior research cites figures from 20 percent to 30 percent:* Ibid., 790.

233 *The intensity of the control:* Ibid.

233 *I didn't realize what big trouble I was in:* Ibid., 791.

233 *As Jennifer Tucker and Leslie Wolfe argue:* *Victims No More* (Washington, DC: Center for Women Policy Studies, National Center for Research on Women, 1997).

233 *the monumental 2000 Justice Department study:* Patricia Tjaden and Nancy Thoennes, *Extent, Nature, and Consequences of Intimate Partner Violence: Findings from the National Violence Against Women Survey* (Washington, DC: National Institute of Justice, United States Department of Justice, 2000).

234 *strong relationship between stalking:* Jeremy Travis, "Stalking: Lessons from Recent Research" (address, annual conference of the National Center for Women and Policing, Orlando, FL, April 14, 1999).

234 *We found a statistically significant association:* Judith McFarlane, Jacquelyn C. Campbell, and Kathy Watson, "Intimate Partner Stalking and Femicide: Urgent Implications for Women's Safety," *Behavioral Sciences & the Law* 20, no. 1–2 (2002): 55.

234 *Maggie Wardle was one of 1,195 women in the United States:* Patricia

Tjaden and Nancy Thoennes, *Extent, Nature, and Consequences of Intimate Partner Violence: Findings from the National Violence Against Women Survey* (Washington, DC: National Institute of Justice, United States Department of Justice, 2000).

235 *Jacquelyn Campbell of Johns Hopkins University:* Qtd. in Marie Tessier, "Study Indicates Jobless Abusers Most Apt to Kill," *Women's e News,* July 24, 2003, www.feminist.com/news/vaw2.html.

235 *violence against women must be understood as different:* Jeremy Travis, "Stalking: Lessons from Recent Research"(address, annual conference of the National Center for Women and Policing, Orlando, FL, April 14, 1999).

235 *Violence against women is predominantly intimate partner violence:* Tjaden and Thoennes, *Extent, Nature, and Consequences of Intimate Partner Violence: Findings from the National Violence Against Women Survey,* iv (Washington, DC: National Institute of Justice, United States Department of Justice, 2000).

235 *In general, 70 percent of intimate partner homicides:* Daniel G. Saunders and Angela Browne, "Intimate Partner Homicide," in *Case Studies in Family Violence,* 2nd ed., ed. Robert T. Ammerman and Michel Hersen, 418 (New York: Kluwer Academic/Plenum Publishers, 2000).

235 *A significant portion of partner homicides:* Ibid., 419.

236 *Femicide is the leading cause of death:* Margaret Morganroth Gullette, "Then and Now: What Have the Sexual 'Revolutions' Wrought?" *Women's Review of Books* 25, no. 1 (2008): 23; Jennifer Tucker and Leslie Wolfe, "Victims No More—Girls Fight Back Against Male Violence" (policy paper, Center for Women Policy Studies, 1997); Gregory Kerry, "Understanding and Predicting Intimate Femicide: An Analysis of Men Who Kill Their Intimate Female Partners," (PhD diss., Carleton University, 2001) 4; K. Stout, "Intimate Femicide: A National Demographic Overview," *Journal of Interpersonal Violence* 6 (1991): 476–85.

236 *that either threats of separation:* Tjaden and Thoennes, *Extent, Nature, and Consequences of Intimate Partner Violence,* 37.

236 *violence against women is particularly likely:* Ann Oakley, *Gender on Planet Earth* (New York: The New Press, 2002) 38.

236 *Separation or threat of separation:* Saunders and Browne, "Intimate Partner Homicide," 421.

237 *comprise a substantial minority of cases:* Ibid., 422.

237 *The pattern of suicide following homicide:* Jacquelyn Campbell, "'If I Can't Have You, No One Can,'" in *Femicide,* ed. Jill Radford and Diana E. H. Russell, 107 (New York: Twayne Publishers, 1992).

237 *Whenever a person threatens suicide:* Alan McEvoy, "Murder-Suicide by Students," *School Intervention Report* 13, no. 2 (2000): 5.

237 *Myrna Dawson distinguishes between the suicide that occurs:* "Intimate Femicide Followed by Suicide: Examining the Role of Premeditation."

Suicide and Life-Threatening Behavior 35, no. 1 (2005): 76–90.

237 *the perpetrator often leaves evidence, such as a note:* M. Daly and M. Wilson, *Homicide* (New York: Aldine de Gruyter, 1988), 219.

238 *there is a long legal and cultural tradition:* Saunders and Browne, "Intimate Partner Homicide," 433.

238 *If the motive is outlined:* Minna Nikunen, "Murder-suicide: Cultural Categorizations in the Crime News," abstract (PhD diss., Tampere University, 2005).

239 *Even when told that the case had a lethal outcome:* Saunders and Browne, "Intimate Partner Homicide," 440.

239 *many of the significant risk factors for femicide-suicide:* Jane Koziol-McLain, et al., "Risk Factors for Femicide-Suicide in Abusive Relationships: Results from a Multisite Case Control Study" *Violence and Victims* 21 (February 1, 2006), www.ncbi.nlm.nih.gov/pubmed/16494130.

241 *A 2008 mtvU-Associated Press poll discovered:* "Executive Summary," *mtvU and Associated Press College Stress and Mental Health Poll,* Spring 2008, www.halfofus.com/_media/_pr/mtvU_AP_College_Stress_and_Mental_Health_Poll_executive_summary.pdf.

241 *suicide was the second leading cause:* Kevin Caruso, "Suicide Statistics," *Suicide.org,* www.suicide.org/suicide-statistics.html.

241 *according to 2006 statistics from the National Institute of Mental Health:* "Suicide in the U.S.: Statistics and Prevention," National Institutes of Health, 2009, www.nimh.nih.gov/health/publications/suicide-in-the-us-statistics-and-prevention/index.shtml#risk.

241 *In 1999, when Neenef died, the ratio:* "Suicide Facts, Suicide Statistics," *HealthyPlace: America's Mental Health Channel,* 2010, www.healthyplace.com/depression/suicide/suicide-facts-suicide-statistics/menu-id-68.

241 *For the general U.S. population, suicide:* Caruso, "Suicide Statistics."

242 *The psychoanalytic concepts of suicide:* M. Rosenbaum, "The Role of Depression in Couples Involved in Murder-Suicide and Homicide," *American Journal of Psychiatry* 147 (August 1990): 1039.

243 *A 1997 study of homicide-suicide perpetrators:* Steven Stack, "Homicide Followed by Suicide: An Analysis of Chicago Data," *Criminology* 35, no. 3: 435–53.

243 *A pivotal 1994 study:* Saunders and Browne, "Intimate Partner Homicide," 422.

243 *While he might be quite psychologically abusive:* Ibid.

244 *Another version of this personality is what George Palermo identified:* "Murder-suicide: An Extended Suicide," *International Journal of Offender Therapy and Comparative Criminology* 31, no. 3: 207.

244 *a history of jealous suspicion:* Ibid., 208.

244 *pathological attachment toward the mother-partner:* Ibid., 213.

244 *the presence of morbid jealousy:* M. Rosenbaum, "The Role of Depres-

sion in Couples," 1038.

244 *In Daniel Saunders' interviews:* Daniel Saunders, in discussion with the author, February 2008.

245 *according to Rosenbaum and Leisring:* A. Rosenbaum and P. A. Leisring, "Beyond Power and Control: Towards an Understanding of Partner Abusive Men," *Journal of Comparative Family Studies* 34, no. 1 (2003): 1.

245 *In their exploration of femicide, Martin Daly and Margo Wilson:* "Till Death Do Us Part," in *Femicide: The Politics of Woman Killing,* ed. Jill Radford and Diana E. H. Russell, 85 (New York: Twayne, 1992).

245 *Anglo-American law is replete:* Ibid.

245 *overly concerned about their masculine image:* Daniel G. Saunders, "Husbands Who Assault: Multiple Profiles Requiring Multiple Responses," in *Legal Responses to Wife Assault,* ed. N. Zoe Hilton, 13 (Newbury Park, CA: Sage Publications, 1993).

245 *identify strongly with the patriarchal narrative:* Julia T. Wood, "Gender, Power, and Violence in Heterosexual Relationships," in *Sex Differences and Similarities in Communications,* 2nd ed., ed. Kathryn Dindia and Daniel J. Canary, 403 (New York: Routledge, 2006).

246 *two contradictory, although not entirely independent, views:* Ibid., 402.

246 *share the assumption of male superiority:* Ibid., 404.

246 *Western culture's romance narratives:* Ibid., 398.

247 *to identify the satisfying of others' needs:* Luise Eichenbaum and Susie Orbach, *Understanding Women: A Feminist, Psychoanalytic Approach* (New York: Basic Books, 1987), 61.

247 *based on all of the available research:* Cited in Gregory Kerry, "Understanding and Predicting Intimate Femicide."

247 *the single greatest danger:* Qtd. in Mary Dickson. "A Woman's Worst Nightmare," *No Safe Place: Violence Against Women,* Public Broadcasting Service, 1996, www.pbs.org/kued/nosafeplace/articles/nightmare.html.

247 *because of what Ann Oakley calls:* Oakley, *Gender on Planet Earth,* 45.

248 *Not all men are abusers:* Lorraine Radford, "Programmed or Licensed to Kill?" in *The New Brain Sciences: Perils and Prospects,* ed. Dai Rees and Steven Rose, 135 (Cambridge, MA: Cambridge University Press, 2004).

Conclusion

256 *And he had access to a gun:* The emphasis here is original to Rick's manuscript.

256 *Remember what happened to two lives:* Rick Omilian, "Reduce Gun Violence in Memory of Slain Student," *Kalamazoo Gazette,* October 24, 2000.

256 *that the addition of dating relationships:* YWCA Domestic Violence

Program staff notes in the possession of Rick and Martha Omilian.

256 *The parents of that young lady:* Qtd. in "New Law Redefines Domestic Violence," *Kalamazoo Gazette,* April 1, 2002.

258 *we live the stories we tell:* Mark Doty, *Firebird: A Memoir* (New York: HarperCollins, 1999), 183.

264 *I heard survivors asking:* Sara Church, "Victim Advocacy in the Legal System: Breaking the Cycle of Domestic Violence," Senior Individualized Project, Kalamazoo College, Fall 2001, 4–5.

264 *before the morning of October 18:* Ibid., 41.

268 *Our strength lies in a philosophy:* The mission statement of the St. John's Home comes from its Web site, www.stjohnshome.org/about.aspx.

273 *Hunting isn't necessary:* Qtd. in John Lahr, "Citizen Penn," *The New Yorker,* April 3, 2006, 48.

274 *I pointed the gun at her head:* The *Prairie Home Companion* episode featuring Billy Collins was broadcast December 16, 2006.

274 *One of the best ways of looking:* The *Writer's Chronicle* 39, no. 3 (2006): 67–68.

Quotations in the text come from the following sources unless otherwise attributed in the chapter notes.

Interviews

(*Indicates electronic communications. Other interviews were in person or by telephone.)

Maggie Wardle's family and friends:

Rick and Martha Omilian, July 18, 2007
Katherine Chamberlain, June 20, 2007
Sara Church, September 4, 2006
Nick Duiker, September 7, 2007
Heidi Fahrenbacher, July 28, 2006; *January 22, 2008
Leza Frederickson, July 19, 2007
*Jeff Hopcian, September 4, 2006
Brooke Nobis, July 6, 2006
*Dan Poskey, January 13, 2009
Kelly Schulte, August 24, 2007
Nandini Sonnad, June 30, 2007
J'nai Leafers Wallace, September 24, 2006
Erin Rome Zabel, June 19, 2007

Neenef Odah's friends:

Navin Anthony, July 10, 2007
*LaVange Barth, October 4, 2006
Frank Church, July 12, 2007
Nancy El-Shamaa, July 19, 2007
Caitlin Gilmet, July 23, 2006; *July 26, 2006; *March 10, 2008
*Stephanie Miller, November 4, 2007
*Kirsten Fritsch Paulson, June 16, 2007
Chris Wilson, August 23, 2007

Other Kalamazoo students:

Simone Lutz, July 13, 2007
Stephanie Schrift, September 16, 2007
*Jennie Toner, July 19, 2006

Kalamazoo College faculty and staff:

Marigene Arnold, July 15, 2006
David Barclay, July 25, 2008
Karyn Boatwright, July 21, 2006
Alyce Brady, September 15, 2006
*Peggy Cauchy, August 22, 2008
*Hardy Fuchs, June 20, 2006
*Robert Grossman, June 22, 2007
Alan Hill, September 29, 2006
Ahmed Hussen, August 20, 2008
*James F. Jones Jr., June 29, 2006; September 4, 2006
Gregory Mahler, June 13, 2007
*Paul Manstrom, January 6, 2007
Glenn Nevelle, August 9, 2006
Patricia Ponto, September 29, 2006
Diane Seuss, March 25, 2006
Gail Simpson, July 18, 2006
Danny Sledge, March 3, 2006

And:

*Sue Youngs, Kalamazoo Department of Public Safety, July 16, 2007

Memorial Service

Written remarks at the memorial service for Maggie Wardle, Stetson Chapel, Kalamazoo College, January 14, 2000:
C. Kim Cummings
Emily Ford
Marilyn Maurer
Corey Spearman

Public Safety Report

Kalamazoo Department of Public Safety
Case #99–33575, October 18, 1999
All quotations attributed to residents of DeWaters Hall whom I did not inter-

view personally come from this source, including those of Heather Barnes and Eric Page.

Visual and Written Materials

Jessica Emhoff Fowle, videotape of Neenef's performance in Frelon, 1999.
Martha and Rick Omilian, scrapbooks containing mementos of Maggie.
Jim Van Sweden, notes from administrative meetings, 1999–2000.

I have listed here some of the sources I found especially helpful while writing this book. This bibliography is by no means, however, a complete record of all the sources I have consulted.

Bernard, J. L., and M. L. Bernard. "The Abusive Male Seeking Treatment: Jekyll and Hyde." *Family Relations* 33, no. 4 (1984): 543–47.

Berman, A. L. "Dyadic death: A typology." *Suicide & Life-Threatening Behavior* 26: 342–50.

Brock, K. *American Roulette*. Washington, DC: Violence Policy Center, 2002.

Campbell, Jacquelyn C. "'If I Can't Have You, No One Can': Power and Control in Homicide of Female Partners." In *Femicide: The Politics of Woman-Killing*, edited by Jill Radford and Diana E. H. Russell, 99–113. New York: Twayne Publishers, 1992.

Carr, Joetta L. *Campus Violence White Paper*. Baltimore: American College Health Association, 2005.

Copeland, Lois, and Leslie R. Wolfe. *Violence Against Women as Bias-Motivated Hate Crime*. Center for Women Policy Studies, National Council for Research on Women, 1991.

Dawson, Myrna. "Intimate Femicide Followed by Suicide: Examining the Role of Premeditation." *Suicide and Life-Threatening Behavior* 35, no. 1 (2005): 76–90.

Foley, Megan K. "Locating 'Difficulty': A Multi-site Model of Intimate Terrorism." In *Relating Difficulty: The Processes of Constructing and Managing Difficult Interaction*, edited by D. Charles Kirkpatrick, Steven Duck, and Megan K. Foley, 43–59. New York: Routledge, 2006.

Gilligan, Carol. *In a Different Voice: Psychological Theory and Women's Development*. Cambridge, MA: Harvard University Press, 1993.

Gullette, Margaret Morganroth. "Then and Now: What Have the Sexual 'Revolutions' Wrought?" *Women's Review of Books* 25, no. 1 (2008): 22–24.

Hart, Barbara. *Assessing Whether Batterers Will Kill*. Pennsylvania Coalition Against Domestic Violence, 1990. In *Barbara J. Hart's Collected Writings*, Minnesota Center Against Violence and Abuse. www.mincava.umn.edu/hart/lethali.htm.

Harway, Michèle, and Marsali Hansen. "Therapist Perceptions of Family Violence." In *Battering and Family Therapy: A Feminist Perspective*, edited by Marsali Hansen and Michèle Harway, 42–53. Thousand Oaks, CA: Sage Publications, 1993.

Holmes, Ronald M., and Stephen T. Holmes. *Suicide: Theory, Practice, and Investigation*. Thousand Oaks, CA: Sage Publications, 2005.

Holtzworth-Munroe, Amy, and Gregory L. Stuart. "Typologies of Male Batterers: Three Subtypes and Differences Among Them." *Psychological Bulletin* 116, no. 3 (1994): 476–97.

Koziol-McLain, Jane, Daniel Webster, Judith McFarlane, Carolyn Rebecca Block, Yvonne Ulrich, Nancy Glass, Jacquelyn C. Campbell, et al. "Risk Factors for Femicide-Suicide in Abusive Relationships: Results from a Multisite Case Control Study." *Violence and Victims* 21 (February 1, 2006): 3–22.

Lund, Laura E., and Svetlana Smorodinsky. "Violent Deaths Among Intimate Partners: A Comparison of Homicide and Homicide Followed by Suicide in California." *Suicide and Life-Threatening Behavior* 31, no. 4 (2001): 451–59.

Lundeberg, Kirsten, Sandra M. Stith, Carrie E. Penn, and David B. Ward. "A Comparison of Nonviolent, Psychologically Violent, and Physically Violent Male College Daters." *Journal of Interpersonal Violence* 19, no. 10 (2004): 1191–1200.

McEvoy, Alan. "Murder-Suicide by Students." *School Intervention Report* 13, no. 2 (2000): 1–5.

McFarlane, Judith, Jacquelyn C. Campbell, and Kathy Watson. "Intimate Partner Stalking and Femicide: Urgent Implications for Women's Safety." *Behavioral Sciences & the Law* 20, no. 1–2: 51–68.

Nicolaidis, Christina, Mary Ann Curry, Yvonne Ulrich, Phyllis Sharps, Judith McFarlane, Doris Campbell, Faye Gary, et al. "Could We Have Known? A Qualitative Analysis of Data from Women Who Survived an Attempted Homicide by an Intimate Partner." *Journal of General Internal Medicine* 18, no. 10: 788–94.

Palermo, George B. "Murder-suicide: An Extended Suicide." *International Journal of Offender Therapy and Comparative Criminology* 31, no. 3: 205–16.

Petrosian, Vahram. "Assyrians in Iraq." *Iran and the Caucasus* 10, no. 1 (2006): 113–47.

Porter, Tony. "How 'Well-meaning Men' Can Get Involved." *Voice Male*, Fall 2006: 9–10.

Radford, Lorraine. "Programmed or Licensed to Kill? The New Biology of Femicide." In *The New Brain Sciences: Perils and Prospects*, edited by Dai Rees and Steven Rose, 132–48. Cambridge, MA: Cambridge University Press, 2004.

Radford, Jill, and Diana E. H. Russell. *Femicide: The Politics of Woman-Kill-*

ing. New York: Twayne Publishers, 1992.

Rosenbaum, Alan, and Penny A. Leisring. "Beyond Power and Control: Towards an Understanding of Partner Abusive Men." *Journal of Comparative Family Studies* 34, no. 1 (2003): 7–22.

Rosenbaum, M. "The Role of Depression in Couples Involved in Murder-suicide and Homicide." *American Journal of Psychiatry* 147 (August 1990): 1036–39.

Rosenbaum, M., and B. Bennett. "Homicide and Depression." *American Journal of Psychiatry* 143 (March 1986): 367–70.

Saunders, Daniel G. "Husbands Who Assault: Multiple Profiles Requiring Multiple Responses." In *Legal Responses to Wife Assault*, edited by N. Zoe Hilton, 9–34. Newbury Park, CA: Sage Publications, 1993.

Saunders, Daniel G., and Angela Brown. "Intimate Partner Homicide." In *Case Studies in Family Violence*, 2nd edition, edited by Robert T. Ammerman and Michel Hersen, 415–49. New York: Kluwer Academic/Plenum Publishers, 2000.

Sellers, C. S., and M. L. Bromley. "Violent Behavior in College Student Dating Relationships." *Journal of Contemporary Justice* 12, no. 1: 1–27.

Stack, Steven. "Homicide Followed by Suicide: An Analysis of Chicago Data." *Criminology* 35, no. 3 (1997): 435–53.

Stout, Karen D. "Intimate Femicide: A National Demographic Overview." *Journal of Interpersonal Violence* 6, no. 4 (1991): 476–85.

West, D. J. *Murder Followed by Suicide*. Cambridge, MA: Harvard University Press, 1993.

Witte, Tricia H., David A. Schroeder, and Jeffrey M. Lohr. "Blame for Intimate Partner Violence: An Attributional Analysis." *Journal of Social and Clinical Psychology* 25, no. 6 (2006), 647–67.

Wood, Julia T. "Gender, Power, and Violence in Heterosexual Relationships." In *Sex Differences and Similarities in Communication*, 2nd edition, edited by Kathryn Dindia and Daniel J. Canary, 397–411. Mahwah, NJ: Lawrence Erlbaum Associates, 2006.